The Culture of Learning

The Culture of Learning

Access, Retention, and Mobility of Minority Students in Nursing

Virginia Macken Fitzsimons
and
Mary Lebreck Kelley

NLN Press • New York

Pub. No. 14-2699

Copyright © 1996
National League for Nursing
350 Hudson Street, New York, NY 10014

The views expressed in this book reflect those of the
authors and do not necessarily reflect the official views
of the National League for Nursing.

Library of Congress Cataloging-in-Publication Data

Fitzsimons, Virginia Macken.
    The culture of learning : access, retention, and mobility of
minority students in nursing / Virginia Macken Fitzsimons and Mary
Lebreck Kelley.
        p.   cm.
    Includes bibliographical references.
    ISBN 0-88737-659-2
    1. Nursing students.   2. Minorities in nursing.   I. Kelley, Mary
Lebreck.   II. Title.
RT73.F485   1996
610.73'071'5—dc20   95-49578
                                                        CIP

This book was set in Garamond by Publications Development Company, Crock-
ett, Texas. The designer was Allan Graubard, and the editor was Maryan Malone.
The printer was Clarkwood Corp. The cover was designed by Lauren Stevens.

Printed in the United States of America.

To Neil and Christine Fitzsimons

and to

Ted, Todd, and Michael Kelley.

There is nothing more difficult to take in hand, more perilous to conduct, or more uncertain in its success than to take [the] lead in the introduction of a new order of things.

Nicholas Machiavelli (1519)

Contents

Part Two: Addressing Student Life Needs and Successes

Part Three: Educational Biculturalism Plus

Part Four: Various Modes and Approaches of Economic Support for Minority and At-Risk Students

Part Five: Preparation for a Master of Science in Nursing: Moving Minority Nurses Toward Leadership Positions

Contributors

Betty W. Barber, PhD, RN
Dean
School of Natural Sciences,
    Nursing and Mathematics
Kean College of New Jersey
Union, New Jersey

David M. Bossman, PhD
Professor
Graduate Department of Jewish-
    Christian Studies
Seton Hall University
South Orange, New Jersey

Carol Conti, MSN, RN
Faculty
Cooperative Nursing Program
Elizabeth General Medical Center
School of Nursing-Union County
    College
Elizabeth, New Jersey

Virginia Macken Fitzsimons, EdD,
    RNC
Professor
Chairperson
Department of Nursing
Kean College of New Jersey
Union, New Jersey

David M. Gibson, EdD
Dean
School of Health Related
    Professions
University of Medicine and
    Dentistry of New Jersey
Newark, New Jersey

Gail Hein, BA
Director
Academic Learning Centers
Union County College
Cranford, New Jersey

Karen Joho, MS, RN
Faculty
Cooperative Nursing Program
Elizabeth General Medical Center
School of Nursing-Union County
    College
Elizabeth, New Jersey

Henry L. Kaplowitz, PhD
Professor
Department of Psychology
Kean College of New Jersey
Union, New Jersey

Myrna Morales Keklak, BSN, RN
Coordinator
Nursing Academic Support Center
Cooperative Nursing Program—
    Union County College
Cranford, New Jersey

Mary Lebreck Kelley, MSN,
    MEd, RN
Dean
Clinical Associate Professor
Cooperative Nursing Program
Elizabeth General Medical Center
School of Nursing-Union County
    College
Elizabeth, New Jersey

Michael E. Knight, PhD
Professor
Early Childhood and Family
    Studies
Kean College of New Jersey
Union, New Jersey

Lisa Carhart Lontai, MS, RNCS
Clinical Assistant Professor
Cooperative Nursing Program
Elizabeth General Medical Center
School of Nursing-Union County
    College
Elizabeth, New Jersey

Judith Mathews, MA, RN
Dean-Clinical Associate Professor
Cooperative Nursing Program
Muhlenberg Regional Medical
    Center
Schools of Nursing and Allied
    Health-Union County College
Plainfield, New Jersey

Lynne R. Nelson, BSN, RN
Work/Study Coordinator
Director of Tutorial Services
Cooperative Nursing Program
Elizabeth General Medical Center
School of Nursing-Union County
    College
Elizabeth, New Jersey

Anne Ormsby, MSN, RNC
Clinical Assistant Professor
Cooperative Nursing Program
Elizabeth General Medical Center
School of Nursing-Union County
    College
Elizabeth, New Jersey

Dula F. Pacquiao, EdD, RN
Assistant Professor
Department of Nursing
Kean College of New Jersey
Union, New Jersey

Teresita Proctor, MS, RNCS
Clinical Assistant Professor
Cooperative Nursing Program
Elizabeth General Medical Center
School of Nursing-Union County
    College
Elizabeth, New Jersey

Susan Warner Salmond, EdD, RNC
Associate Professor
Department of Nursing
Director of Graduate Program
Kean College of New Jersey
Union, New Jersey

Florence G. Sitelman, MA
Consultant
New York

Robert Sitelman, PhD
Professor
Department of
    Philosophy-Religion
Kean College of New Jersey
Union, New Jersey

Paula Dunn Tropello, MSN, RNC
Clinical Assistant Professor
Cooperative Nursing Program
Elizabeth General Medical Center
School of Nursing-Union County
    College
Elizabeth, New Jersey

Acknowledgments

*P*rojects with the scope and complexity of the Transcultural Leadership Continuum (TLC) are impossible without extensive conceptual and financial support. We are grateful to the Robert Wood Johnson Foundation, Inc., for its generosity and its recognition of minority nurse access, retention, and mobility as essential to building a dynamic and effective health care system. We thank its staff of professionals for their support throughout the various stages of this project.

The BARD Foundation, Inc. provided early seed money as our master's program in clinical administration with a transcultural nursing perspective was being developed. It was the question, "Where will our minority master's candidates come from?" that began our search for student access and retention mechanisms. The Helene Fuld Health Trust, long a supporter of nursing students and education, provided much needed financial assistance for computers, interactive video computers, and computer software programs for our students.

Four schools collaborated in this undertaking—Elizabeth General Medical Center School of Nursing, Kean College of New Jersey, Muhlenberg Regional Medical Center School of Nursing, and Union County College (UCC). Our thanks to the consistent support of the Union County College Administration—Dr. Thomas Brown, President, and Dr. Ernest Cronan, Vice President for Academic Affairs. They both recognized the value of exploration and change and told us to go ahead and "just do it."

Special thanks to Professor William Dunscombe of UCC who provided support early in the development of this project and who has contributed to its ongoing progress.

Special thanks to Mr. John Kopicki and Mr. Philip Brown of Muhlenberg Regional Medical Center and Mr. David A. Fletcher and Mr. Anthony H. Bliss of Elizabeth General Medical Center for their consistent support and encouragement.

Our Project TLC Co-Directors Judith Mathews and Gail Hein need particular recognition. Many meetings and negotiations are necessary to move faculty groups and 1600 students in a new direction. Their flexibility and understanding made it possible. Dot Hellenbrecht, our administrative assistant took the notes, kept the office running, and facilitated recommendations—essential work—and we thank her.

Kean College's Governor's Challenge Grant laid the framework for student access and mobility efforts. Bob Sitelman, President of the Kean College Federation of Teachers, mobilized the faculty for this endeavor. Dr. Nathan Welss and Dr. Hank Ross, former and current Presidents of Kean College, guided administrative policies to facilitate the Challenge Grant. Dr. Hank Kaplowitz and Dr. Mike Knight have received national attention for their contributions.

With the assistance of Mrs. Lyle Brehm of the Kean College Foundation and Dr. Ernest May, our communications and relationship with the Robert Wood Johnson Foundation, Inc., became a reality. Thank you.

To all of the faculty, staff, and students of our programs, our grateful thanks for your very hard work and professional willingness to implement new ideas. You took risks and achieved success.

To Nancy Pohl, Gloria Washington, Tanya Whitney, and Joanne Rogoz for your long days and late hours of technical support, thank you.

To Patricia Munhall, expert and colleague, we extend our grateful recognition and appreciation for serving as a primary consultant to the project. And to Allan Graubard, director of the NLN Press, who gave our project a title, *The Culture of Learning,* and a forum for national dissemination, our deep appreciation.

VIRGINIA MACKEN FITZSIMONS
MARY LEBRECK KELLEY

Prologue

*B*y chance one evening, two nurses met over a salad bar in a fast-food restaurant. As their children talked and played with their french fries, the women reminisced about the years they had worked as teachers and administrators. They ended by saying, "There is so much to be done for students. Let's do a project together." That project is the *Transcultural Leadership Continuum* initiative. It is currently funded by the Robert Wood Johnson Foundation, Inc., for the four-year period, 1992 to 1996. And it changed the nature, and so the "Culture of Learning," in our nursing programs.

> *Why should higher education be concerned with diversity? If the goals of higher education include teaching people to think critically, to be socially responsible, to communicate effectively, and to value differences, diversity becomes a necessity. Diversity is the spice that adds to the quality of life and culture. And if we are to effectively cope with rapid social, political and economic changes, we must be able to appreciate and include people who are different from us. (Santovec, M. (1994) Recruitment and retention in higher education. Madison, WI: Magna Publications, Inc.)*

Foreword

Exegi monument'aere perrenius
(Horace)

*T*he bard's boast that he had "built a monument more lasting than bronze" may or should be every teacher's aspiration. The stuff of education is, after all, the transition of past knowledge and skills as well as their advancement through study and research. In a very real sense, education is a monument never quite completed. Education is, however, a fragile enterprise, more easily dismantled than monuments of bronze. Unlike bronze statues hewn or hammered into shapes that capture and freeze some moment of time or place, education somewhat like the amoeba needs to bend and twist, retract and expand to survive and flourish in changing environments.

As artists are rendered great by their ability to interpret and represent perennial values or deep human emotions, so too are educators. Whether the knowledge and skills they transmit are newly discovered or collected from the past, their greatness as teachers is founded precisely on their abilities to lead their students to discover past and present in their own context of time, place, and culture. In no small way is this the intent of this book. An underlying belief is that each student and each teacher is conditioned by a multiplicity of factors, all of which in some way impinge on the teaching-learning contract.

This book is about education in the concrete but it is constructed on a foundation of values, beliefs, and assumptions that veteran educators (both past and present) have culled from experience, study, and, perhaps, even from quiet pensive moments in which they have wondered about this process we call "education."

It is a book for all educators but it is also unabashedly dedicated to teachers in the health professions. There are few human enterprises in which the quality of an education can affect the lives of individuals as quickly as in the health professions. Graduates of nursing and allied health programs are expected to have mastered a set of skills or competencies that have direct bearing on the well-being of those they serve. Yet technology and the explosion of biomedical research findings challenge educators to find new and better ways to integrate essential core knowledge, new technologies of diagnosis, and therapeutic treatments and skills with an increasing demand for affective behaviors that are sensitive to peoples from the many cultures which now constitute our nation. Increasingly, too, do our classrooms and laboratories mirror the face of a culturally myriad populace. The authors have attempted to shape a balance between the individual student's need for customized instruction and methodologies that encourage group intersupported learning.

There is little doubt that the teaching/learning process is not easily separable, one part from the other. In this regard, the chapters that follow attempt to focus on the faculty as both teachers and learners. So, too, do the authors recognize the uniqueness of each student in this process. They recognize that there is simply no cookie-cutter approach that will mold students into successful health professionals.

In many respects, this book honors the difficult balance required by our society. The authors recognize the nip and tuck inherent in its demands and expectations, articulated so well by Bell more than 20 years ago:

> *Analytically, society may be divided into three parts: The social structure, the polity and the culture. The social structure comprises the economy, technology and occupational system. The polity regulates the distribution of power and adjudicates the conflicting claims and demands of individuals and groups. The culture is the realm of expressive symbolism and meaning. It is useful to divide society in this way because each aspect is ruled by a different axial principle. In modern Western society the axial principle of the social structure is* economizing—*a way of allocating resources according to principles of least cost, substitutability, optimization, maximization, and the like. The axial principle of the modern polity is* participation, *sometimes mobilized and controlled, sometimes demanded from below. The axial principle of culture is the desire for the* fulfillment and enhancement of self. *(Daniel Bell, (1973) The Coming of post industralist society: A venture in social forecasting. New York: Basic Books)*

The authors, recognizing that the social structure of health care in our society has very much been bent to economizing, make substantive suggestions and create workable blueprints for the recruitment and retention of students. In the mix of managed care and health professions' education, there is little room for the expense, *human, financial, social,* and *educational,* borne by students who fail to complete their education successfully and in a timely manner.

DAVID M. GIBSON

Introduction

Virginia M. Fitzsimons and Mary L. Kelley

The major social issue facing the U.S. is whether this nation can embrace a new generation of Americans and build a renewed sense of national unity while rejoicing in diversity. . . . Our response to this urgent and persistent challenge will have an impact far beyond the classroom and will reach into the future as far as anyone can see.

Ernest Boyer (1983)

As we move to the close of this last decade of the century, it is ever more necessary to prepare minority nurses at advanced practice levels who understand the cultural and health care beliefs of a diverse population and who are prepared to care for them (Finocchio & O'Neill, 1994; Leininger, 1994; Rosella, Regan-Kubinski, & Albrecht, 1994). Without minority nurses in our baccalaureate and graduate degree pools, there will be no minority leadership as we move into the new millennium.

NATIONAL, STATE, AND LOCAL PICTURE

The emerging pattern in nursing education is also seen in all areas of higher education. Minority students gain admission and enroll, but are the least successful in graduating. Over the past five years, the national picture for minority graduations from nursing programs has been disconcerting.

1

Graduations of minority students from all programs declined during this period from 14.7% to 12.7%. In 1993, African American students accounted for 6.8%, and Hispanic students 2.6%, of the graduations from all generic nursing programs. Minority enrollments show no significant change. Figures I.1 and I.2 illustrate national minority admission and graduation data from generic nursing programs during 1992 and 1993 (National League for Nursing [NLN], 1994).

Data from our state, New Jersey, mirror the national picture. Of the African American students who were admitted to a basic nursing program in 1992, 11% were enrolled in a generic BSN and 89% were enrolled in an AD/Diploma program. Fewer than 5% of African American and Hispanic nurses hold baccalaureate degrees. One percent of our nurses with master's degrees are African American or Hispanic. The need to develop minority leadership is dramatic. Figures I.3 and I.4 illustrate minority admission and graduation date from generic nursing programs during 1992 and 1993.

At the same time, 60% of incoming students at the associate level are enrolled in remedial courses. Only one in six, or 16%, of the students complete a program at the associate level. In our nursing programs at the associate level, attrition rates at the remedial level approach 50%. Up to another 50% are lost at the science and early nursing course levels.

Attrition is a tragic waste of human and fiscal resources. The time, energy, and money invested in each student's education is significant and

Figure I.1   Admissions 1992–1993—All Basic Nursing
Programs—United States

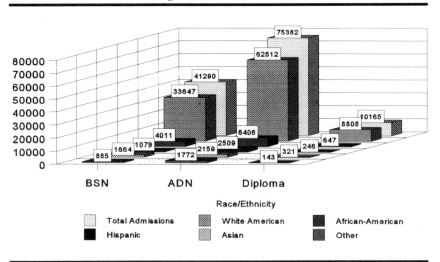

Figure I.2 Graduations 1992–1993—All Basic Nursing
Programs—United States

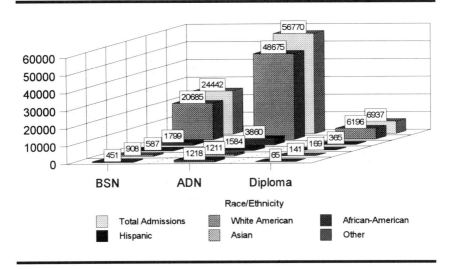

Figure I.3 Admissions 1992–1993—All Basic Nursing
Programs—New Jersey

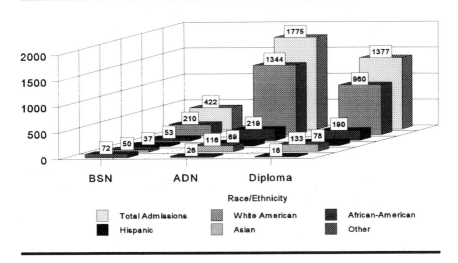

Figure I.4   Graduations 1992–1993—All Basic Nursing
Programs—New Jersey

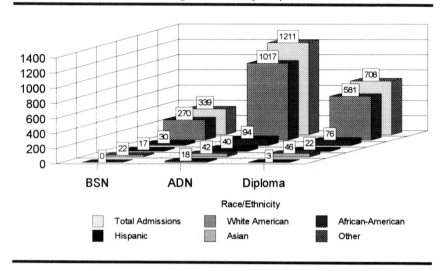

too frequently results in pain, failure, and lowered self-esteem and self-confidence. This phenomenon is also occurring with students who can least afford it. Dewey (1969) might have cited these failed educational experiences as "miseducative"—they arrest and distort the individual's growth. Because miseducative experiences are repeated across this country at alarming rates and in all settings, no greater priority exists for educators than the significant enhancement of students', particularly minority students', rates of success. What is going on? Why are remediation programs failing?

WE SAW IT COMING

As early as the mid-1970s, nursing faculties recognized the implications of the changing health status and demographic data. Programs made a public commitment to recruiting, enrolling, and graduating minority students. Program changes were mobilized. Increasing program access through flexibility, open admissions, and curricula initiatives would accommodate the needs of the new, older, working, economically disadvantaged, more culturally diverse, and less academically prepared student. Standard retention and remediation strategies were in place or were developed and put in place. Our programs offered day, evening, weekend, and accelerated divisions. There were opportunities for full- and part-time study. Seamless articulation, AD/Diploma to BSN, existed. Within two years, minority enrollment increased by 50%. However, attrition rates skyrocketed. By the mid-1980s, it was clear that traditional retention strategies were not working and that the unprecedented complexity of the students' needs demanded a more comprehensive and in-depth approach. As our schools became revolving doors, important moral and ethical questions became apparent as well (Urban, 1993). Can a school enroll students and promise access to a discipline, knowing that the student's level of mastery is limited? How much is enough remediation in the presence of open admissions? Could we deliver the practitioner we promised?

Our moral obligation to students is to provide them with sufficient academic support to graduate. Our moral obligation to the profession and the community is to graduate a competent and accountable nursing practitioner.

Students continued to fail. Without a clear understanding of what is expected of them and of the rigors of the curriculum, underprepared students are set up for failure. For faculty, witnessing such predictable failure is morally repugnant. Failure is a loss.

Our entering students have an average age of 28 years; all hold high school or equivalency diplomas. Remediation on a college level can refine skills somewhat, but growth in comprehension and synthesis of the mathematics and reading levels are difficult to achieve in a short period. Major academic limitations for our learners are the inability to organize for class and homework assignments, to recognize priority learning material, and to realize a sufficient-time-on-task/successful-exam-outcome ratio.

CONTINUING THE SEARCH FOR ANSWERS

We continue to recruit and enroll minority candidates into our programs successfully, but attrition rates remain unacceptable. Focus groups have revealed that the major reasons for high attrition are family responsibilities, financial needs, academic habits, work hours interfering with class and study time, and language difficulties. Many students had completed their primary and secondary education in other countries. English as a second language (ESL) was a solid beginning, but the students still struggled with the major courses—anatomy, physiology, chemistry, microbiology, and nursing. Mastery of the required content demanded a reading comprehension level higher than many of our students possessed.

Cultural expectations of an educational environment differ widely. Aspects of this educational culture include learning styles and organization. As important as these variables may be, student variables of age, gender, and time availability are what account for substantial differences in expectations between the learner and the faculty (Griggs, Griggs, Dunn, & Ingham, 1994). Recruitment of adult candidates was an artifact of the precipitous decline in traditional, 18-year-old, high school graduates in the mid-1980s. The familiar first-time, full-time student base was not available. Frantic in the face of plummeting enrollments, many higher education programs moved to the larger pool of non-college-educated adults, who were seen as mature, motivated, and goal-directed. They possessed all these attributes. They also came fully loaded with the responsibilities of adults: full-time jobs, families, housing, child-care, and transportation needs. In single parent households, one person bears the burden of responsibility for the household, parenting, and economic support. And these single parents (mostly women) often look to nursing for career development and economic mobility.

The major difference between the traditional college student and the adult learner is the complexity of their lives. Curricula have been written for the 24-hour day of the traditional college student whose family or student loan program is providing support over a two- or four-year period. Because of job and home responsibilities, few middle-class or lower-socioeconomic-status adults can be available for authentic full-time study. Working full time, or many hours part time, substantially erodes time for class and study. Part-time study doubles the number of years needed to complete a program evoking stressors on goal-directiveness, physical stamina, family roles, time issues, work situations, and social relationships.

Students who work all day and attend class on weekends or until 8 or 10 p.m. several evenings a week change family roles and child-parent relationships. But, the classes away from home are only the beginning. Preparation for class, clinical rotations, papers, and exams consume many additional hours, leaving little time for socialization, recreation, and relaxation. If the time issues are not addressed, academic success is at high risk and the stressors in these students' lives can become overwhelming, as evidenced by the wide range of pronounced stress-related symptoms that are being observed.

The adult learners who must first spend a number of semesters in remediation study move the time frame for the program out even further, testing mightily their ability to tolerate delay and frustration. The learner needs a clear vision of the goal and consistent support to problem-solve and persist. Persistence to goal must be a prime variable in the teaching strategies because that is the primary characteristic at risk. Traditional curricula focus on the content and not on the learner. Time and money management are behavioral imperatives, because in most instances both are scarce resources.

DEFINING CULTURE

Attrition rates documented that standard curricula, conventional teaching strategies, traditional retention strategies, and support systems did not "see" the culture of the new learner. Change was needed—in the administrators, curricula, methods, faculty, students, and viewpoints. We define learning as a change in behavior, more or less consistent over time. The faculty, who were already committed to preparing minority nurses for leadership in minority communities, were ready to do the most difficult thing: to change and, therefore, to learn.

Culture, multicultural populations, and multicultural curricula—the buzz words of the 1990s—have been covered widely in the press and general media. However, ethnic culture, which is the standard notion of culture, is geographically grounded; it is a "Where are you from?" point of reference. The stereotyping of groups that emerges from such a model has inherent limitations. Broader definitions of culture suggest appropriately complex views and include the group's particular beliefs, customs, arts, and institutions at a particular time. Culture implies refinement in intellectual and artistic taste. Such a perspective addresses the development of intellectual faculties through education. Another, and rather attractive, derivation of the word *culture* is the term *cultivation,* which means tillage of the soil. So when we speak of education, we are cultivating the fertile minds of the students. Actually, ancient metaphors relate higher education to the cultivation of the plush olive grove of the academy.

The term *culture shock,* to the contrary, addresses a condition of anxiety and disorientation that can affect someone suddenly exposed to a new culture. Preparing a person to enter a professional culture requires the development of the highest level of cognitive and affective domains. Critical thinking skills concern the ability to judge the value of material for a particular purpose. Professional judgments are based on definite and defined criteria, which may be internal (organization) or external (relevance to the purpose). The person may determine these criteria or be given them. Learning outcomes in this area are highest in the affective and cognitive domains because they contain elements of all lower categories, plus conscious value judgments based on defined criteria.

Affective domain behaviors are characterized by a value or value complex. At this level of the domain, the individual's value system has controlled his or her behavior long enough to produce a characteristic lifestyle or mode of pervasive, consistent, and predictable behaviors. Learning outcomes at this level cover a broad range of activities, but overall behavior will be typical or characteristic of that student. The most appropriate instruction techniques will consider the learner's general patterns of personal, social, or emotional adjustment (Gronland, 1976).

A culture is a group of people who share common beliefs, attitudes, and behaviors. In effect, a nursing education curriculum is really an introduction to, and some level of mastery of, the culture of the profession. A value is a belief that is acted on in a consistently frequent manner; it is expressed as a behavior. Valuing addresses the worth or value a student attaches to a particular object, phenomenon, or behavior. Values are central organizing forces in any society or group providing direction to peoples' behavior and giving it meaning. Students and teachers bring to any new learning situation a body of knowledge, ideas, and concepts developed from their prior learning experiences. Such an understanding of the world is deeply rooted in the personality and drives its affective, temperamental, and motivational structure.

WHEN CULTURES CLASH

The post-op surgical patient began to hemorrhage. The nurse turned to the student and firmly ordered, "Get me the dressing cart. Get me some towels." The African American student turned to the faculty member and responded in anger, "No one is going to talk to me like that. I'm leaving." That student left the nursing unit, and left nursing.

The patient's intravenous was dry. The instructor told the student, "You have put your patient in jeopardy. This is the second time this has occurred this week. You are on clinical warning. The written warning will be ready tomorrow." The student never returned to the clinical area or to the nursing course. Whereas the instructor viewed the warning as a "wake-up call to emphasize safety," the Asian student viewed it as a humiliating loss of face.

Routine situations can become cultural clashes when experienced by persons from differing cultural perspectives. Each of the students felt devalued and offended. The African American student was responding to the voice tone of the Caucasian nurse, who had used an immediate imperative sentence, reflecting the urgency of the situation. To the student's ear, the tone sounded disrespectful, and she would not stay in such a situation. The Asian student had lost face; she felt shamed. Both situations were intolerable to the self-respect of these students, and yet in both cases their responses stunned the nurse/faculty, who believed they were communicating necessary and important information. The attrition of each student added to the low minority graduation rates from the programs. This attrition is unrelated to classroom academic success and illustrates why staff, faculty, and students must gain insight into cultural differences.

EDUCATIONAL BICULTURALISM PLUS

The concept of educational biculturalism addresses both the noncognitive and cognitive aspects of student learning (Kornguth, Frisch, Shovein, & Williams, 1994). Its intent is to redirect the standard focus of content development to incorporate self-esteem, perception, enhancement, and concrete application of principles as a teaching strategy. This model demonstrates that the following seven noncognitive areas can assist the learner in comprehending material:

1. Positive self-concept or confidence.
2. Realistic self-appraisal.
3. Understanding racism and strategies to deal with racism.
4. Preference for long-range goals to short-term or immediate needs.
5. Availability of strong support systems.
6. Successful leadership experience.
7. Knowledge acquired for a particular field.

There are also four vehicles for cognitive growth:

1. Learning styles.
2. Motivational styles.
3. Reasoning development.
4. Error analysis.

When we speak of culture, therefore, we are addressing more than ethnic/racial culture. We move from a focus on the two-culture ethnic system—the minority student and the middle-class faculty—to a more complex model that incorporates theoretical perspectives from a broad range of liberal arts and science disciplines. Educational development and the growth of the neophyte professional demand more than an analysis of cognitive and noncognitive areas. We must humanize and operationalize these areas to understand how the minority student is the same as and yet different from the traditional student and professor.

Mobilization of the mentoring and role modeling activities had us explore additional aspects of culture. We address the meaning and effects of social class differences and of verbal language styles as they relate to the student-teacher relationship. Professional development has traditionally been accomplished through mentoring and role modeling whereby the experienced professional passes the torch (professional role) to the new professional generation through education and preparation for practice. In the mentoring process today, social class and cultural differences are added variables, but in the end, the same product—a competent, ethical, and clear-thinking professional person—is the hoped-for result.

Cognitive learning styles (Griggs et al., 1994; Hodges, 1988) determine the way people take in, process, and use information from their environment. Students with different cultural backgrounds enter the classroom experiencing a great deal of anxiety because their learning styles differ from standard "American" learning methods. To learn effectively, however, these students need emotional security that will enable them to be available for the necessary changes.

MOVE TO A TRANSCULTURAL LEADERSHIP MODEL

We knew that a graduate program was necessary to increase the percentage of minority representation and to create a critical supply of credentialed minority nurses at the administrative, advanced clinical practice, and faculty levels. The intent was to move the associate degree nurses, especially minority nurses, through our undergraduate BSN program and then right into a graduate level program. To accomplish this, we planned and initiated a master of science in nursing with a focus in clinical nursing administration, including an orientation to the continued development of the concept of transcultural nursing.

As we quickly learned from addressing the needs of minority students, transcultural is exactly what the word implies; it incorporates the broadest meaning of culture: race, ethnicity, gender, economic/social class, and even groups of persons with common health problems. Any group that shares common beliefs and behaviors constitutes a culture or cultural subgroup. Our MSN graduates would thus be educated in a cohort designed to represent different ethnic groups, ages, genders, and work experiences. Each cohort in turn would use a curriculum immersed in transcultural theory at every level. Activities and clinical practice would uniformly address patient and staff issues that rotate around culture. When changing demographics result in clients, staff, faculty, and students with differing perspectives, it's time to approach culture and cultural issues within a framework built on science and discussion. It is too easy to let personal perspectives, feelings, and experiences move into the equation. Using the disciplines of sociology, philosophy, nursing, and anthropology facilitates understanding. We have found that discussions grounded in a theory base assisted us to move into very delicate areas of cultural differences. Personal worldviews based on one's own experience (with an N of 1) and stereotyping are put into perspective when balanced against literature developed from authenticated research and replication.

CAREER GOAL DEVELOPMENT—RAISING CAREER EXPECTATIONS

Focus groups with minority associate degree graduates identified the specific need to target career goal development as a primary activity with the African American and Hispanic registered nurses. Many of these women and men are the first in their families to graduate from a college program. They identified the associate degree and registered nurse license as the end of a long road allowing them to be associate degree nurses in their communities. The faculty agreed with the nurses that the attainment of the associate degree and registered nurse status was indeed a fine accomplishment. However, career advancement, salary improvement, and leadership positions were held captive to the attainment of at least a bachelor of science in nursing degree and preferably a master of science in nursing degree. We always opened expectations to the doctoral level. The communities that we serve need the expertise of baccalaureate and higher degree nurses to exert leadership in solving the complex health maintenance and disease prevention realities of today's world.

Communities of color are hardest hit in the areas of communicable diseases, as well as in neonatal and maternal morbidity and mortality. The quality of life in many such communities is gravely affected by the tragic sequelae of chronic diseases left untreated or treated at late stages (Dunston & Siegel, 1991; U.S. Department of Health and Human Services, 1992). Communities of color need and deserve nurses who understand the lives of persons in their communities and who are prepared to provide community-based care, prevention services, lifestyle adaptation teaching, and community health assessment and planning (Finocchio & O'Neill, 1994; Leininger, 1994; Moccia, 1994; Rosella, Regan-Kubinski, & Albrecht, 1994). To achieve these baccalaureate and higher degree competencies, the nursing profession must raise the career expectations of minority nurses and facilitate access to educational mobility.

The communities in which our programs reside have a "rich mosaic of peoples and cultures" (Essex and Union Advisory Board for Health Planning, Inc., 1993). There are dramatic unmet health needs within our region, which is rated as high risk in relation to health status (Dunston & Siegel, 1991; Essex and Union Advisory Board for Health Planning, Inc., 1993). Our mandate is clear.

OUR PLAN

The primary goal of our project and activities is to increase the number of minority nurses who are prepared for nursing leadership positions and who can positively impact the quality of the health care of the citizens in our communities.

We have four major objectives:

1. To increase the retention rate of minority students through:
    a. Increasing the success rate in the early preclinical courses.
    b. Addressing student life needs.
2. To educate the faculty regarding the concept of "Educational Biculturalism."
3. To develop various modes and approaches for economic support during the progression through the programs.
4. To increase minority representation in nursing at the administrative, clinical practice, and faculty levels through mobility to BSN and MSN levels.

The following chapters detail the processes, activities, research projects, and people that have moved our four schools toward achieving these goals and objectives.

REFERENCES

Boyer, E. (1983). *A nation at risk: The imperative for educational reform.* Washington, DC: U.S. Department of Education.

Dewey, J. (1969). *Pedagogical creed in education today.* Westport, CN: Greendwood Press.

Dunston, F. J., & Siegel, B. (1991). *Healthy New Jersey 2000, A public health agenda for the 1990s.* Trenton, NJ: New Jersey State Department of Health.

Essex and Union Advisory Board for Health Planning, Inc. (1993). *Needs assessment for Region III.* Essex and Union Counties, planning report No. 3. South Orange, NJ.

Finocchio, L. J., & O'Neill, E. H. (1994). Strategies for state health workforce reform. *Pew Health Professions Commission* (2), 1-17.

Garbin, M. (Ed.). (1991). *Assessing educational outcomes.* New York: National League for Nursing Press.

Griggs, D., Griggs, S. A., Dunn, R., & Ingham, J. (1994). Accommodating nursing students' diverse learning styles. *Nurse Educator, 19*(6), 41-45.

Gronland, N. (1976). *Measurement & evaluation in teaching.* New York: Macmillan.

Hodges, L. C. (1988). Students entering professional nursing: Learning style, personality type and sex-role identification. *Nurse Education Today, 8,* 68-76.

Knight, M. E., Lumsden, D. L., & Gallaro, D. (1991). *Outcomes assessment at Kean College of New Jersey.* Lanham, MD: University Press of America.

Kornguth, M., Frisch, N., Shovein, J., & Williams, R. (1994). Noncognitive factors that put students at academic risk in nursing programs. *Nurse Educator, 19*(5), 24-27.

Leininger, M. (1994). Transcultural nursing education a worldwide imperative. *Nursing & Health Care, 15*(5), 254-261.

Louden, M. (1994, August). *News from NLN.* New York: National League for Nursing Press.

Magna Publications, Inc. (1988). *Making changes: 27 strategies from recruitment & retention.* Madison, WS: Author.

Moccia, P. (1993). *A vision for nursing education.* New York: National League for Nursing Press.

Moccia, P. (1994). *Trends in contemporary nursing education.* Nursing Datasource. New York: National League for Nursing Press.

Molina, C. W., & Molina-Aguirre, M. (1994). *Latino health in the US: A growing challenge.* Washington, DC: American Public Health Association.

Munhall, P. L., (1994). *Qualitative research, proposals and reports: A guide.* New York: National League for Nursing Press.

Rosella, J. D., Regan-Kubinski, M., & Albrecht, S. A. (1994). The need for multicultural diversity among health professionals. *Nursing & Health Care, 15*(5), 242-246.

Santovec, M. (Ed.). (1994). *Recruitment and retention in higher education.* Madison, WI: Magna Publications.

Sherrod, R., & Harrison, L. (1994). Evaluation of a comprehensive advisement program designed to enhance student retention. *Nurse Education, 19*(6), 29-33.

Urban, C. (1993). Disadvantaged professionals: Implications for education and practice. *Nursing Connections, 6*(2), 24-28.

U.S. Department of Health and Human Services. (1992). *Healthy people 2000. National health promotion and disease prevention objectives. Summary report.* Boston: Jones & Bartlett.

Watson, J. (Ed.). (1994). *Applying the art and science of human caring.* New York: National League for Nursing Press.

Part One

Increasing Minority Student Retention

The Humanistic Edge:
Teaching and Learning from
the Cultures of Our Society

David M. Gibson

Individuals can and will learn that which they perceive to be important
to their lives: survival and success in the family, in social situations and
in earning a livelihood. When students can see a relationship between
knowledge, cognitive skills, surviving and success, there will be a moti-
vation to learn. Success is seen as empowering individuals to function to
their maximum capacity in the various arenas of life.

(John Dewey, 1969)

We are a nation of minorities. Indeed, it may be more accurate to describe our soon-to-be society as minority free. American culture will be
pluralized and the true work of integration will be intercultural. In most
respects, the efforts to bring diverse cultures into dialogue will be the lot
of educational institutions. How well these institutions cope with this
task will depend largely on the preparation and readiness of their leaders

and faculty to change the ways they instruct students. Success will not be the result of proselytizing in the manner in which Horace Mann preached the Common School Movement. Its past, and perhaps continuing error, has been the presumption that different cultures should be fully incorporated into a majority culture. In reality, the "melting pot" has always remained just a theory. In current American society, for instance, how would you determine which group really defines the majority?

On the other hand, Dewey's empowerment consequent to success is belied by many of our citizens' feelings of disenfranchisement. The exclusion of whole groups of peoples from access to educational opportunities brings only a sense of alienation and disempowerment. Moreover, such exclusion hampers the integration of new groups into our society and tears the fabric of common sense. Whether they are new citizens on our shores or members of groups that have been here for centuries, those who are excluded from the benefits of society are most likely to disdain it. In this regard, Eugene Brody writes:

> *Contemporary migrants include large numbers of refugees who have typically been subject to diverse and repeated trauma and loss, both in their home countries and in transit. Their culturally alien, minority status combined with a lack of knowledge, skills and confidence result, furthermore, in rejection by the host society. Vulnerable to illness, and without the support of familiar context, including language, they are targets of discrimination, excluded from full participation in the cultural process of their new society and access to the benefits available to its native members. (Brody, 1993)*

Educators in the health professions have an excellent opportunity to provide students with relational correlations between earning a livelihood and the knowledge, cognitive skills, and affective skills requisite for practice. Designed for student success, these educational programs integrate students from culturally diverse backgrounds into the common cause of healing and caring through clinical experiences that best mirror the workplace to which the students will eventually contribute and where they have, at least in part, "the support of a familiar context." Education's finest challenge is to help mold the generations that ensue, epitomizing in many respects the Jeffersonian construct to provide an informed citizenry. It is uniquely so for health professions' educators, who also impart knowledge, skills, and competencies that will add dignity to their students' lives and to those they serve.

As our students become ever more culturally diverse, our educational programs must at once provide integrative experiences and comfort with differences. Nursing education, nonetheless, along with other career and professional educational programs, has been narrowly focused to assure competencies within our profession. We can hardly argue with the appropriateness of this construct, for to fail in the heart of the mission would be to mislead the students entirely. Professional competence, however, is but one component of a student's education. We expect our students to graduate with more than technical or professional skills and knowledge. We want them to have some broad understanding of the world in which they will work and play, even though professional education has been woefully lacking in the integration of the liberal arts and humanities. Yet, however much we may complain about the current encroachment of career or technical training into the academy's curriculum, the tension between career education and liberal arts education is not new. Indeed, there has been widespread, consistent concern that the professional curriculum has gradually crowded out liberal learning opportunities (Bennet, 1984; Bloom, 1987; Bok, 1985; Rudolph, 1984; Stark & Lowther, 1988). Professional curricula have also been criticized for their narrowness of focus, with overemphasis on problem solving and little or no emphasis on problem framing (Elam & Lynton, 1985). The perennial tensions between vocational and liberal education in the American higher education enterprise have been well documented by Veysey (1965). This chapter provides all educators in the health professions with a clear blueprint of ways in which our institutions may best meet the challenge of supporting and sustaining our students through the integration of services, curricula, and culturally driven differences.

Health professions' educators have other good reasons for preparing a culturally diverse cohort of future practitioners. For one thing, we simply need to prepare a more diverse workforce to care for an increasingly diverse patient population; for another, as health care shifts from acute care settings into community-based, ambulatory care, or home health care settings, patients will show far less tolerance for cultural insensitivity than they do now in institutional settings. To ensure success, faculties need to learn new ways of interacting with students and of refocusing their research. Qualitative research methods lend themselves to the study of human actions and interactions in a way that supports the needs of both the researchers and their subjects. It allows entry for the nonquantitative aspects of students' or, indeed, patients' experiences. Qualitative research allows investigators to listen to and record their subjects' cares, concerns, joys, sufferings, and triumphs, as in the following passage:

> *. . . relief of suffering comes most often by changing the meaning of the experience for the sufferer and restoring the disrupted connectiveness of the sufferer with herself and those around her. (Brody, 1987)*

The emphasis on qualitative research for health professions' faculty should help integrate the students' learning experience and may also strengthen their program of study, as Dewey suggested.

In recognition of some constrictions of professional nursing curricula, the American Association of Colleges of Nursing (1986) recommended a series of steps to broaden the education of nursing students. Among the major abilities students should achieve, the following capacities are germane to this work:

> *Understand a second language, at least at an elementary level, in order to widen access to the diversity of world cultures.*
>
> *Understand other cultural traditions in order to gain a perspective on personal values and the similarities and differences between individuals and groups.*
>
> *Comprehend the meaning of human spirituality in order to recognize the relationship of beliefs to culture, behavior, health and healing.*
>
> *Understand the nature of human values and develop a personal philosophy in order to make ethical judgments in both personal and professional life. (Essentials of College and University Education for Professional Nursing: Final Report, pp. 4–5)*

In our increasingly intermixed culture, it is patent that our educational programs need to broaden students' experiences and foster diversity. By providing a philosophical basis through a phenomenological approach to biculturalism or through strategies to mentor and retain a diverse student population, we can create a yardstick for measuring success. So, too, the emphasis on preprofessional course work is an important and integrative component of the total nursing educational experience. In a larger sense, a responsive curriculum recognizes the changing demographics of our nation by making every effort to incorporate today's minorities into tomorrow's collaborative workforce. The onus of such change is rightly placed on the educational institutions and their faculties with the clear recognition that true leadership is not hierarchically anointed but rather allotted from the governed. The focus, however, is squarely on the students' unique conditions, cultures, and learning styles. Such a focus is not new. Aquinas said, *Quidquid recipitur, recipitur secundum modum recipientis* (That which is received is received through the conditioning of the receiver). In taking some liberties with both translation and the English language, we might note that we learn from and through our "ownness." The wisdom of the two Thomases, Dewey and Aquinas, tells us that teaching and curriculum need to meet the empowerment needs of our students and their cultural "ownness," through which they, as do we, condition learning.

REFERENCES

Bennett, W. (1984). *To reclaim a legacy: A report on the humanities in higher education.* (NEH Report 636). Washington, DC: U.S. Government Printing Office.

Bloom, A. (1987). *The closing of the American mind.* New York: Doubleday.

Bok, D. (1985, Fall). Looking into education's high tech future. *EDUCOM Bulletin, 3.*

Brody, E. (1993). *Biomedical technology and human rights,* p. 215. England: Dartmouth Publishing.

Brody, H. (1987). *Stories of sickness.* New Haven, CN: Yale University Press.

Dewey, J. (1969). My pedagogical creed. In J. Ratner (Ed.), *In education today.* New York: Greenwood Press. (Original work published 1901)

Elam, E. S., & Lynton, E. A. (1985, October). *Assessment of professional education.* Paper presented at the American Association for Higher Education, Columbia, SC.

Rudolph, F. (1984, May/June). The power of the professions: The impact of specialization and professionalization on the curriculum. *Change, 16*(4), 12-16.

Stark, J., & Lowther, M. (1988). *Strengthening the ties that bind: Integrating undergraduate liberal and professional study.* Report of the Professional Preparation Network, BDH639. Ann Arbor, MI: University of Michigan, School of Education, National Center for Research to Improve Postsecondary Teaching and Learning.

Veysey, L. (1965). *The emergence of the American university.* Chicago: University of Chicago Press.

2

Infusing Philosophical Thought into Transcultural Nursing Understanding

Dula F. Pacquiao

MULTICULTURALISM AND HEALTH CARE

As forecasts of increasing demographic heterogeneity in the United States are fast becoming a reality, debates have intensified over how to promote a community out of naturally different and often discordant student populations. Society generally views education as a major force in transforming these differences in people into a cohesive whole with common sets of assumptions for decisions and actions in dealing with life's experiences. Such a task, however, has essentially remained a vision rather than reality. Evidence persists that the gap is widening in school achievement of ethnically diverse students compared with their white American peers.

In professional schools, whose aims include socialization of students into a common culture of the discipline, measures to recruit and retain ethnically diverse students have generated disappointing results. Among all categories of health professionals, only a small percentage are of diverse backgrounds. And based on recent enrollment figures, not much change can be expected in the near future.

Although educators agree on the virtues of developing a culturally diverse workforce and accept initial diversity, norms in school and in the workplace are standardized and skewed toward the dominant culture. Hence, for ethnically diverse students, school achievement goes beyond learning new knowledge and skills. They need to acquiesce to school norms that may not mesh well with values taught at home. For a majority of these students, schooling is a dissonant experience and an exercise in self-denial that creates havoc in their personal life. Self-expression is counterproductive to school achievement. Success in school demands an ability to exist in a strange world, mimicking adaptations that have no meaning or sense to their being.

SELF, SCHOOL, AND SOCIETY

The philosophical works of Merleau-Ponty and Heidegger underscore the primacy of the individual's unique perceptions of experience that invest it with meaning. In sociology, Karl Mannheim has extended this concept in his formulation of socially reconstructed reality. Indeed, many studies support the idea that the individual perceives and interprets phenomena in a highly personal and subjective process that reflects previous life experience. The meaning, value, and significance of schooling, therefore, depend on the learner's framework of past lived experiences.

The seminal work of Gilligan (1982) and Belenky and her associates (1986) on women's ways of knowing, suggests that the individual's validation of her natural ways of knowing the world is an initial necessary step before she can construct a new and different way of thinking. Self-affirmation rather than denial is critical in moving into another world or realms of meaning defined by others. Nearly 60 years ago, John Dewey articulated the same tenet. Speaking of schoolchildren, he posited that learning is an active process involving the child's interaction with the subject matter that begins and ends with the child's own experience. According to Dewey, each child senses and moves to a deeper and wider realm of meaning by building on his or her innate capacities, interests, and predispositions.

Anthropologists have long argued for the centrality of value orientations in conditioning thoughts and behaviors of groups of people, because such values tend to create long-lasting effects on the individual's personality. Goldschmidt (1954) has theorized that values are the central organizing force providing direction to people's lives as well as meaning for their actions. According to Ruth Benedict (1934), in every culture *characteristic purposes* provide a consistent pattern of thought and action for members that other societies do not share. C. Kluckhohn (1949) has recognized that values constitute the significant *cognitive configuration* in determining behaviors of members of a cultural group. Values are interwoven in the unconscious matrix of the individual's personality, unfolding as the cognitive map for interpreting human experiences and guiding actions or decisions about such experiences.

Learning, which is primarily a cognitive process, is organized and constructed within the framework of the person's life experience and, for that matter, cultural background. In fact, life-course theories for human experiences such as aging propose the significance of analyzing the phenomenological and collective experiences of individuals to understand their present life ways as well as to predict their future integration. Hence, discussions about human experience must include the cultural, psychological, historical, and sociological forces that have been integrated into people's lives.

According to F. R. Kluckhohn (1976), every human group has a dominant value orientation as well as variant patterns of values. The dominant value premises largely determine the status and prestige of members within mainstream society. In a pluralistic society such as the United States, the dominant American ethos is superimposed on varying and sometimes conflicting value orientations. The interplay of these variables is significant in understanding the academic plight of ethnic minority students. It is where discussions should begin regarding prescriptions about recruitment, retention, and promotion strategies for culturally diverse students.

The eminent sociologist Talcott Parsons (1968), has posited that school norms support the dominant societal norms. Parsons views the school system as a potent instrument for socializing members to the valued norms of society, breaking continuity from norms at home when conflicts exist. In fact, a great number of sociological studies have documented that schools perpetuate class structure in society and that cultural experiences of many poor and racial minority students are incompatible and in conflict with school norms. Similarly, ethnographic studies of schools have found that students bring into any new learning situation an integrated body of ideas, predispositions, and values developed from prior experiences that become an organized structure for interpreting, connecting, and processing new information.

VALUE ORIENTATION AND COGNITION

Several anthropologists contend that the dominant American ethos exemplifies the values held by middle-class white Americans rooted in the Puritan value system of the early colonial period. Such values place a premium on the uniqueness of the individual, glorifying his or her ability to control destiny by mastering the environment through science, rationality, and self-discipline (Hsu, 1961; F. R. Kluckhohn, 1976). The corollary values of autonomy, self-responsibility, and self-control support the core ethos of individualism and self-reliance. Parsons (1968) theorizes that the norms of *instrumental activism* that place high value on individual achievement underlie early socialization of many Americans.

In this theory of a social system, Parsons (1951) has conceptualized five pairs of alternative patterns of actions within a bipolar continuum. Every component of each pair is a corollary premise of related action alternatives. Parsons' concept of self-orientation with its corollary premises of instrumental, achievement, universalistic, and specificity orientations is congruent with values of individualism and self-reliance. By contrast, his formulation of collectivity and its corresponding expressive, ascriptive, particularistic, and diffuse norms is congruent with values of group-centeredness and mutual dependence. Self-orientation legitimizes pursuit of individualistic, private interests, whereas collective orientation subordinates such interests to those of the group or the primary collectivity to which an individual belongs. Instrumental orientation is centered on attaining goals without experiencing relational or expressive gratification. Achievement orientation uses distinct standards of actual and anticipated specific performance based on universalistic norms independent of ascriptive ties or an individual's particular relationship with others. Specificity segregates standards of role performance vis-à-vis diffuseness, which places primacy on ascriptive and relational criteria in role expectations.

Dahrendorf (1979) has formulated the concept of "life chances . . . [as] the manner and extent by which human capacities are molded and extended in society" (p. 11). The author posits the interplay between society and human beings in terms of how the former provides a balance between an individual's choices (options) and relations with others (ligatures) within a given social context (space) and social time (history). The individual's realization of full potential is embedded in the alternatives made possible in a given society. Certain societies tend to place more emphasis on one over the other. In fact, Levine and White (1986) find that Western societies espouse values of individual options vis-à-vis ligatures or social attachments in the Third World.

Schools are a microcosm of a society. Life chances or academic survival for students are intertwined with the opportunities for growth and success made available to them. Their success potential is probable when schooling practices allow for a balance between values they have and those values espoused in the school. Phillips (1983) has found that the academic achievement among Native Americans in the Warm Springs reservation went down when the teachers used white middle-class norms to evaluate their performance. The author has noted marked differences when school norms paralleled those at home.

It is still necessary to explain how differences in cognitive operations between student groups can affect school performance. Several studies indicate that members of same ethnic groups tend to have greater similarities than differences relevant to their thinking, motivation, and temperament. My study (see Chapter 14) of adult nursing students suggests a cultural conditioning of cognition that goes beyond language differences.

Anthropologists such as Kluckhohn have developed a paradigm for examining how several value orientations support the salient cultural premises of a group. Values evolve as cognitive orientations from generations of dealing with basic human problems for survival within a specific context of time and space. Such values condition a particular group's life ways and worldviews. Value orientations create a cohesive cognitive map that becomes the leitmotif for thoughts, feelings, and actions of group members in a particular society.

In cultures where group-centeredness and mutual interdependence are central value premises, interactive patterns are based on the relationship between participants and their positions in the social hierarchy. Hence, for groups where positional authority is highly determinant of persons' status in society, interactions are governed not by the content of the interchange but by the structure of the relationship. A student is not at the same level in the hierarchy as the teacher. Thus, communication is expected to be from teacher to student. Such students have a natural predisposition toward a highly structured, teacher-directed, and teacher-initiated learning rather than toward self-directed and independent thinking. In contrast, groups with individualistic ethos demand clear, elaborate, self-reflective, and critical interactions regardless of the context of the exchange. A person does not take for granted that others understand his or her own thoughts since this is a highly individualized and self-determined process. This interactive style underlines the emphasis on analysis and reflective application demanded in American schools and expected in standardized exams.

Members of group-centered societies develop a strong sense of in-group versus out-group consciousness (Hsu, 1961) and are strongly influenced by the context of social interactions. Members are more likely to emphasize their similarities than their differences. They need to have a sense of belonging to the group rather than of being separated and competing with others. Competition is acceptable between groups, not between individuals in the same group. In contrast, individualistic societies tend to emphasize differences between persons and prefer competitive modes of interaction. When this approach is applied to schooling practices, evaluations are focused on differentiating student abilities and acceptance of individual competitiveness regardless of the group. On the other hand, group-centered students prefer group mastery of predetermined levels of achievement instead of tests of performance by individual students competing with each other. School evaluation strategies in the United States reflect partiality toward the individualistic orientation.

Another premise of group-centeredness is the distinction given to members of the in-group as against outsiders. The individual is likely to interact with outsiders differently than with others from the same group. Hence, development of a reference group is limited to members of the in-group. Particularistic ties govern interactions and guide investment of trust in others. Group-centered students may view teachers, administrators, other students, and the whole school environment as part of a strange, uncomfortable atmosphere, and may react to behavior patterning initiated by outsiders with initial suspicion, resistance, and in-group protectiveness. In a teaching-learning situation, outsiders will likely fail to penetrate the worldview of these students unless they are given time and appropriate nurturance of group cohesiveness. Schooling practices based on an individualistic ethos provide universalistic standards for achievement with deliberate minimization of group differences. To address differences among students is antithetical to this egalitarian ideal, which assumes that, given a set of rules, it is up to the individual to create his or her own pathway for success. In contrast, group-centered schooling practices will likely stress active guidance of individual group members to achieve rather than set universalistic rules for achievement. In this context, the teacher is an integral part of the group who will exercise patience, repetition, and active guidance for the whole group. Achievement is by the group and not limited to any particular individual.

When maintaining smooth interpersonal relations is paramount, students are likely to be euphemistic and less analytical or critical of one another. Emphasis is on tolerance and acceptance of others rather than on asserting individualized thoughts and desires. Such a value premise predisposes acceptance of facts, avoidance of conflict, and sensitivity to others. On the other hand, groups that place high value on individualism motivate the person to seek self-distinction from all others. Hence, students elaborate their assertive, self-determined thoughts among others and show a natural preference for discussions, criticisms, and disagreements. Statements are inherently scrutinized so that the individual's distinct ability becomes evident to others. The same cognitive and interactive skill is upheld in school norms and standardized exams.

A congruent premise of group-centeredness is an emphasis on relationships that may contradict the precepts of achievement orientation. Where group harmony superimposes individualized thoughts and desires, the person is likely to focus on present harmony rather than on the future accomplishment of specific outcomes. Hence, time orientation may not be driven by future goals but by past or present circumstances. Present-oriented groups do not accentuate prioritizing to achieve a future goal when such purposes create conflicts. The status quo maintenance of relationship far outweighs future-oriented tasks because the group is greater than the individual. Self-directed determination of priorities and decision making are not supportive of group goals. In contrast, individualized decision making and self-directed focusing on outcomes unencumbered by group norms are indigenous to members of societies that stress self-reliance. School examinations place a premium on a student's ability to analyze situations, determine priorities, and make individualized decisions.

Dominant American values glorify human beings' ability to use, control, and master their natural environment. Phenomena are to be examined and explained in a rational and reflective way. Maintenance of status quo is contradictory to progress. Hence, schools emphasize scientific thought process, empiricism, and achievement of tangible outcomes. However, societies that view nature as greater than those who live in it tend to be fatalistic, accept status quo readily, and do not require rational explanation of uncommon phenomena. Individuals are not predisposed necessarily to investing time and energy to discover and explain events that are accepted as natural characteristics of the bigger universe and of life. Emphasis centers on promotion of harmonious relationships with nature rather than on the domination of nature for human purposes. However, American schools stress the value of independent problem solving and initiative in achieving tangible explanations for phenomena and in taking examinations, which places those unfamiliar with this worldview at a disadvantage.

BICULTURALISM IN NURSING EDUCATION

In nursing school, the ultimate measure of students' cognitive ability is through application of learning rather than passive accumulation of facts and rote learning. Whereas faculty esteem independent, creative, reflective, and highly individualized thought patterns and behaviors, students on the other hand, may uphold relational, other-directed learning styles compatible with their innate value orientations. In negotiating with their new environment, these students tend to mimic persons in authority, whose word they take as absolute, because they are unfamiliar with school norms and are using behaviors that have effectively worked for them at home and elsewhere most of their lives.

Instructors should make the dominant norms visible and teach them in school rather than assume they are inherent capacities of students who need guidance and nurturance in coping with these new expectations. Basic assumptions about abilities of adult learners in institutions of higher education fall short in accounting for the initial diversity in pre-dispositional capacities that can affect school achievement. The egalitarian model of measuring achievement with standardized exams fails to consider differences in cognitive operations conditioned by cultural norms that indirectly create a bias against those whose indigenous value premises do not reflect mainstream norms.

In a study of women's epistemological development, Belenky and her associates (1986) found that subjects had to achieve validation and affirmation of their innate, personalized, intuitive way of knowing before they could move toward the highly abstract, empirical way of thinking indigenous to most men. Like the subjects in my study, these predominantly female students required that important step of validating their natural worldview as a prerequisite to constructing a new way of thinking and behaving to mediate the demands of a different environment.

To help ethnic minority students succeed in school and become competent advocates for culturally diverse clients, schooling practices should nurture and sustain their unique self-image rather than abrogate these differences that compose the matrix of their being. Assimilationist teaching, which presupposes a monocultural value orientation at the expense of students' esteemed values from home, creates total disorganization in students' self-concept and leads to academic failure. Hence, educational goals and processes need to be reconceptualized to realize increased and meaningful ethnic minority participation in health care.

School practices need to promote biculturalism among students instead of a monocultural value orientation that ignores the multicultural constituency of student and client populations. In *biculturalism,* the individual affirms his or her unique self while learning to address the needs of others who may have different values. In contrast, *monoculturalism* upholds a singular value orientation that minimizes or negates diversity.

The literature is replete with recommendations for the education of multicultural student populations. These suggestions need to begin with an understanding and appreciation of these students' indigenous values and predispositions, which significantly influence the way they will negotiate in a world different from their own. The process of biculturalism is facilitated by valuing and affirming the self. Imposing another set of values before students complete this initial process of self-affirmation plunges them into a world where the self is virtually nonexistent.

The process of education transforms the individual's origins and sense of being to a state of active interaction with what is learned and requires the ability to find oneself and make sense of life events. This notion remains valid for adult students in higher education. Having gone through years of elementary and secondary schooling does not guarantee homogeneity in students. Schooling is a component of an individual's life course and, like any other component, is integrated with previous patterns to negotiate with the present and prepare for the future.

Teaching multicultural students the values of any discipline requires special knowledge and skills about them apart from the subject matter. The transcultural approach to teaching applies cultural knowledge and skills about the student and the population we serve in designing and implementing the curriculum. This is underscored by the students' use of their own cultural model (Ogbu, 1991) in dealing with the school environment and in processing the subject matter.

A significant issue for instructors is how best to measure student achievement. School examinations aimed at measuring achievement of universal standards may be biased in requiring cognitive operational skills that are skewed toward values of the dominant group. Minimizing cultural bias in school examinations should not be limited to language but must include an examination of values inherent in cognitive operations expected.

A strong argument for the availability of skilled mentors for culturally diverse students is in order. Mentors make sense of the strange environment by modeling behavioral norms that are otherwise oblivious to students from another cultural perspective. Values embedded in the cognitive configuration result in highly spontaneous, implicitly influenced, and unconsciously conditioned thoughts and behaviors. Values presumed to exist may not be taught, and outsiders to the culture learn such nuances from observing and mimicking others. Bicultural mentors provide a link between their own world and that of the student.

REFERENCES

Belenky, M. F., Clinchy, B. M., Goldberger, N. R., & Tarule, J. M. (1986). *Women's ways of knowing: The development of self, voice and mind.* New York: Basic Books.

Benedict, R. (1934). *Patterns of culture.* Boston: Houghton Mifflin.

Dahrendorf, R. (1979). *Life chances: Approaches to social and political theory.* Chicago: University of Chicago Press.

Dewey, J. (1938). *Experience and education.* New York: Macmillan.

Gilligan, C. (1982). *In a different voice: Psychological theory and women's development.* Cambridge, MA: Harvard University Press.

Goldschmidt, W. (1954). *Ways of mankind.* Boston: Beacon Press.

Hsu, F. L. (1961). American core value and national character. In F. L. Hsu (Ed.), *Psychological anthropology: Approaches to culture and personality* (pp. 209-230). Homewood, IL: Dorsey Press.

Kluckhohn, C. (1949). *The mirror of man: The relation of anthropology to modern life.* New York: Whittlesey House.

Kluckhohn, F. R. (1976). Dominant and variant value orientations. In P. J. Brink (Ed.), *Transcultural nursing: A book of readings* (pp. 63-81). Englewood Cliffs, NJ: Prentice-Hall.

Levine, R. A., & White, M. I. (1986). *Human conditions: The cultural basis of educational development.* New York: Routledge and Kegan Paul.

Ogbu, J. U. (1991). Immigrant and involuntary minorities in comparative perspective. In M. A. Gibson & J. U. Ogbu (Eds.), *Minority status and schooling: A comparative study of immigrant and involuntary minorities* (pp. 3-33). New York: Garland.

Parsons, T. (1951). *The social system.* New York: Free Press.

Parsons, T. (1968). The school as a social system. In *Socialization and schools.* Reprint series No. 1: 69-90. Cambridge, MA: Harvard Educational Review.

Phillips, S. U. (1983). *The invisible culture: Communication in the classroom and community in Warm Springs Indian Reservation.* New York: Longman.

3

The Academic Learning Center (ALC): Building a Culture for Learning

Gail Hein

OPEN FOR LEARNING

*T*he need was obvious. The retention of students had to be our primary objective. We could see two dramatic trends: Our student body was becoming increasingly diverse and too few of our students were retained until graduation. With retention, our multidiscipline focus and our proceeding solutions have worked for us. A county college's purpose is to open the door of academic advancement to all students, to offer students a chance to succeed, and to develop a college-level career field.

Before our Academic Learning Center (ALC) opened, we offered a number of small developmental department-run programs with a common objective: improving the performance of academically underprepared students by providing access to educational ideas, missed or neglected. These programs, however, were scattered across the campus, had few open hours, and used faculty or professional tutors. Too often, students found the doors closed and hours posted on a note. Regular faculty, and adjunct faculty in particular, were simply not available often enough for a structured tutoring laboratory.

To answer these needs, we created a centralized tutoring center. Data tracking the progress of our students indicated that we should focus on the needs of the marginal student who did not necessarily fail, but who did not reregister and simply faded away. We wanted to support students with documented academic difficulties who sought our assistance.

One-to-one tutoring is a logical approach for academic support. Many tutoring programs directed toward the developmental student offer assistance by scheduled appointments and are a result of faculty referrals. Usually, students who have demonstrated difficulties with classroom material are referred to the tutoring center, where they make an appointment with the center staff. After interviews with these referred students, staff members decide whether supplemental support is appropriate. This is an undesirable arrangement because precious time is lost as students make their way through an unnecessary maze of bureaucracy. Our "no appointments" approach saves mountains of paperwork, recording, reminding, and follow-up. It frees us to tutor. No time is wasted with bureaucratic busywork.

DEVELOPMENT OF THE ACADEMIC LEARNING CENTER (ALC)

Although cost was a concern, we decided not to limit the population to developmental students. We wanted the atmosphere for the ALC to be that of a place for learning. Students should find it easy to join in. It should be an "in" place to be, a place to meet others. In a culture for learning, the group approves of raising grades, preparing for exams, studying with friends, and asking questions. If a group's culture is its attitudes, beliefs, and behaviors, then learning is a culture with predictable variables. We chose to implement these variables. Our primary objective has been to replace negative notions of tutoring with positive images that connote learning, success, and growth. Tutoring is a proactive measure that successful students take to achieve and to maintain good grades. Tutoring is also a semester activity, not a sporadic crisis measure to rush to at exam time. Difficult courses are targeted for special attention. Faculty assist with course outlines and materials, and students are invited to come, socialize, and study.

AMBIENCE

The challenge was to create a new atmosphere, to engineer a new way of thinking about learning. Accessible tutoring would permit the student to take the responsibility for his or her own use of the center.

Some complained that without an appointment system we would be paying students—peer tutors—just for sitting around. They had a good point. We reflected that a culture for learning has the component of industriousness, a nonverbal but an overt environmental factor. The common refrain, "I'm bored," rises from lack of meaningful and purposeful activity. A cultural environment supporting learning is charged by the energy of engaged people.

When hired, student peer tutors agree to do clerical, receptionist, and other types of general office work when not tutoring. An unintended consequence of this decision is the busyness around the center. There is no evidence of boredom or hanging around. Everyone is occupied. The air buzzes with conversation and activity. The positive mood of the environment is palpable.

Open hours make a statement about our attitudes and beliefs regarding learning. We are like a 7-Eleven shop (or emergency room), open for 14 hours every school day. Students are responsible and assertive on their own behalf, and we are here on a walk-in basis when they need us.

For many students, the ALC has become a quasi-social life. Students with free time wander in, join a study group, and become acquainted with one another. They form informal support groups, compare notes, and share valuable (and sometimes invaluable) information. There is safety in numbers as well as in the comfortable atmosphere. Studying takes discipline and concentration. Social networking takes the edge off and diffuses the anxiety associated with new behaviors by enabling students to bond with others on campus and to join in campus life. A connection is being developed; the ALC has become "the place to be." Student attrition occurs more often from lack of social bonding than from academic failure. When the student fails to make friends in class, attendance drops, and academic failure ensues. An important student social connection with the institution emerged through the physical location and open floor plan of the center. Rectangular tables accommodating 8 to 10 students are available in abundance. Signs on each table denote the subject or course tutoring that is available at that location. In addition to student peer tutors, professional staff members serve as supervisors. Conversation flows easily. The center is a pleasant place to be.

LOCATION, LOCATION, LOCATION

As with buying real estate, location is the primary variable for success when planning an ALC. On our campus, the central, most accessible, and visible building is the library. So, the library became the physical location for our ALC. The atmosphere of the library, which was infused into the center, proved very helpful because the behaviors expected in a library are purposefulness, serious activity, and high regard for learning. The scholarly search for knowledge is the hallmark of the library. It is very moving to walk up the broad staircase and witness the sea of human beings bent over books in full concentration, or working in tutoring groups. The usual call for library quiet is replaced by the humming sounds of persons fully engaged in learning. This atmosphere sets up an environment with clear and certain messages and expectations. It demonstrates a culture of learning.

Consolidating the existing subject-oriented assistance centers scattered across the campus was necessary because each had been supported by an individual department. The new centralized ALC was responsible for fostering a sense of collegiality among the various segments of the college. The individual departments participate in the ALC Liaison Committee and faculty members recommend potential peer tutors. Each faculty member responding to the request for names of potential tutors receives an acknowledgment. Recommended students also receive a letter of congratulations informing them who submitted their names for this honor. Students appreciate such academic recognition from their professors. The culture of learning arises from positive reinforcement and public praise. The success and recognition of learning should feel good.

PEER TUTORING

Informal peer tutoring is a college tradition. Small clusters of students working together in the cafeteria, the library, empty classrooms, and outside on the lawn and steps serve as social networks. Because commuting students do not have the luxury of the social life of on-campus students, music and sporting events are planned to enhance school spirit. We decided our center would focus on socialization, too.

Our aim is to institutionalize self-direction in studying. The peer tutor approach fosters independence by peer modeling. Tutoring is a prestigious position on campus and has high visibility. These students must have earned an overall 2.5 GPA and a 3.0 in their subject. Students tapped to be tutors feel honored and often identify it as a memorable college event. The tutors get a strong value message for learning and good grades. They showcase excellence and enthusiasm for learning. Having achieved academic success themselves, the tutors have the learning values, beliefs, and behaviors for success. They have defined their own culture of learning.

In addition to earning minimum wage or better, peer tutors report that tutoring improves their own grades. Each tutor has a veteran mentor who guides the new tutor after orientation. The tutors foster cooperative learning by demonstrating to weaker students the study habits of successful students. Tutors have developed workshops on college life, study habits, and exam skills. They become sophisticated in the ways of academic life and mature in their own learning self-direction.

Ongoing tutor training ensures quality and uniform format in the tutoring sessions. Tutors are evaluated each semester, and while there is considerable turnover because it is a two-year college, the consistent training, the tutor manual, and the close supervision assure a high level of tutor competency.

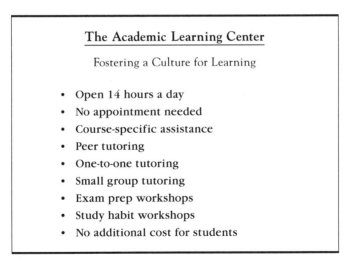

The Academic Learning Center

Fostering a Culture for Learning

- Open 14 hours a day
- No appointment needed
- Course-specific assistance
- Peer tutoring
- One-to-one tutoring
- Small group tutoring
- Exam prep workshops
- Study habit workshops
- No additional cost for students

A MODEL FOR LEARNING

The ALC system is a paradigm for an effective learning environment. Efficient, dynamic, open, humanistic, thorough, current—it speaks to learning and self-development with clear and precise messages. We planned and implemented the Nursing Academic Support Center within this setting. The Transcultural Leadership Continuum (TLC) initiative to improve minority progression was launched with great enthusiasm.

REFERENCES

Bruner, J. (1960). *The process of education.* Cambridge, MA: Harvard University Press.

Genter, D., & Stevens, A. L. (Eds.). (1983). *Mental models.* Hillsdale, NJ: Erlbaum.

Heiman, M. (1991). In A. Costa (Ed.), *"Learning to learn" in developing minds: A resource book on thinking skills.* Washington, DC: Association for Supervision and Curriculum Development.

Heiman, M., & Slomianko, J. (1988). *Methods of inquiry.* Cambridge, MA: Learning to Learn, Inc.

Heiman, M., & Slomainko, J. (1992). *Success in college and beyond.* Allston, MA: Learning to Learn, Inc.

4

The Nursing Academic Support Center (NASC): High Visibility for an Hispanic Nurse Mentor

Myrna Morales Keklak

*T*he Nursing Academic Support Center (NASC) is situated in the Academic Learning Center (ALC), the tutoring center of the college, on the second floor of the college library. Its placement in the ALC is appropriate. Our services incorporate all the tutoring activities of the ALC with the added advantage of the depth of a single discipline. Students' needs vary from academic to social and sometimes require nothing more than a sympathetic ear. In all, the NASC brings nursing to life for hundreds of prospective nursing majors who are in the pre-nursing course phase. The early courses—remedial and basic sciences—are high failure rate courses. Minority students were particularly vulnerable to attrition at this level. The NASC was initiated as a major intervention strategy to improve retention early in the curriculum. We served over 700 nursing students in the 1994–1995 school year. This chapter describes the Center's origin and present development.

AN HISPANIC NURSE MENTOR SPEAKS

The Kean College Alumni newsletter arrived one mid-December morning. The cover story for this issue was an overview of an important grant recently secured by the Kean College Nursing Department in cooperation with the Cooperative Nursing Program of Union County College. The story began with an emphasis on the need for an increase in the racial and ethnic makeup of the leadership in the nursing profession and described the grant's potential impact on the profession's future leaders and on the preparation of a larger number of minority nurses for leadership positions in their communities.

I read the article with no particular interest. It was not the first time, since entering nursing in the 1970s, that I had read about the need for greater numbers of minorities in nursing. It was not until I read the statistical information in the article that I realized how dramatically low minority representation in nursing actually was. And most of these minority nurses were concentrated at the practical nursing, diploma, and associate degree levels. Very few minority nurses possessed the educational credentials needed to emerge as leaders in nursing itself and in minority communities.

I called for more information the following day. The only thing on my mind was my personal desire to further my own education. That phone call changed my nursing career. I asked for information about graduate programs in nursing and the role that this new grant would take in helping nurses attain advanced credentials for leadership positions. I wanted to be a nursing leader. Reviewing the grant's objectives, it was clear that given the opportunity, minority nurses with advanced education could fill the gap that existed in the health care of minority clients. It made me think of why I became a registered nurse.

I am Hispanic. I was surprised how closely my life story mirrored that of many of the students who were to be assisted through this grant. I could feel the passion in me growing. Someone was actually interested in assisting more people like me to enter nursing.

I still remember not being able to envision myself as a nurse. All the nurses I had ever seen were born in the United States and none had to struggle with English as their second language. I had been unable to imagine how someone who had difficulty pronouncing unfamiliar words ever could become a nurse. I wondered out loud how many minority students believed that of themselves and, as a result, were not considering nursing as a career. Would students profit from knowing a nurse who understood their doubts? As an Hispanic, I had experienced them and had still succeeded in becoming a nurse, in spite of it all.

I thought this grant could make a difference and that I needed to be a part of it. Several telephone conversations later, I was offered a position within the grant if I was interested. I was so interested I could not contain myself. I would have a four-hour round-trip—a long commute—and did not know how I was going to fulfill the grant's objectives, but I believed in this project and wanted to be a part of it.

The grant, referred to as the TLC (*Transcultural Leadership Continuum*) by its authors, called for a central goal of minority student access, retention, and mobility in nursing. One of the specific aspects called for the creation of the Nursing Academic Support Center, to be coordinated by a minority registered nurse. This minority nurse, by serving as a mentor and role model for minority nursing majors, would impact on minority nursing major retention in a positive way. Two months after my initial review of the grant, I became one of the minority nursing mentors and coordinator.

STARTING FROM SCRATCH

There I was that early March morning, all prepared to save as many minority nursing majors as possible, with no real idea how it was to be done. All I really had was my own experience. Becoming a nurse was one of the greatest things that had ever happened to me and from that vantage point, I found I could successfully reach students. The most surprising part is that my experiences spoke to all students, simply because feeling out of place and unsure of oneself translates for all human beings, regardless of race, ethnicity, or gender.

We decided that we would introduce the grant to the students through large informal sessions. All nursing majors were invited to a location on the main campus of the college. Several sessions were held, to reach as many students as possible.

With the North lecture room secured, the refreshments ordered, and the letters mailed, the day of the first session finally arrived. I knew that I would be expected to speak and should be prepared. All day I found myself not being able to do that. Something inside me told me what it was that I should do, so I did, and I simply told my story. My story is not always an easy one to tell, and there have been many times when I wish I could go back and change some of the details. Yet for many of my students, it is my story and my honesty in telling it, that helps to keep them believing in themselves. I remember being surprised the first time a student confided in me about her life after explaining that she felt she could trust me, all because I had told my story.

THE NURSING ACADEMIC SUPPORT CENTER BEGINS

The initial sessions were completed and the word was out on the campus. It was obvious by the student turnout at our information sessions that there was need for our center on the campus; the challenge was how to address these needs.

Our students face formidable odds. They are older adults, sometimes returning to school after a number of years; many are single parents; often they are unsure of themselves; some lack strong study and testing skills; and many have extreme language and financial limitations. Some of them have to overcome all these problems.

It took a semester to establish the NASC physical facility and activities. Making nursing very visible was a priority. Lots of nursing pictures and symbols were hung on the walls and doors. Our official opening ceremony with many dignitaries and politicians was a huge success. With extensive publicity, the goals of our project were widely public—and our students were drawn to us. Weekly advertisements in the student newspaper and displays near the biology and chemistry classes invited students, and minority students in particular, to the NASC.

Students arrive at the NASC with all sorts of needs. Sometimes, these needs can be handled with a telephone call to a particular agency of the college or the school of nursing. Often, the student does not recognize a specific need. Many times, anger is a cover for insecurity and confusion. A question about the number of courses a student should carry per semester becomes a way for students to confide that they cannot keep up with the required workload.

Gina

Gina arrived at my door one late afternoon. Small, with dark hair and eyes, she appears meek, but is very self-directed, and although she speaks with a heavy foreign accent, is quite articulate. She is enrolled in a required non-nursing course and, after having requested assistance from her professor with her current course work, was told that her dream of becoming a nurse "may not be realistic." According to Gina, the professor has decided that her difficulties with this course are due to her deficits with the English language and that these deficits will translate into later difficulty with her nursing courses. All this had been decided by the professor without having examined Gina's academic transcript. She has stopped by my office for an opinion on her professor's comments and for my assistance with the course. The course, I know, carries a very high attrition and failure rate among all nursing majors.

Listening to Gina's story without showing emotion was a difficult task for me. At that moment, Gina's story conjured up the many negative experiences my family and I have had to live through: the time in the department store, when the clerk refused to wait on us, claiming in a loud voice that she could not understand a word my mother was saying; . . . the time we stopped for directions while driving to Maryland, and the gas station attendant walked away claiming he could not understand anything my father had said (he never gave my father a chance to repeat himself); . . . I managed to compose myself, asked Gina for her permission to run a copy of her current transcript, and wasn't surprised by what I found. Her grades are excellent, including her English grades. Gina, as is required for all students for which English is a second language, had registered and attended the first few weeks of the English composition and conversation classes designed for the non-native student. She was found to be so advanced that her English professors had her placed in the equivalent college-level class. She proceeded to earn straight A's.

I decided that the only way to help Gina was by letting her know that I believed in her ability and to assure her that her being an Hispanic was neither a negative nor a deficit. It was not until I shared with her my own personal experiences that she began to believe me. Only after she realized that English was not my native language and that I have still managed to be successful in nursing, did she again begin to believe in herself and her goal.

Maria

Maria and I met at an open house for new students. There, she asked me three or four times if I am Hispanic—"Do you speak Spanish?" and "Are you a real nurse?" Since that initial meeting, Maria has stopped by my office regularly, as she puts it, "to make sure you are still there and to look at you." It seems I'm the only "real" Puerto Rican nurse she knows.

TRANSMITTING THE PROFESSIONAL CULTURE

Nursing education's principle goal is to instill in students not only the behaviors but, even more important, the norms and values deemed imperative to growth and to success within the profession. Every day, nurse educators, leaders, administrators, and staff nurses struggle with the challenge of how to transmit the best of professional behaviors and modes of success to the next generation of nurses. This new generation is filled with diversity in both culture and ethnicity. Hispanic students comprise 3% of the country's RN nursing majors. Less than half of this number will successfully complete their studies and meet their goals of obtaining nursing degrees.

As mentor and coordinator of the NASC for the Cooperative Nursing Program majors, I have worked closely with our Hispanic students and have found that my personal experiences as an Hispanic woman and a nurse have contributed to my effectiveness. Because of the large numbers of students the NASC services, I have not been able to be a personal mentor to all students. However, I have become a visible role model for the ethnic students coming to the NASC.

TEACHING THE PROFESSIONAL CULTURE

Both role modeling and mentoring enhance student learning and overall success within the profession. The use of the role model has been accepted as a method for teaching professional attitudes and behaviors. A profession portrays its basic values through its practitioners—its role models. We are all three things: the nurse we think we are; the one we would like to be; the nurse that others see. It is the latter that is the modeled role (Kramer, 1968).

Critics of the role models used in nursing education believe that while students learn from the role model, this type of learning is passive and limited (Hamilton & Smoyak, 1978). Nevertheless, it is an accepted strategy for transmitting professional attitudes and behaviors from faculty to students. Role modeling is idealistic and imitative (Bidweol, 1989).

The effective role model realistically demonstrates the role to the neophyte. Self-perception of the role grows as the learner acts in the role. Discussions of personal and affective aspects of the role experiences enhance learning and insight for both the role model and the learner. Role models motivate, encourage, and direct the learner toward higher goals. As a role model and mentor, I am innovative, empower others, and assist them to be goal directed. By being caring and understanding, identification and attachment occur with the learner. Being a minority nurse facilitates the identification and attachment process for minority students, who can learn from me, a seasoned practitioner. Goals and values have congruency when life experiences are seen as similar. Things become possible because I am real to them and from their world. They can become like me. I elicit appropriate behaviors and attitudes in the learner who is observing me. By replicating my behavior patterns, the learners' current and future behaviors merge into desired professional behaviors (communication style, aseptic technique, safety, study skills). As mentor/role model to minority students at our NASC, I have bridged the gap between cultures through familiarity with and understanding of the cultural differences.

A model has a greater impact on the individual student through actions and behaviors than through spoken words. Mentor and role model, which are similar concepts, share many of the same attributes. As a result, people often use these concepts interchangeably. Mentoring, however, is a long-term, active process between an experienced individual and a neophyte. Through the developing relationship, the professional provides sponsorship, guidance, education, and personal assistance. The goal of this relationship is the advancement of the neophyte's career. The mentor role is a strategy for transmitting knowledge, attitudes, and professional behavior from the experienced to the nonexperienced, which requires active participation on the part of both individuals. The mentor/neophyte relationship is a long-term, one-to-one, emotional involvement that is not available to all, but is reserved for the few who are identified as having special potential (Bidwell & Brasler, 1989). Being the mentor/role model in the NASC has a multiplier effect. My high visibility, accessibility, and overtly Hispanic identification make me very public. Minority students are welcome and they know it.

MENTORING HISPANIC STUDENTS

Hispanics graduate from nursing programs in the smallest number of all ethnic groups. Hispanic communities rank highest in health care needs. Do Hispanic students have particular mentoring needs, and as an Hispanic nurse, what are the implications for me personally and professionally?

Ethnic minorities are geographically stable after graduation. They return to their communities as nurses. These indigenous nurses are known to their communities. They communicate positive health values as well as serve as an effective force to improve health services (Werning, 1992).

Hispanic students often have English as a second language, feel very loyal to their own culture and have limited experience in higher education. Does an Hispanic student need a Hispanic mentor or role model? In the Hispanic culture, trust is reserved for the immediate family and then is earned slowly by a limited outside circle. My being Hispanic and Spanish speaking is a catalyst in the mentoring relationship. I have experienced the cultural evolution needed. They ask me, "How much of my culture must I forfeit to be in an American college, learning how to be a professional nurse?" I can tell them that it is not so much shedding one culture for another. One is not "better" than another. Rather, the culture of nursing—how to act, think, and talk like a nurse—is the process of learning and interpreting new behaviors into the total personality of the person.

The NASC is a vehicle for me to be a visible minority—an Hispanic nurse. By far, my role is that of education. But my name is Morales, and it gives me the freedom to introduce delicate topics of ethnicity and differences. My story is one of perseverance and growth and it will fall on eager ears. If my face looks familiar and it makes me more approachable—all the better. The purpose of the NASC is clear: more well-educated nurses for communities in need. Role modeling and mentoring for each student, one by one, moves each closer to the community and professional practice.

HISPANIC NEEDS

Hispanics constitute 8.2% of the U.S. population. Less than half have access to adequate health care. Morbidity and mortality rates are higher than those of the white majority (Werning, 1992). Less than 50% of Hispanic adults have completed a high school education. This is reflected in the Hispanic unemployment rate, which is double that of the nation's average (Cresce, 1992).

It is estimated that by the year 2030, minorities will account for about 40% of the U.S. population; Hispanics, currently the fastest growing minority group, are predicted to be a large part of this number (Exter, 1993). If nursing wants to impact on the quality of life of minorities, such as the Hispanic population, efforts must be made to reach this population and what better way than through mentors and role models. Minority health care providers are more likely to return to their own communities, and are able to bond and communicate with the minority clients they serve. Having minority representation, in the form of more Hispanic nurses, can reduce the misconceptions that exist about the minority groups. Negative stereotyping diminishes through personal interactions with ethnic groups. Hispanic students enter the nursing programs with significant needs. The most common educational needs are difficulties with the English language, a lower level and quality of prior education, and problems in accepting the realities of cultural changes.

The issues of language and education can vary greatly, depending on the amount of time the individual has spent in this country, the length and quality of the education both here and in the country of origin, and the individual's level of acculturation.

Hispanics view cultural changes with great concern and in contrast to their feelings of loyalty to their own culture. Cultural change is a needed process in ensuring the student's success in nursing. There is some merit to this concern shown by Hispanics. It is a reality that there is pressure to assume some dominant American values. Knowing an Hispanic nurse who has lived, experienced, and made the transition into the professional culture facilitates change.

Trust is the cornerstone of a role model-mentor and neophyte relationship, and as previously stated, Hispanics extend trust cautiously. They also attach great significance to showing respect for their language and culture. The role model and mentor must know and honor these attributes.

The use of Hispanic nurses to mentor and to serve as role models for Hispanic nursing majors has advantages. These nurses, by virtue of their own transitional experiences, are more aware of and sensitive to the special needs of these students. They can support the cultural shifts that the students must accomplish. Trust can be addressed because it is understood by the Hispanic nurse who has lived the experience.

There are also potential disadvantages in using Hispanic nurses to mentor Hispanic students. A dependent relationship may develop between the role model or mentor and student. Hispanics are not a homogeneous group. Significant cultural differences exist among Hispanic groups from different Spanish-speaking countries, and they have diverse histories of immigration to the United States. Thus, an Hispanic nurse with similar cultural background is not always available for mentoring or to serve as a role model.

Nevertheless, the advantages outweigh the apparent disadvantages, and Hispanic nurses should be utilized to assist students, especially in areas of acculturation that require the understanding of different value systems. Examples of value system differences that exist between Hispanic and white, middle-class Americans are the issue of trust, a group rather than individual orientation toward success, and the reluctance of Hispanics to focus group attention on oneself. Who then to better to assist Hispanic nursing majors with these conflicts of value systems than a nurse who understands and shares the student's value system but also knows the need for openness to realize success?

REFERENCES

Bandura, A. (1977). *Social learning theory*. Englewood Cliffs, NJ: Prentice-Hall.

Beck, C. (1991). How students perceive faculty caring: A phenomenological study. *Nurse Educator, 16*(5), 18-22.

Bidwell, A., & Brasler, M. (1989). Role modeling versus mentoring in nursing education. *Image: Journal of Nursing Education, 21*(1), 23-25.

Cresce, A. R. (1992). Hispanic workforce characteristics. In S. B. Knouse, P. Rosenfeld, & A. L. Culbertson (Eds.), *Hispanics in the workplace* (pp. 9-28). Newbury Park, CA: Sage.

Davis, J., & Rodella, E. S. (1992). Mentoring for the Hispanics: Mapping emotional support. In S. B. Knouse, P. Rosenfeld, & A. L. Culbertson (Eds.), *Hispanics in the workplace* (pp. 151-169). Newbury Park, CA: Sage.

Exter, T. G. (1993, February). The largest minority. *American Demographics,* 59.

Hamilton, M. (1981). Mentorhood: A key to nursing leadership. *Nursing Leadership, 4*(1), 4-13.

Kitchener, K. (1992). Psychologist as teacher and mentor: Affirming ethical values throughout the curriculum. *Professional Psychology: Research and Practice, 23*(3), 190-195.

Knouse, S. B. (1992). The mentoring process for Hispanics. In S. B. Knouse, P. Rosenfeld, & A. L. Culbertson (Eds.), *Hispanics in the workplace* (pp. 137-150). Newbury Park, CA: Sage.

Kramer, M. (1968). Role models, role conception, and role deprivation. *Nursing Research, 17*(2), 115-120.

La Rosa, M. D. (1989, May). Health care needs of Hispanic Americans and the responsiveness of the health care system. *Health and Social Work,* 104-113.

McNeese-Smith, D. (1992). The impact of leadership upon productivity. *Nursing Economics, 10*(6), 393-396.

Morrison, P. (1989). Nursing and caring: A personal construct theory study of some nurses' self-perceptions. *Journal of Advanced Nursing, 14,* 421-426.

Parathian, A., & Taylor, F. (1993). Can we insulate trainee nurses from exposure to bad practice? A study of role play in communicating bad news to patients. *Journal of Advanced Nursing, 18,* 801-807.

Thomas, I. M. (1995, August). First steps. *Hispanic,* 64-66.

Werning, S. C. (1992). The challenge to make a difference: Minorities in health care today. *Health Care Trends & Transition, 4*(1), 33-46.

5

Learning to Learn* (LTL): Offering the Student Academic Behaviors That Work

Henry Kaplowitz and Suzanne Bousget

*W*e needed a common language for learning. With so many students doing poorly, it seemed reckless not to attend to the process of learning.

Our students struggled in several ways. Many had difficulty with organization and priority setting. They wanted to memorize everything. Many had never really studied and had no idea how to begin. Some students getting the lowest grades on the exams claimed they were spending many hours studying. Students born abroad had difficulty with multiple-choice questions in particular and paper-and-pencil or computer exams overall. Success on such exams is essential because it is the major form of evaluation in the United States. Most professional board and licensing examinations require paper-and-pencil or computer skills.

---

*Learning to Learn, Inc.®, P.O. Box 38-1351, Cambridge, MA 02238 (1-800-28THINK), was developed by Marcia Heiman and Joshua Slomianko.

We chose Learning to Learn (LTL) for our students because exam preparation can be simply and systematically mastered. Student retention is linked to exam success. Evolving a culture for learning required that we provide our heterogeneous students with a homogeneous approach to learning.

We also needed a method suitable for diverse students. The United States Department of Education found that LTL is the only college-level program that has been demonstrated as:

- Effective for both average and nontraditional students.
- Significant in improving college students' grade point average and retention in college.
- Not requiring subject matter tutoring.
- Having a significant impact on students' retention through graduation.

The combination of behaviors, material organization, and asking questions was what we needed. Learning to Learn prepares students for active, high-level learning. Professional development demanded that the students be able to apply, synthesize, and evaluate what they were learning. Learning to Learn gives the students conceptually sound, accessible strategies that lead to productive critical thinking and intellectual development.

Our low graduation rate, common in community colleges, indicated a more structured approach would be helpful. Language, behaviors, attitudes, and beliefs—the LTL package offered each. There are many study methods. Choosing a very effective one and then making it a part of the curriculum of our programs forced and shaped the learning environment.

GENERAL OVERVIEW OF LEARNING TO LEARN

Learning to Learn was developed by Dr. Marcia Heiman and Joshua Slomianko. The LTL system has its genesis in the theory and practice of behavioral psychology. Nearly 30 years ago, Dr. Heiman was part of a group of graduate students at the University of Michigan. The group used techniques of behavioral analysis to identify critical learning skills common to successful learners. Rather than focusing on the traditional techniques of diagnosis and remediation of unsuccessful students, the group sought to discover what was systematic and predictable about successful students' learning. By studying behaviors common to good learners, an attempt was made to isolate skills that could be taught to failing students in a relatively short period of time. These behaviors were identified by asking the successful student to make internal events external and explicit—to talk aloud their thoughts as they engaged in a variety of academic tasks.

The Michigan group found that successful students commonly use the following major learning tools:

- They ask questions of new materials, engaging in an overt dialogue with the author or lecturer, forming hypotheses, reading or listing for confirmation.
- They identify the component parts of complex principles and ideas, breaking down major tasks into smaller units.
- They devise informal feedback mechanisms to assess their own progress in learning.
- They focus on instructional objectives, identifying and directing their study behaviors to meet course objectives.

These skills were translated into a set of exercises that failing students could apply directly to their academic work, and formed the basis of LTL.

THE LEARNING TO LEARN SYSTEM

Learning to Learn contains general learning skills, which apply to all subject-matter-areas, and subject-specific skills, which relate to the structure of complex academic disciplines, like economics or chemistry. Students begin using learning LTL skills by systematically generating questions from lecture notes and reading materials. By generating questions that directly reflect the material under study, students begin to ask themselves the kinds of questions addressed by the fields they are studying.

The LTL system contains a number of skills that are subject specific, determined by a given field's structure, by the kinds of questions it raises and by the kinds of behaviors and subskills required of the student. For example, both history and economics ask cause/effect questions. However, Heiman and Slomianko's' work on the questions asked by differing fields suggest that history as a discipline often focuses on the effects of sequential events, whereas economics emphasizes the effects of simultaneous events. In order to clarify the interactions among simultaneous events, economics uses a variety of graphs. Thus, the structure of economics dictates the need for a subject-specific learning skill: teaching students to translate from prose to graphs, and back to prose. Again, the major principles in Learning to Learn form the basis of the strategies used: Students learn how to break down complex problems into component parts and to form ongoing questions about the material—in this case, about material presented in both prose and graphic form. In sum, a determination of the relevant subject-specific LTL skills is not deduced from a general theory of cognition, but varies according to the explicit characteristics of the field under study.

LEARNING TO LEARN STRATEGIES

Questioning new material is a strategy that promotes comprehension. It may be effective because students are provided a format or structure for new material and are forced to think meaningfully about what they read or hear. From research in cognitive psychology, we know that structure enhances comprehension and memory. Furthermore, questioning promotes deeper and more complex thoughts about new material. This "deep processing" provides for a longer lasting memory. Thus, research conducted under more sterile laboratory conditions in cognitive psychology is consistent with predicting that questioning will be an effective learning strategy in promoting greater comprehension and memory.

Devising informal feedback mechanisms is an important "metacognitive" activity—that is, students must reflect on their own thinking and learning process. Again, researchers in cognitive psychology have demonstrated that fast learners know where to look for learning deficits. Fast learners can assess deficits and are more likely to correct a deficit immediately. Thus, the prediction is that if students can be trained to identify and correct learning deficits, to tease apart what they know from what they do not, they will become more effective learners.

Focusing on objectives or being knowledgeable about the criterion task is critical if a student must correctly choose one learning strategy over alternatives. A student who can accurately assess the criterion task (be it multiple-choice exam, essay exam, or written paper) can select the most effective learning strategy. In laboratory demonstrations that compare informed and uninformed students' performance, informed students outperform the uninformed. Training in assessing the criterion task and selecting an appropriate learning strategy will improve student performance.

Dividing a complex task into smaller segments is an important success skill. Few would argue with this strategy, yet this strategy has had less research attention in cognitive psychology than the others.

Each of these activities that "good" students engage in is used in each LTL technique. Some of the major LTL techniques as they relate to the stages of information processing follow:

1. *Input Skills.* Generating questions from lecture notes and assigned readings.
2. *Organization Skills.* Information maps and task management.
3. *Output Skills.* Exam preparation.

HISTORY OF LEARNING TO LEARN AT KEAN COLLEGE

Traditionally, learning assistance efforts focus on tutoring. However, innovative learning assistance efforts are necessary when providing a comprehensive learning support system for the academic success and ultimate persistence of today's student. During the summer of 1987, Kean College introduced a three-credit LTL course that was designed to enhance student academic success by modeling a variety of learning strategies that are used by successful students. These strategies include ways to learn new material effectively, to organize information, and to enhance memory for information. The learning strategies represent applications of behavioral psychology. Learning to Learn courses are used at over 100 colleges nationally, and are marketed by Learning to Learn, Inc. through the textbooks *Success in College and Beyond* and *College—A New Beginning.* Students enrolled in the course are taught the strategies, which they then apply in their other academic courses at Kean College. The course is required of all entering Equal Education Opportunity (EEO) students at the college, and EEO students placed on academic probation. At the discretion of each school's dean, the course may be required of regularly admitted students placed on academic probation. The course is recommended to all freshmen, but freshmen admitted to the college under the category of "Special Admission," whose Scholastic Aptitude Test (SAT) scores or high school performance fall short of standard admission criteria, are strongly encouraged during advisement to enroll in the course. To serve the college's Spanish-speaking population, at least two sections of the course are taught in Spanish each semester.

LEARNING TO LEARN SUCCESS

Evaluations of the effectiveness of the LTL course have been conducted for the Equal Education Opportunity (EEO) population. EEO students who took the LTL course significantly improved their academic performance as indexed by their grade point average (GPA). The improvement was statistically significant at the $p < .01$ level.

Another way to examine the effectiveness of the LTL course was to compare the EEO cohort (students who enrolled at the college prior to the offering of the course) with an earlier cohort. During the spring semester, average GPA for the cohort was 2.32 (standard deviation = .75), whereas the average GPA for the experimental group was 2.57 (standard deviation = .85). The difference in average GPA was statistically significant [$t(152) = 1.82$, $p < .05$]. Thus, EEO students who have had the benefit of the LTL course show a higher GPA than those students who have not taken the course.

LEARNING TO LEARN TRAINING

There are annual internal training initiatives in which Kean College faculty, administrators, and professional staff are trained to teach the LTL course. In addition, statewide training initiatives were implemented early in the history of LTL at Kean College. In June 1989, the New Jersey State Department of Higher Education provided funds for a Summer Institute, an intensive training experience, that was open to faculty, administrators, and staff of New Jersey public and private colleges and universities. Since then, training has also been conducted for secondary, middle, and elementary school educators and administrators from a variety of New Jersey cities and townships.

Training involves introducing faculty, staff, and administrators to the particular LTL strategy by asking them to actively engage in the learning process. Hands-on experience is provided for each LTL strategy. For example, those being trained are asked to take actual notes during a brief college-level lecture. Those who receive training are asked to participate as if they were students taking the LTL course. Furthermore, materials selected for use during training represent the typical content of a course (e.g., faculty who teach nursing students work with materials selected from the nursing field).

Typical training involves a team of faculty members who have all received extensive training in LTL strategy instruction. At Kean College, those who train other faculty have also taught the LTL course. The team approach enriches the training process because each faculty member can provide a particular perspective from his or her own academic discipline. While one faculty trainer presents a skill during the training procedure, other faculty trainers can join those who are participating in the training activity and answer questions, clarify procedures, and offer support.

With the support of the Robert Wood Johnson Foundation grant, arrangements were made for a team of trainers from Kean College to

Figure 5.1   Student Notes from a Class on Cardiac
            Assessment Non-LTL Style

Lecture 9/10/94

Cardiac Assessment
A. History - inquire about chief complaint for priority nursing
        intervention.
   Common S + S - chest pain, dyspnea, fatigue, palpitation,
        syncope, weight gain + edema
   1. chest pain - common ocurrence in cardiac disorder such
      as MI, myocardial, ischemia, pericardites. Also in
      pulmonary diseases such as pleurisy, pneumonia, pulm
      embolism. May be associated with anxiety - often a result
      of myocardial ischemia i.e., lack of blood supply to myocar-
      dial tissues. highly variable in nature characteristics-
      maybe described as "strange feeling" indigestion, dull,
      heavy pressure, burning, crushing, constricting, vise-like,
      aching, stabbing Usually substernal. or precordial
      May radiate to shoulders, arms Note time when pain
      begins + ends. M.J. chest pain lasts longer than 1/2 hr.
      or till intervention is done. Anginal pain lasts less than
      20-30 min. + relieved by rest or nitroglycerin.

provide training in LTL techniques to faculty and staff members of the
institutions involved in the grant during the Spring 1993 semester. This
included separate sessions for the day, evening, and weekend nursing
faculty and support staff of the Cooperative Nursing Program; the faculty at Union College who are primarily members of the English, Biology, and Mathematics Departments; the staff of the Academic Learning
Center (ALC) and the Nursing Academic Support Center (NASC), and
the nursing department faculty at Kean College.

Each training program lasted the equivalent of two days and took the
form of a hands-on workshop. For example, participants were required to
take notes on a lecture and develop questions from their notes using the
LTL method. Likewise, they not only learned the LTL method for reading

Figure 5.2   Student Notes from a Class on Cardiac Assessment LTL Style

Lecture 9/4/95
Cardiac Assessment

Why is it important
to identify pt's
chief complaint?

History - Inquire re: chief complaint to est.
   priorities for nursing intervention: to
   evaluate pt's understanding of condition

Common S+S: 1) chest pain

What are the common
presenting complaints
of pts c̄ cardiac
disorders?

   2) dyspnea
   3) fatigue
   4) palpitation
   5) syncope
   6) weight gain - edema

Explain the basic
pathophysiology of
chest pain due to
cardiac disorders?

1) Chest pain - commonly occurs in cardiac disorders
   but can be present in pulmonary diseases; may
   also be associated with anxiety
   - often a result of myocardial ischemia, i.e.,
     lack of blood supply to myocardial tissues

Why is it important
to assess chest
pain thoroughly

   - highly variable in nature due to diff. causes.
     Therefore, needs to be evaluated thoroughly using
     descriptive data:

How might a pt.
describe his/her
chest pain?

   Characteristics - "strange feeling", dull, heavy
   pressure, "indigestion", burning, crushing, con-
   stricting, vise-like, stabbing, burning tightness
   Location - usually substernal or precordial,
   may radiate to neck, jaw, teeth, one or both
   arms, shoulders, back

Differentiate between
M.I. chest pain
and anginal chest
pain.

   Duration - note time when pain begins + ends,
   generally M.I. chest pain lasts longer than
   ½ hour or till intervention is instituted. Anginal
   pain usually lasts less than 20-30 min & relieved by

Figure 5.3   A Student Generated Information Map on Chest Pain

Chest pain of:

	Myocardial Infection	Angina Pectoris
What is the etiology of the chest pain	Unrelieved ischemia due to complete obstruction of coronary artery-causing irreversible damage.	Temporary ischemia due to partially obstructed coronary artery.
What are the characteristics of the pain?	More severe, prolonged crushing, radiating to one or both arms, neck + back. Sharp, Knife-like. Lasts more than 30 min.	Mild to moderate, short duration 5-15 min. "indigestion", "gas", burning, squeezing not sharp.
What relieves the pain?	Unrelieved by rest or nitroglycerin. Responds to narcotics e.g. morphine.	Usually relieved by rest (sitting or lying down) and nitroglycerin.

textbooks, but applied it to texts in their own field. With regard to organizational strategies, nursing school faculty in particular vied with one another to come up with the most useful applications of information maps.

Throughout the sessions, a dialogue ensued between the Kean College trainers and the respective faculty trainees regarding the difficulties they perceive in teaching relatively underprepared students such difficult courses as anatomy and physiology, pharmacology, and the various clinical nursing courses. Most of the faculty assumed that the very high failure and attrition rates that they experienced in their courses were inevitable. The trainers, however, had all worked with similarly underprepared students in the LTL classes at Kean College. They had watched most of their students develop information-processing skills and become competent, successful students. By trading anecdotes and war stories, and by encouraging an open and frank discussion of problems, the endorsement of the LTL methodology by the trainers became more credible. At the end of each training program, most of the faculty left enthused and even the most cynical felt it was worth a try. The administrators of the nursing schools capitalized on the enthusiasm of their faculties and set up teams to integrate the LTL techniques into the curriculum.

TEACHING AND LEARNING CHANGES IN THE CLASSROOM

To facilitate integrating LTL across our programs, a remedial course, IDS 095, was chosen as the vehicle to teach the method. LTL saturation was attempted. Our nurse mentors, the faculties, the NASC staff, even bulletin boards, talked LTL. Faculty rewrote lectures and developed new assignments to implement LTL in their courses. While LTL is not subject dependent, faculty wanted to support the methodology in each course. Learning to Learn strategies enabled learning as a behavioral system to be discussed. Faculty checked the students' notebooks. Classes generated questions and developed information maps.

CHANGING LEARNING BEHAVIORS

Students found it extremely difficult to change learning styles. We were asking them to change their learning culture, their beliefs, and behaviors, and resistance was formidable. Even in the face of success (better grades on exams), students sometimes dropped back from using LTL.

Witnessing these behaviors, we have become aware that when a student moves from failure to success, many equations in his or her life are shaken. Wished-for goals might be achieved, roles in marriages and families are altered, and relationships shift. The student is being asked to think on a higher cognitive level, to move to an inquiry method of exploring content, and to problem solve. The cultural shift needed to assume new professional beliefs, behaviors, and language causes students to move through the rigors of evaluation of their ethnic, cultural, and socioeconomic class norms. Success means a better job, higher family income, and a college degree. Success means change in the entire social constellation of the student.

Learning to Learn and its success has become the fulcrum for cultural change in our programs. Learning to Learn makes success possible because it offers organization where there was chaos. It has become the academic language to a diverse, multicultural group of students and faculty.

REFERENCES

Andre, T., & Sola, J. (1976). Imagery, verbatim and paraphrased questions, and retention of meaningful sentences. *Journal of Educational Psychology, 68,* 661-669.

Brown, S. I., & Walter, M. I. (1983). *The art of problem posing.* The Franklin Institute Press.

Heiman, M. (1987). "Learning to learn: A behavioral approach to improving thinking," in D. Perkins et al., (Eds.), pp. 431-452. *Thinking: The second international conference.* Hillsdale, NJ: Erlbaum.

Heiman, M., & Slomianko, J. (1992). *Success in college and beyond.* Allston, MA: Learning to Learn, Inc.

Peck, J. E. (1981). *Critical thinking and education.* New York: St. Martin's Press.

Wilen, W. W. (1982). *Questioning skills for teachers.* Washington, DC: National Education Association.

6

Learning to Learn (LTL) Finds Critical Placement in a Preclinical Sequence

Paula D. Tropello

GOIN' FISHING

*P*articipatory learning—which actively involves both the teacher and student—is dynamic learning: This interactive process is limited when the student is struggling academically and doesn't understand why achievement is so elusive. Although basic skills courses identify and remediate some problem areas, students enter the core curricula still at risk.

Especially at risk are students from other cultures, primarily recent immigrants with English as a second language. Often they come without having mastered critical thinking and organizational strategies. Often they learn by rote memory. Also at risk are the students who have been marginally successful in local secondary school systems, graduating with limited academic strengths. They enter our college and find that they are in need of basic math, writing, and reading skills.

Academic early intervention is best for at-risk students, who are open to change and are more willing to adopt new behaviors as they begin college courses. Learning to Learn is an overt thinking program that teaches the students to organize, to think, to analyze, and to be ready for exams. They are proactive behaviors for independence and success. Give a man a fish and you feed him for a day. Teach a man to fish and you feed him for a lifetime. Our students are ready to fish.

EARLY AND OFTEN

Learning to Learn works for diverse groups of students. We find that it is best to introduce LTL skills very early in the prenursing curriculum before the demands of the heavy sciences. Later, students are reluctant to relinquish even unsuccessful habits; they are less open to change.

We placed LTL in an early, noncredit, interdisciplinary course. It is a nonthreatening setting, and students are immersed in the new learning strategies. They get a continuous cycle of modeling, dialogue, practice, and confirmation in LTL. Faculty are mentors moving the students into the academic context of the college.

Learning to Learn is mandatory for all students doing English remediation courses. Saturation in these skills is accomplished and overrides the students' fear of another failure. Mandatory attendance emphasizes and prioritizes the importance of the content.

NARROWING CULTURAL GAPS

There is an American classroom. Teachers expect participation, individualism, questioning, and an ability to do paper-and-pencil tests. This is how we do it here. Other cultures have far different norms. For them, being quiet, reticent, nonassertive, and deferential to others represents appropriate behavior. Cultural differences in our classrooms influence how the teachers view the students. When the teacher wants the student to ask questions, and the student views questioning as an affront to an authority figure, the cultural gap may preclude effective learning.

Learning to Learn serves as a bridge between cultures. It gives the new student permission to speak out and participate in discussions. Comfort levels rose when we introduced LTL questioning methods. Using lecture notes to generate questions is less threatening. The student

Table 6.1   Sample: Information Map

	How Many Years to Achieve?	What Type of Education?	How Much Salary Is Earned?
LPN	1 year	Certificate	20–30K
RN	2–3 years	Diploma and/or Associate	30–40K
BSN	4 years	Bachelor of Science	35–50K
MSN	1–2 years beyond BSN	Master of Science	40–60K

is not questioning or challenging the teacher but rather is doing required homework and, in fact, only questioning him- or herself.

Using ethical dilemmas and career development examples serve as energizing formats. Our students generated topics, for example, clarifying the various levels of nursing. They used the computer search CD-ROM to gather data, assembled abstracts, and in small groups constructed information maps. Table 6.1 illustrates how the students began.

As faculty, we were taken aback that one important focus for the students was nurses' salaries. But, the topic got everyone talking. The students were very articulate—economic and social mobility were priorities for them. Students lengthened the chart, asked many questions, and increased the chart's complexity.

ASKING IS OK

Learning to use the college facilities orients students to the campus. Why was I astonished when a student confided in me that to ask for directions to the library or bookstore was a "losing face" experience for her? Cultural differences assault self-perception. Humanistic teaching demands that we gain insight into the experiences and feelings of our diverse students. Students wrestle with feelings of humiliation because of limited vocabulary skills. Both international and American-educated students need the LTL glossary development methods. As questions are formulated, unfamiliar words are added to the notebook glossary. Word definitions are broad enough for clarity. Visualizing and using the words are strong reinforcers. When students do not understand words in test question stems, they miss the entire question. Writing skill practice helps to polish vocabulary development and dovetails with LTL's question format. It makes sense to ask what is the main idea, what are the relevant facts, because these are basic LTL questions.

EXAM TERROR

Haitian- and Jamaican-born students talked at length about the difficult transition they experience with American written exams. They had never taken multiple-choice exams. Test anxiety was pronounced. Again LTL gave them skills training. Item stems were analyzed and irrelevant distractors discussed. The women gained confidence when they felt a sense of mastery.

Relaxation techniques and guided imagery were helpful. So was giving permission to tape-record lectures. The day the Haitian students had me take notes as they spoke French Creole was the day I understood their world. We also asked their professors to keep blackboard notes up longer so that the ESL (English as a second language) students could copy them at a slower pace. It was necessary to practice exams with the students to balance the time spent and the weight placed on exams.

THE READING KEY

Learning to Learn's focus on reading for meaning and writing key questions served students in their critical reading skills. Formulating questions gave the students pride in mastering information organization. The classes moved from lower level "mirror" questions to higher level summary questions that demonstrated an interpretation of information on an analysis level. We capitalized on cultural group norms supporting cooperation rather than competition by using a class structure of consistent small groups.

Our groups were struggling academically because of limited fluency with graphs, charts, focused writing, and the ability to compare and contrast facts and information. Repeated LTL exercises interpreting graphs, charts, and maps cut from newspapers increased skill and confidence. They learned to read readings and summaries for meaning. Scanning, a simple yet essential reading comprehension tool, is LTL work also.

SKILLS FOR FITTING IN

Students who learned to use the tools of organization and analysis felt more comfortable in college classes. They expressed this as being the way they felt when they knew how to skate or ride a bike when neighborhood children wanted to play. It's necessary to feel comfortable and competent in order to participate.

Students needing additional work with English explained that they don't feel as if they are "really in college" until they have completed the basic skill courses. Feeling part of college life supports academic success. Students feel excitement, revitalization, and gratitude when they have mastered tools for structure and feedback.

Learning to Learn offered all minority and foreign-born at-risk students precise methods to think like a college student. Exposure to the LTL class format very early in the students' curriculum simplifies their complex needs and breaks the sophisticated levels of academic skills into learnable and logical phases. The processes of LTL refine essential communication and interpersonal skills. Understanding, planning, and developing alliances respect cultural differences and support the language and behaviors of the college arena.

REFERENCES

Adler, M. J. (1982). *The Paideia Proposal: An education manifesto.* New York: Macmillan.

Boyer, E. (1989). Connection through liberal education. *Journal of Professional Nursing, 5*(2), 102–107.

Heiman, M., & Slomainko, J. (1988). *Methods of inquiry.* Cambridge, MA: Learning to Learn, Inc.

Heiman, M., & Slomainko, J. (1992). *Success in college and beyond.* Allston, MA: Learning to Learn, Inc.

Nursing Remediation Task Force Report. (1995, June). Union County College/Elizabeth General Medical Center School of Nursing, Elizabeth, NJ.

7

Infusing Learning to Learn (LTL) in a Clinical Nursing Course

Carol Conti, Lisa Carhart Lontai, and Teresita Proctor

TARGETING MINORITY STUDENT RETENTION

*M*inority student retention takes a big hit in two places in the curriculum. Half the group is lost in developmental courses. When literacy and math skills are too weak (below 10th-grade level), the developmental lag is too great to recover in a year or two. Fluency in reading and math are imperative and irreplaceable. They are cumulative skills that take repetition and time to refine. Minority students with limited high school success are caught with literacy skills too underdeveloped to manage the sciences.

Another 50% of minority students are lost in the second nursing clinical course. Faculty trained in Learning to Learn (LTL) targeted these students for special attention. That the students were ethnic minorities seemed both irrelevant and relevant. In analyzing the students' needs, learning style is an issue. Learning the behaviors, attitudes, and beliefs of professional nursing meant initiating the students into a new culture. Faculty were educating the students to be nurses. To become nurses, students had to master certain content, behaviors, and skills. The ethnicity of the student was irrelevant to having a safe, competent practitioner. A safe practitioner is a safe practitioner.

On the other hand, because we had a commitment to improving minority student retention rates, an attrition rate of 50% for minority students in this particular course posed a challenge. If we could improve minority retention in this clinical course, overall minority retention to graduation rates would improve. Our outcomes assessment processes indicated that LTL would be a useful strategy. Faculty had been trained in LTL, and we decided to have the first major, across-the-board implementation of LTL in this second clinical course. Learning to Learn offered a concrete, systematic way to talk about learning. Learning to Learn had been demonstrated as most effective with minority students. Learning to Learn was introduced into the targeted course.

STUDENTS USE THE LEARNING TO LEARN METHODS

It was difficult for the students as they grappled with a new way of learning, but they liked the integration of the techniques into the classroom learning activities. Many were eager and enthusiastic to begin using the LTL strategies. The strategy that received the most time and attention was generating questions from lecture notes. A sample lecture on cardiovascular assessment was provided to every student in class during the first day of school and the instructor showed the class how to generate critical thinking questions. The students were encouraged to ask WHY and HOW questions. They were required to look for reasons and relationships. By the fourth week of the semester, the students were getting quite efficient at critical thinking questions. Instructors praised and encouraged the students, but the best reinforcement came from the ability to anticipate exam questions. "A couple of the questions I generated were actually asked in the test, not the exact words but the idea was exactly the same. I was so excited!" happy students exclaimed.

The students were excited and the instructors were elated. Learning to Learn was paying off. Successful students took class notes in LTL style. They began to design questions relating to lecture content. Questions moved from mirror questions (directly reflecting information in the notes) to summary questions (identifying main ideas), "What if . . . ?"

questions (showing variations in the information being learned), and creative questions (going beyond the information given). Notes were better organized, key points were identified quickly, and at the same time the students were preparing for exams.

SOCRATES IN THE CLASSROOM

Our classroom became a Socratic forum. Teachers and students were engaged in question-answer dialogue. Even in a class of 30 students, an internal dialogue went on as students asked questions and sought confirmation or denial of hypotheses while listening to a lecture or reading a book. The students were learning to use the scientific method as well as the subject matter. Hypotheses were confirmed or denied by the data. Questions were providing a frame of reference to organize facts. Isolated facts are difficult to retain. Information organized into patterns and trends is more easily recalled and applied. The question approach helped the students to think and to act like nurses. It assisted them to move into the professional role—to assume the cultural beliefs, behaviors, and attitudes of a nurse. Learning to Learn students were able to read for meaning, information, relevance, and patterns.

PREPARING FOR EXAMS

Our students believe that our objective exams are difficult and often impossible to study for. They see questions as being minor details chosen at random to trick the students. Learning to Learn question charts enabled the students to predict and to prepare for multiple-choice test questions. Learning to Learn students developed a glossary of terms—and so learned the language of nursing. They were able to compare and to contrast information. Question charts became information maps, precise summaries of the content. Quiz grades were improving—students began to see their success. Students were doing better on exams and they reported feeling in control of their learning. For faculty involved in the project, it was gratifying to see some students beginning to succeed in a difficult course. Some students, however, didn't use LTL.

SOME STUDENTS FAILED

For some students, enthusiasm for LTL was short-lived. They did not give themselves a chance to gain any positive outcome from the strategies.

Some of the reasons given for not continuing to use LTL were lack of time due to family or personal responsibilities, difficulty in coming up with "good" questions (those that require more knowledge than recall), and lack of immediate positive results for their efforts (passing or getting a good grade on a test or quiz).

The faculty kept asking each other "Why?" What was it that kept some students from successfully using LTL strategies? The search for explanations became imperative for everyone involved. Leininger (1991) pointed out the need to explore the culture care practices of nursing service and education administrators. This exploration could also be extended to how the culture of learning is perceived and practiced by nursing faculty vis-à-vis nursing students. Faculty perceived LTL as a good method of studying that would bring positive results to any student who adhered faithfully to the strategies long enough for them to become a habit. Students might have had a similar perception but the method required them to establish new ways of studying and learning, a task that required a lot of time and a lot of effort. Many students had little energy left after they finished their jobs, played out their roles as parent and spouse, and dealt with educational cultural shifts.

For many students coming into the program, critical thinking was a new way of learning: They realized that rote learning would get them nowhere, that their old way of studying was no longer effective. They felt the pressure of the cultural shift. The situation they were in was like the one that occurs when a colonizer tries to replace the culture of the invaded people with "civilized" ways of doing and thinking, according to the colonizer's own cultural practices and values (Lawlor, 1991). As one student pointed out during a discussion, she had a hard time applying LTL because it was very different from the way she used to study and to take notes. The incongruence between the new and the old ways of studying was too insurmountable, resulting in noncompliance.

Another explanation for the difficulty in applying LTL strategies came from a lack of a higher level learner maturity in some students. This lack of learner maturity prevented unsuccessful students from moving from a simple to a more complex type of learning. Nursing requires students to move beyond item and directive learning to rationale and contextual learning to give intelligent, positive, and compassionate care to clients (Bevis, 1988). In rationale learning, theory supports practice. Students learn the basis of their nursing actions and why one is more appropriate than the other. Learners are able to put together the information received with their own feelings and ideas and put them into action. What they learn eventually influences the process of decision making and their ability to make judgments. As students move up to a higher level of learning, they gain a higher level of learner maturity. Many of our students are still at the item and directive learning level and need to achieve rationale learning to become critical thinkers. One student expressed this need during a discussion in which she stated that item learning, which was adequate in studying for her science courses, was no longer useful because now she had to "think about it." The word *think* is crucial because it demands more effort and more time. Learning to Learn is initially time consuming for both student and instructor. And in a society that wants quick results and immediate gratification, it can be very frustrating. Learning to Learn must be constantly reinforced for the students until it becomes their own. Therefore, we strove to maintain a positive and supportive atmosphere with the students.

These were the students who invested the time and the energy to achieve positive outcomes. For them, LTL has become a habit and culture of learning with a proven track record for ensuring success. The implementation of the LTL project provided many avenues for the development of a helping relationship between student and teacher. Learning to Learn promoted growth, development, maturity, and improved functioning. As teachers, we have always been aware that providing information is not our main function. What is more vital is establishing a relationship with our students that will facilitate learning. Thus, we took the LTL project as a good opportunity to strengthen this relationship.

The weekly notebook checks, the discussions, the individual one-to-one sessions that occurred on a regular basis provided a fertile ground for developing feelings of connection and reciprocity between students and instructors. Through such contacts, student and teacher discovered the worth and uniqueness of each other. The scheduled, as well as the impromptu, small group and individual meetings were utilized fully by faculty to elicit sharing of thoughts and feelings that otherwise might be impossible in a large class situation. For example, many students expressed personal reasons for failing to follow through with the LTL strategies; their frustration at their failure—and at times their anger—were apparent. Yet, at the end of the session, they also expressed gratitude for the resources that were available to them, including the chance to verbalize their feelings to their instructors. During these meetings, the instructor was not just a passive listener. She provided open, honest communication through mutual self-disclosure. By sharing her own experiences during her student days and correlating them with her students' experiences, the instructor demonstrated empathetic understanding. Also, authentic personal communication provides students with some personal knowledge about the teacher that allows them to get a little closer to her. With open communication and interest in their students' learning, the faculty members facilitate the students' positive self-concept and enhance their cognitive abilities. Every small accomplishment eventually leads to a bigger success. By recognizing each student's accomplishment, no matter how small, we kept them positively motivated, optimistic, and confident about their own learning. Students whose motivation was flagging received special attention. For instance, one student who stopped formulating questions about her lecture notes stated that it took her so much time to think of questions. She also admitted that it took her a long time to read and understand the material, so that by the time she finished reading a chapter she had no time left to generate questions from her notes. The instructor reassured her that this was also a learning strategy. The student resumed using LTL and became more proficient in managing her time with the help of the LTL mentor. By acknowledging students' efforts and progress, we also salute their status as successful learners.

MEASURING SUCCESS

The LTL method will continue to be integrated into the curriculum because the faculty believes in the benefits it gains for students and teachers alike. Learning to Learn creates an atmosphere of social support for the students with the message that they are cared about—esteemed and valued in a network of mutual communication and obligation. Being part of this network encourages students to assume responsibility for their own learning; they feel they are in control of their own fate, which undoubtedly reinforces their positive self-concept. One of the students summed up this correlation in a moving statement, "It's good to know that someone believed in me at a time when I didn't have much belief in myself." This student attributed her success in the course to LTL strategies and the supportive environment provided by her peers and instructors.

The learner and the teacher are in a relationship that is almost akin to symbiosis. They are interdependent. One cannot exist without the other. Those of us who are willing to take the mandate of keeping the culture of learning alive and strong must affirm this relationship and work together with our students to give them the necessary tools for success in their chosen profession.

Results were good even the first semester we implemented LTL. Table 7.1 demonstrates the increase in the number of successful minority students from one to nine. We are pleased with this early success.

Table 7.1   Nurse 132 LTL Project Results

	Number of Students	Number of Students Passing	Number of Minority Students Passing
Control Group	34	16 (47.07)	1 (6.27)
LTL Group	33	19 (57.5)	9 (47.3)

Learning to Learn puts the students and faculty at the center of an educative process that empowers both the learner and the teacher. Student and teacher may be from two distinct cultures, but they both strive for the same goal, the student's success in the program. Awareness of having a common goal facilitates the acculturation process. The student's acceptance of new ways and the faculty recognition that old ways can be incorporated into new ways, preserves the students' self-identity in the process of learning.

REFERENCES

Abraham, I. L. (1982). Support groups for nursing students in psychiatric rotation. *Issues in Mental Health Nursing, 4,* 159-165.

Bevis, E. O. (1988). New directions for a new age. In (Ed.), *Curriculum revolution: Mandate for change.* New York: National League for Nursing Press.

Cobb, S. (1976). Social support as a moderator of life stress. *Psychosomatic Medicine, 38*(5), 300-314.

DiMinno, M., & Thompson, E. (1980). An interactional support group for graduate nursing students: A report. *Journal of Nursing Education, 19*(3), 16-22.

Griffith, J. Q., & Bakanauskos, A. J. (1983). Student-Instructor relationships in nursing education. *Journal of Nursing Education, 22*(3), 104-107.

Heiman, M., & Slomianko, J. (1988). *Methods of inquiry.* Cambridge, MA: Learning to Learn, Inc.

Heiman, M., & Slomianko, J. (1992). *Success in college and beyond.* Allston, MA: Learning to Learn, Inc.

Hilbert, G. A., & Allen, L. R. (1985). The effect of social support on educational outcomes. *Journal of Nursing Education, 24*(2), 48-52.

Lawlor, R. (1991). *Voices of the first day: Awakening the aboriginal dreamtime.* Rochester, VT: Inner Traditions International.

Leininger, N. (Ed.). (1991). *Culture care diversity and universality: A theory of nursing.* New York: National League for Nursing Press.

McKay, S. R. (1980). A peer group counseling model in nursing education. *Journal of Nursing Education, 19*(3), 4-10.

Middlemiss, M. A., & Van Neste-Kenny, J. (1994). Curriculum revolution: Reflective minds and empowering relationships. *Nursing and Health Care, 19*(7), 350-353.

Rogers, C. (1977). The characteristics of a helping relationship. In D. L. Avila, A. W. Combs, & W. W. Purkey (Eds.), *Helping relationships sourcebook.* Boston: Allyn and Bacon.

8

The Male Student Nurse Subgroup: Learning to Learn Maps Perinatal Practice

Karen Joho and Anne Ormsby

*B*lue is for boys and pink is for girls. The conceptualization of gender begins in pregnancy. This vivid reminder of societal roles and expectations greets all male nursing students on their arrival on the perinatal clinical rotation. An essential outcome of perinatal nursing is the delivery of a healthy mother and infant. Male student nurses bring to this experience a personal belief system that incorporates cultural exposure, life experiences, and societal stereotyping. Not all men can move into this unique clinical experience with ease. As the number of men entering nursing schools increases, a responsibility of the perinatal faculty is to address the significance of the societal male and nursing student role expectations and to work to provide this subculture, the male nursing student, with a challenging and exciting clinical experience. An additional responsibility of the perinatal faculty is to assess the male students subculture within the clinical setting. When problems develop, society's perception of the intrusion of the male nurse into a predominantly female health care domain may be what is operating, not the male student's inability to do certain procedures and skills.

FACTORS THAT CHALLENGE MALE STUDENT NURSES

It has been our experience that the inclusion of male nursing students on the perinatal unit generates various viewpoints and levels of comfort by staff, physicians, clients, families, other nursing students, and faculty members. The quandary is not related to conflicting sex role ideologies among the various groups but rather represents conflict between generations (Kritek, 1988). Male students have demonstrated behaviors uncharacteristic of female nursing students, including self-isolation on the clinical unit or overly demonstrative nurturing behaviors. Self-isolation is seen in young males who have limited life experiences in dealing with women and young children. On the other hand, if the male student shows excessive feminine attributes, concerns arise over the male student's negative perceptions of his own maleness within the perinatal environment.

Male nursing students are often confused with students of medicine. This confusion is not limited to the client-student relationship. It also expands into the family-student, staff-student, and physician-student relationships. This occurs in spite of androgynous dress and the use of titling identification. This confusion results in repetitive re-introduction of the male student and the continuous need to clarify the role of the male student nurse.

THE CLIENT ASSESSMENT

Part of the postpartum physical assessment focuses on the examination of the breasts and genitalia. This may be the student's first opportunity to palpate a fundus, or inspect a lacerated perineum. Clinical performance anxiety is even more heightened by the student's preconceived role of the male student nurse. Unmarried adolescent mothers experience role conflicts when the perinatal nurse is male. The challenge results when young unmarried mothers view the male nursing student as a male first and then as a student. This is different from the reaction of older married mothers who view the student as a nurse who happens to be male.

Patient education, an essential and large part of nursing, can pose as another anxiety-provoking experience for the male student. Topics such as family planning, menstruation, self-breast examination, infant care, and the family role changes that occur with childbirth may be very new to the male student. Additional reading and research may be required.

Attitudes of clients and families contribute to the challenge of the male nursing student on the obstetrical unit. Some clients have verbalized the traditional opinion that a nurse is more credible and knowledgeable if a person has experienced a health care need. This sex role stereotyping attitude separates the male nurse from his female counterparts. The male nurse does not have the experiences of a woman or even the possibility to experience pregnancy, birth, and breast feeding. But then the female nurse never has prostate or scrotal problems.

THE STUDENT ASSESSMENT

Prior to starting Learning to Learn (LTL) strategies, the instructor's multifaceted assessment of each male student can facilitate a clinical rotation appropriate for the distinct learning experience by providing insight and knowledge about the individual student's attitudes and behavioral norms. To obtain this information, the perinatal faculty member can observe the male student's interactions with female students and faculty, and promote a classwide discussion on societal roles, expectations, and gender attributes. A personal talk in a confidential setting addressing the particular concerns of each male is also helpful. This student assessment should be ongoing throughout the course.

CLINICAL STRATEGIES

The following strategies may be incorporated into the clinical setting at any time. To alleviate the male student's clinical performance anxiety, the instructor may provide a skills laboratory experience using simulated genitalia and breasts. This opportunity for practice will empower the male student to perform his assessment at an increased comfort level. Encouraging the male student to focus on previously learned professional behavior will help to compensate for his uneasiness and possible self-consciousness in performing intimate assessments on young healthy females. Role-playing is an invaluable tool for reducing the student's anxiety. A faculty member who suspects self-isolation as a form of disengagement from the clinical experience must initiate a discussion with the student to determine whether his lack of experience with the female gender is creating problems. Disengagement is seen in young males, married and unmarried, whose cultural norms promote and demand female modesty.

LEARNING TO LEARN STRATEGIES

Developing an information map to analyze cultures and their diverse beliefs about perinatal nursing provides insight into the male student's personal perspective. Additional information maps may be developed for topics such as female-male relationships, family planning, the birth

Table 8.1   Information Map of Cultural Beliefs and Topics
Related to Perinatal Nursing

		Cultural Groups		
		Orthodox Jewish	Asian	Indian	Black American
B	Position of Women in Culture	Patriarchal, patrilineal, male oriented	Reverence based on age not gender	Female rank below male with few rights	Matriarchal, matrifocal
E	Procreation	Responsibility of marital couples	Preference for sons prevalent		One's worth is proven through childbearing
L	Family Planning	Males forbidden to use condoms or masturbate	No laws or mores preventing use of any method	Males reject vasectomies	Female sterilization is dominant form of birth control
I	Breast-feeding	Large number breast-feed— a weaning ceremony is held	Do not breast-feed until "true milk" is evident	No laws or mores preventing or encouraging	Not practiced frequently
E	Circumcision	All male children due to religious laws	No religious or cultural views	No religious or cultural views	Commonly practiced
F					
S	Presence of spouse at birth	Cannot view genitalia; cannot touch female after evidence of blood	Generally female attended	Female oriented with predominant use of female health care providers	No cultural bias—varies within each family

process and postpartum period, breast feeding, sexual practices, and gender-specific role expectations in different cultures. Creating information maps as a group activity encourages dialogue between male and female students, enlightening students, not only with their own cultural beliefs, but with the beliefs held by other societies.

Table 8.1 illustrates an information map of cultural beliefs related to perinatal nursing. The information in this map also can help students develop nursing diagnoses and care plans based on cultural beliefs. Information maps generate critical thinking behaviors and ultimately guide clinical practice. This LTL strategy assists male students in their professional role development and transition to perinatal nursing practice. The benefits of using LTL strategies in the classroom and clinical area are recognized. The creative application of these strategies to assist the male student in his professional role development is a bonus.

REFERENCES

Begany, T. (1994). Your image is brighter than ever. *RN, 57*(10), 28-34.

Bobak, I., Lowdermilk, D., & Jensen, M. (1995). *Maternity nursing* (4th ed.). St. Louis, MO: Mosby.

Brenda, E. (1981). When the postpartum nursing student is male—A challenge to maternity instructors. *Journal of Nursing Education, 20*(4), 5-8.

Heiman, M., & Slomianko, J. (1988). *Methods of inquiry.* Cambridge, MA.: Learning to Learn, Inc.

Kritek, P. B. (1988). Gender roles and the health professional. In M. E. Hardy & M. E. Conway (Eds.), *Role theory perspectives for health professionals* (2nd ed., pp. 309-341). Norwalk, CT: Appleton & Lange.

Letizia, B. (1994). Ban on male nurses in labor and delivery is upheld RN Newswatch, *Professional Update. RN, 57*(12), 16.

Squires, T. (1995). Men in nursing. *RN, 58*(7), 26-28.

Trandel-Korenchuk, K. M., & Trandel-Korenchuk, D. M. (1981, Fall). Restrictions on male nurse employment in obstetric care. *Nursing Administration Quarterly,* 87-90.

Tuminia, P. (1981). Teaching problems and strategies with male nursing students. *Nurse Educator, 6*(5), 9.

Part Two

Addressing Student Life Needs and Successes

9

Student Empowerment: Hearing Students' Voices

Lynne R. Nelson

In a universe of open systems, causality is not an option. Energy fields are open, not a little bit or sometimes, but continuously. A universe of open systems explains the infinite nature of energy fields, how the human environment fields are integral with each other, and that causality is invalid. Change then is continuously innovative and creative. Moreover association does not mean causality.

(Rogers, 1992, p. 30)

We grasp external space through our bodily situation. A "corporeal or postural schema" gives us at every moment, a global, practical, and implicit notion of the relation between our body and things, of our hold on them. A system of possible movements or "motor projects" radiates from us to our environment. Our body is not in space like things; it inhabits or haunts space.

(Merleau-Ponty, 1964, p. 5)

Persons and groups strive within an environment to create a world in which meaning and purpose exist and in which social discourse supports self-esteem and enables goals. As unique identities emerge from this interaction, a growing diversity of people and their environments also emerges, and within a sense of pandimensionality (Rogers, 1992).

Pandimensionality, which may describe the nature of multicultural groups in nursing education, is also descriptive of unique interactions, especially of the student and the environment, that are the subject of this chapter. The academic program discussed here is distinguished by three divisions, which exist to address student needs from various sociocultural backgrounds and life styles. The traditional day division is complemented by an evening division for students who must work during the day. A third, weekend division was instituted to create even greater opportunities for potential student populations to attend nursing school. The three divisions function as a whole, with students from multiple cultures, of different ages, gender, socioeconomic backgrounds, ethnicity, language of origin, religion, and political persuasion. With all students granted equal status as members of the student body and the three divisions served by the same curriculum, the school itself offers a unified, dynamic environment characterized by students, faculty, administration, and support services functioning in positive integrality. Seeking as well to enhance the human value of student experiences, the school incorporates several further components here: belonging, reciprocity, mutuality characterized by validation and shared visions and goals, and synchrony—the variable rhythms of "shared movement through time and space."

LIVING ON THE EDGE

Eliciting the involvement of such a diverse group of students was no minor feat. It involved, first off, allowing for the expression of the environmental cultures of which the students were a part. To speed this effort, we developed capacities for an empowerment group. Of special concern were students who seemed to live on the edge of school life either because of heavy familial responsibilities or job commitments outside of school, or who exhibited social alienation through anger, frustration, or emotional absence. Students who exhibited alienation in such ways sometimes felt that they did not have a forum in which to impact their world. Student government, an active component of school life for many students, still did not include participation from persons representing all aspects of the school environment.

Noncognitive patterns of academic experience, such as a lack of a sense of belonging and a lack of affiliation with persons of perceived power in the environment, can contribute to increased attrition rates among students (Jones, 1992; Pacquiao, 1994). Students who do not perceive that they have access to enough social support in the school setting may become overwhelmed by personal responsibilities, and may feel especially powerless and frustrated when they experience academic disappointments. For some students, one more crisis may mean the difference between whether or not they stay in school. An empowerment group provides these and other students with an opportunity to validate or invalidate their perceptions of the world. It is a vehicle by which students can bring themselves from the edge into the center of the student world in interaction with representatives from the differing aspects of the immediate school environment.

THE CONCEPT

Inclusion of representatives from all sectors of school life is a vital conceptual component of the project. This approach achieves the greatest impact on the cultural environment of the school. Students have access as equal partners affecting the human and environmental fields. They further are exposed to the means and to the mechanisms that reshape patterns of being. Figure 9.1 shows the dynamic aspects of the relationship between and among the components of the group. Power, which is conceived as a fluid force in the environment and not inherent in any one individual, enables the whole environment to move in agreed-on directions. Power is shared.

POWER AND EMPOWERMENT:
A NEW FEMINIST PERSPECTIVE

Theories of power from a classical feminist perspective originally included an emphasis on gender differences. From a masculine framework, power included dominance and was characterized as *power-over*. From a feminist perspective, power incorporated the *power-to* including the ability to effect change. Attempts to incorporate concepts of power from African Americans and other ethnic groups did not sustain this classical dualism (Griscom, 1992; Sagrestano, 1992; Yoder & Kahn, 1992). Their experiences within the larger society indicated that power issues are

Figure 9.1   Model of an Empowerment Committee

Environmental Field

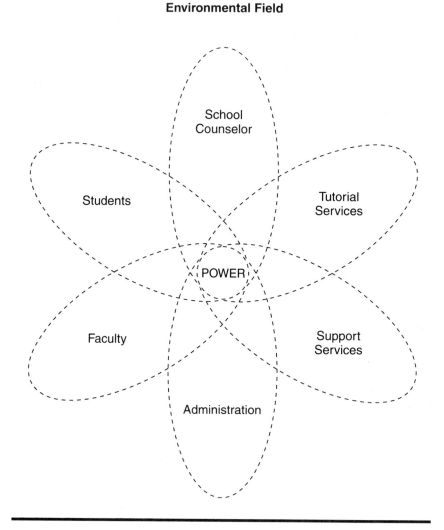

more related to inherent and bestowed positions of strength or weakness within society than to gender distinctions (Griscom, 1992).

The power-to from a feminist perspective has also been linked to personal empowerment and control, a model that does not incorporate treatment of societal issues (Yoder & Kahn, 1992). Recent concepts of empowerment have included sharing for the enhancement of others through responsibility, collectivity, and process (Wheeler & Chin, 1991). These concepts seemed to be linked more closely with the goals of the project—to create positive change in the environment through an empowering process of group interaction and direction. They are also consistent with the goals of nursing, which concerned the health of individuals and their shared environment. The power-to of broad, modern feminism, which encompasses promoting the good of all members of society, male and female, informed the decision making and actions of the committee.

THE EMPOWERMENT COMMITTEE MEETS

The Empowerment Committee included student representatives from all the divisions of the program and from the four clinical nursing courses. Among the issues they discussed about various aspects of school life, two concerns appeared to be paramount: the difficulty and frustration many students experienced trying to deal with the volume of course content and/or objective test taking, and the need to develop greater cohesiveness among classmates in the school's three academic divisions.

Representatives from all components of school life brainstormed about possible directions for coping with these problems. It was agreed that the committee would undertake a study of current themes of empowerment through curriculum change and, based on the committee's conclusions, make recommendations to the faculty, administration, and student body. Students began by examining the precepts of *Student Management Teams* through which students actively participate with faculty in the structure and outcomes of the learning process (Cunningham, Chambers, Howard, & Schenk, 1994). This process reflects current ideas concerning the curriculum revolution, empowerment through teaching, and the new caring groups (Allen, 1990; Beck, 1991; Bevis & Murray, 1990; Chally, 1992; Guynn et al., 1994; Tanner, 1990). The curriculum revolution incorporates major themes of social responsibility, the centrality of caring, an interpretative stance by faculty to continuously discover meanings and to identify assumptions in education and practice. Other themes include the incorporation of theoretical pluralism and diversity in the environment of education and practice while maintaining and enhancing standards. Finally, the relationship between the student and faculty seems central to this revolution of worldview (Tanner, 1990). Students on the committee expressed an interested commitment to engage in the ongoing study, and they have received packets of materials with which to inform their thinking.

The idea of caring, which is central to the concepts being studied by the Empowerment Committee, has characteristics of an ethical principle inherent in social responsibility and in empowering nonviolent behaviors, such as advocacy and cooperation, toward goals to benefit the common good (Munhall, 1988). These principles were evident during an empowerment party in which senior students, acting as caring peers, related strategies for student success. Peer interactions are powerful resources for creating a sense of belonging in the academic environment. Then student goals for success do not appear so impossible (Hughes, 1993; Nichols & Lachat, 1994).

PIZZA AND EMPOWERMENT: ANATOMY OF A GRAND MEETING OF THE STUDENT BODY

Members of the Empowerment Committee worked with students and faculty of the Student Government to hold a pizza empowerment party to which all members of the school community were invited. This was to be an opportunity to introduce the school to the activities of the committee and to elicit ideas, inspiration, and/or complaints from participants. Two parties were planned (for day students and for evening/weekend students), and pizza was supplied by the Student Government.

People gathered in large numbers at the day party. They listened attentively to a presentation of the aims of the committee while eating hearty helpings of pizza. When asked for input, the students began to share, albeit slowly at first, their problems with each of the clinical courses. A constant theme of frustration began to emerge relating to the nature of examinations and the intensity and volume of course content. Student experiences included difficulty with the exams, frustration over conflicting demands of family and home life versus school, and a sense of unfairness that there was not enough time to study successfully and work outside the academic environment. Some said simply that they felt things were wrong in their lives but could not define what the wrong things were. There was a lively, candid, and creative airing of issues.

SENIORS SPEAK

Students were most attentive to the perceptions of the seniors who spoke eloquently of similar struggles through their courses. Seniors identified with the junior students as being in the world of the student, but with successful prior experience. Some of the seniors shared how they had failed a prior nursing course, but that the key to their ultimate success was in perseverance to goal. They encouraged students not to give up, to keep the goal of nursing excellence before them, to seek out instructors and support services, to make the school their own, become involved, not live on the edge, and to have hope. Seniors engaged in a powerful form of caring. They were vulnerable themselves for the sake of their classmates, were collaborative in offering themselves for help and advice when needed, and gave valuable suggestions to enable success. The patterns of interactions became a powerful force for success by diminishing some of the despair in the room and faintly stirring hope within those students present. Each person was to get involved personally or through representatives on the Empowerment Committee. Empowerment means action and involvement. Empowerment equals energy and movement.

PLANS FOR THE FUTURE: NEXT STEPS

The committee continues its explorations of the implications and implementation of the students' recommendations. Brainstorming groups continue. Future plans have included exploration of how joint empowerment events can combine day, evening, and weekend student participation. We have explored ways in which greater connections can be made between seniors and the other classes and the faculty. A process has been set in motion to effect change.

Human beings are on the threshold of a fantastic and unimagined future. (Rogers, 1992)

REFERENCES

Allen, D. G. (1990). The curriculum revolution: Radical re-visioning of nursing education. *Journal of Nursing, 29,* 312-316.

Beck, C. T. (1991). How students perceive faculty caring: A phenomenological study. *Nurse Educator, 16*(5), 18-22.

Bevis, E. O., & Murray, J. P. (1990). The essence of curriculum revolution: Emancipatory teaching. *Journal of Nursing Education, 29,* 326-331.

Chally, P. S. (1992). Empowerment through teaching. *Journal of Nursing Education, 31,* 117-120.

Cunningham, M. E., Chambers, J., Howard, L., & Schenk, S. (1994, Spring). The student management team: A vehicle for empowerment. *Revolution: The Journal of Nurse Empowerment,* 42-46.

Griscom, J. L. (1992). Women and power: Definition, dualism, and difference. *Psychology of Women Quarterly, 16,* 389-414.

Guynn, M., Wilson, C., Bar, B., Rankin, K., Bernhardt, J., & Hickox, C. (1994). Caring groups: A participative teaching/learning experience. *Nursing and Health Care, 15,* 476-479.

Hughes, L. (1993). Peer group interactions and student-perceived climate for caring. *Journal of Nursing Education, 32,* 78-83.

Jones, S. H. (1992). Improving retention and graduation rates for black students in nursing education: A developmental model. *Nursing Outlook, 40*(2), 78-92.

Merleau-Ponty, M. (1964). *The primacy of perception.* (H. L. Dreyfus & P. A. Dreyfus, Trans.). Evanston, IL: Northwestern University Press.

Munhall, P. (1988). Curriculum revolution: A social mandate for change. In *Curriculum revolution: Mandate for change* (Publication No. 15-2224, pp. 217-230). New York: National League for Nursing Press.

Nichols, M. R., & Lachat, M. F. (1994). Senior-led freshman groups: A strategy for professional development. *Nurse Educator, 19*(6), 46-48.

Pacquiao, D. (1994). *Socioculture influences in cognitive styles of African-American, Filipino and Hispanic nursing students.* Unpublished manuscript.

Rogers, M. E. (1992). Nursing science and the space age. *Nursing Science Quarterly, 5*(1), 27-34.

Sagrestano, L. M. (1992). The use of power and influence in a gendered world. *Psychology of Women Quarterly, 16,* 439-447.

Tanner, C. A. (1990). Reflections on the curriculum revolution. *Journal of Nursing Education, 29,* 295-299.

Wheeler, C. E., & Chin, P. L. (1991). *Peace and power: A handbook of feminist process.* (3rd ed.). New York: National League for Nursing Press.

Yoder, J. D., & Kahn, A. S. (1992). Toward a feminist understanding of women and power. *Psychology of Women Quarterly, 16,* 381-388.

10

Mentoring African American Students: One Path to Success

Lynne R. Nelson

*A*frican Americans living at the dawn of a new century reflect significant trends in the growing multicultural climate that has developed during the past decade. The legacy of slavery in the United States continues. Their parents or grandparents may have taken part in the civil rights movement of the 1950s and 1960s, watched the burning of the nation's cities, and listened to Martin Luther King, Jr., Malcolm X, Stokley Carmichael, and Angela Davis. They danced to the jazz of Duke Ellington or the blues of Bessie Smith. They heard the Temptations, know of Iced Tea, and perhaps cried when Marvin Gaye was killed. To them, Aretha's "Respect" marked the beginning of the women's movement. At times, they eat soul food and sit through long church services with ladies all in white. Now, they are part of the coloring of America.

The cultural experience of the African American infuses the world we know with beauty like the facets of an ever-changing kaleidoscope. What is the nature of this commonality beyond skin color and among the multiplicity of African Americans? Immediately there is an experience of racism, institutional or personal, actual or perceived, and which exists like a malevolent will. In this context, mentoring African American students becomes a complex process. For it often involves assisting them to extract meaning from the experiences that they perceive to cause alienation from the educational environment. The lack of available strategies to deal with racism increases a student's risk for academic failure by thwarting academic and personal development. Students who may not know how to navigate the educational system and are reluctant to seek assistance become increasingly alienated (Kornguth, Frisch, Shovein, & Williams, 1994). At this point, academic difficulties may seem an overwhelming indictment of the student's abilities. Blame is projected outward at the system and assistance isn't sought.

For response, the minority mentor assists students in understanding and coping with incidents of actual racism, in reality-testing perceived racism, and in developing personal strategies to overcome adversity. The mentor validates students' experiences but challenges them to allow nothing to deter them from accomplishing their goals.

Ken and Daniel were two African American men who were enrolled in the first introduction course to nursing concepts. I was teaching them study techniques and strategies for test taking. Ken interjected: "We were stopped on our way through the hospital." His eyes held that knowing pain. "I don't think any of the white students were stopped, even the other guys, and no one had IDs with them today." "Did you ask them?" I said. "Yes, we asked them," Daniel said, his voice louder than Ken's and holding in his brimming anger. "You tell me, is that right?" Daniel was angry with me now and upset at the memory. "I think it's awful," I responded. "What do you want to do about it? I'll help you if you want to complain." They looked at each other, calming down a little at my validation of their experience, and asked: "What do you think we should do?"

Without diminishing their right for fair play, I tried to offer perspective: "This time, I think you should let it slide. See if you can recognize the person who stopped you and if it develops into a pattern, then we can do something to change the situation. You will find all kinds of people everywhere you go. A hospital is no different. What you need to see is that this is a good place, the school has had a commitment, as does the hospital, to the education of people from all kinds of ethnic backgrounds. Do not let anything like this prevent you from what you have a right to do." "That seems good to us," they said. "By the way, get your hospital IDs and wear them," I said. A sadness had settled over us as we sat there, a thoughtful silence, but that is sometimes the way things are.

African American students from many backgrounds have difficulty with the structure and functions of the academic environment. Some students from Haiti state they are used to essay questions and find objective tests confusing. It is difficult for them to see how these multiple-choice tests are a real indication of knowledge. Many students feel that you have to learn two things: First you have to learn the material, then you have to learn how to take the tests. This seems very unfair to them. Mentoring the students who are not used to this type of assessment of their knowledge includes validating their concerns. Test-taking is a skill that must be mastered if you intend to best demonstrate your knowledge. Reminding students that this is the way they will be tested in the United States on the licensure exam becomes a powerful motivator to develop good test-taking techniques.

Many African American students exhibit styles of learning that differ from the expected skills of the academic setting (Pacquiao, 1994). Mentoring these students includes assisting them in becoming aware of the differences in their styles. Mentoring is teaching students how to adapt to what is expected while accepting that the style with which they are familiar is a valid way of knowing. Students who come for mentoring are encouraged to become bicultural learners. They are taught the expectations of the academic setting and strategies to demonstrate mastery of the course content. Positive affiliation with students mentored is a deliberate undertaking in helping to create an environment for optimal learning.

Julie comes to see me after every examination and quiz, whether she does well or not. She states that she has been helped not only in learning strategies to assist her in studying but has developed positive and affiliative relations with her clinical instructor through role-playing in my office. "I really know what is expected of me, and if I make a mistake, I just need to get back in the swing of things, learn from what went wrong, and not brood about it," she says. Early in the semester, Julie thought of leaving school because she did not feel a part of things. Students such as Julie may need to be approached by a mentor. Feelings and thoughts can be explored until a safe relationship and trust are established. Then other relationships can be developed.

Mentoring African American students will help to change the face of the nursing profession by enabling minority students to succeed and become nurses who represent within the profession the multicultural world of which they are a part. Our profession will then reflect the diverse world of our times.

REFERENCES

Kornguth, M., Frisch, N., Shovein, J., & Williams, R. (1994). Non-cognitive factors that put students at academic risk in nursing programs. *Nursing Educator, 19*(5), 24–27.

Pacquiao, D. (1994). *Sociocultural influences on cognitive styles of African-American, Filipino and Hispanic nursing students.* Unpublished manuscript.

11

Outcomes Assessment: A Program Imperative for Supporting At-Risk Students

Michael Knight

NO BAD NEWS

*O*utcomes assessment improves student learning and development by creating methods to (a) articulate the goals of each academic program, (b) gain feedback on progress toward those goals, and (c) use the feedback to modify aspects of each academic program to ensure that the goals are being achieved.

Data from assessment should never be used to make comparisons among faculty, departments, schools, or colleges. Outcomes data should not be used for faculty evaluation and, in particular, should not be employed in the retention, tenure, promotion, or merit award processes. Faculty who feel threatened by punishment or rewards have altered assessment perspectives and are skewed toward reporting only positive, upbeat data or not reporting at all. Why should they put themselves in a self-destruct mode?

No-Bad-News is a term used at Kean College to refer to the permission granted to find areas within a program which could use attention and further development. Implied is the principle of no punishment for identification of need within a program or department. The "No-Bad-News" approach enables faculty to deal with reality—even harsh reality—forthrightly. Program change comes only when the real problems are addressed. Fixing what's broken exposes vulnerabilities and challenges personal assumptions. Fixing what's broken improves programs.

Outcomes assessment with a No-Bad-News view freed our faculty to look at minority retention frankly. It worked. Curriculum and instructional methods changed, and the educational culture within the classrooms shifted. Retention of minority students improved and content mastery increased.

ASSESSMENT FOR PROGRAM IMPROVEMENT

The foundation for an effort such as assessing the outcomes of an academic program is not the technical competence of the individuals involved, but rather the perspective they take in approaching the task. Waterman (1988) describes the importance of the attitudes people possess, the resulting attention they give to a particular activity, and the expectations that these two factors create. "Does pride cause quality or does quality cause pride?" (Seymour, 1992). The focus of assessment on the improvement of programs, faculty development, and the developing of our students' talents enabled Kean College to commit to a comprehensive outcomes assessment program. The Transcultural Leadership Continuum (Project TLC) used this expertise as a basis for its program development. Subsequent changes improved minority access, retention, and progression.

A CONTEXT FOR ASSESSMENT

Decisions about assessment require a clear sense of the program's purpose. There are some common reasons why particular outcomes assessment programs are initiated, the types of responses institutions might select, and key issues in determining what and how outcomes can be examined. These factors are developed in the context of the impact a comprehensive outcomes assessment program will make on an institution.

Kean College faculty, experienced in outcomes assessment, worked closely with participating schools as curricular/program changes occurred.

PURPOSES FOR ASSESSMENT

One of the first questions to ask when considering the notion of assessment of student learning outcomes is "Why?"—why would our academic program want to engage in this activity? The decision to implement such a process may include one or more of the following reasons: It is mandated by an external agency; it will enable evaluation of individual student performance; or it will improve the quality in the academic programs. Although these reasons are not necessarily mutually exclusive, conflicts among them may emerge as assessment activities are implemented.

There are accountability mandates. Outcomes assessment may be the direct result of a mandate. Governing boards have issued directives to establish outcomes assessment programs in most states (El-Khawas, 1990). In some states, legislatures have taken the initiative away from state boards and local institutions by passing laws requiring various forms of assessment. Accountability often requires reporting results to an authority. Institutions face the difficulty of balancing and responding to unclear and sometimes conflicting demands. In these circumstances, the question, "What do they want?" drives the college or university's response. Frequently, colleges and universities find accountability and future funding inexorably intertwined, implicitly or explicitly, raising the outcomes assessment ante to high stakes.

Program improvement is a bona fide reason for assessment. Outcomes assessment may be instituted for the sole purpose of improving programs. While this objective is usually presumed in mandated or student assessment approaches, it helps develop and maintain focus if it is viewed as the primary rationale.

For program improvement, learning outcomes are part of a systemized data-based review and revision of the curriculum, classroom teaching techniques, learning processes, and student development activities. Assessment may be an independent process, or it may be part of formal program review and planning activities.

A learning environment or culture for learning is established. Assessment for program improvement develops relationships among learner traits (knowledge, motivations, expectations), learning process characteristics (curriculum, teaching methods, advisement), and outcome measures (test scores, satisfaction measures, performance ratings, postcollegiate success).

It emphasizes the use of the outcomes measures as feedback to the learning process for determining adaptations and changes to increase effectiveness, thereby developing a self-regulating assessment program.

At a more specific level, outcomes assessment may be instituted to find out how individual students are performing. Student assessment seeks to answer questions about individual students. Is he or she learning what we think we are teaching them? Does his or her performance meet specified criteria? When minority students, African American and Hispanic, enter our programs in large numbers and then graduate at a rate of no more than 5%, we must ask, "What variables will make a difference in their learning?" The assessment process may be a vehicle for placement or counseling. Or, the process may serve as a gate to limit access to a higher level of study or, possibly, even graduation.

Student performance is the critical element in any type of outcomes assessment. The emphasis may be on evaluation of students or on evaluation of programs and institutions. Outcomes from programs and institutions can be examined by securing a well-selected sample of student performances; outcomes of individual students require total participation.

Student assessments easily become high-stakes performances—the results have a significant impact on the performer by affecting his or her progress or requiring additional course work.

INSTITUTIONAL RENEWAL

A commitment to outcomes assessment is a commitment to making changes at all levels within the institution. The concerns may begin as student learning questions, but quickly become curriculum development issues. Curriculum development issues move to faculty development concerns. The development of students, curriculum, and faculty requires an organizational development perspective. Approaching decisions about outcomes assessment from this frame of reference provides an opportunity for institutional renewal.

Renewal finds its origins in organizational change. Those directing assessment programs have found that recognizing and preparing for faculty, administration, and staff reactions to change helps enormously to guide the development and implementation of the activities. Outcomes assessment efforts have demonstrated the potential to revitalize the learning environment. There is a delicate balance, however, between those who favor change and those who favor the status quo, between those who perceive assessment as a threat and those who perceive it as an opportunity. Approaches to assessing institutional effectiveness can turn problems presented by mandates into opportunities for positive growth and development, or renewal.

RESISTANCE TO CHANGE

Resistance can be exhibited at any point in the assessment process. The administration can be resistant to the concept of assessment, or it can be the faculty that is recalcitrant. It is necessary to understand the basis of the resistance to overcome it.

Nolan (1982) has listed several reasons people resist change. Much resistance has its foundation in fear—fear of the unknown, of failure, of having to learn new skills, of loss of status or rights in the new situation. It may also have its roots in poor communication of goals, purposes, and reasons for the change. Many may resist change just because it is change and may carry along with it conflicts and/or feelings of discomfort. Involvement in the planning of change, clearly defining the goals and objectives for the change, addressing the personal needs of those involved, designing flexibility into the change, communicating openly and honestly, focusing on the positive aspects of the change, and providing adequate training for those involved are just a few of the measures that can help overcome resistance to change.

Waterman (1988) has detailed criteria of excellence, and developed these variables as essentials for implementing change and growth within organizations. He identifies these aspects as factors for renewal and goes on to state, "Without renewal there can be no excellence." To achieve excellence, colleges and universities that work within this conceptual framework during the implementation of an outcomes assessment program have a greater chance of success in their pursuit of excellence and can contribute positively to the transformation of the institution.

Informed opportunism or the ability to sense opportunities and to act while others hesitate may allow institutions to react positively to the suggestion of implementing an outcomes assessment program when it becomes clear that such a program will require a major organizational change. Waterman looks to the use of facts, whether they are negative or positive, as a vehicle for renewal. He also stresses the use of congenial controls that work along with friendly facts, to reflect realities, but not entangle the people doing the job.

Direction and empowerment illustrate that boundaries need clear definition, but at the same time allow people the flexibility to work within them. Enlisting faculty members from each department to serve as liaisons to the assessment project is a first step toward direction and empowerment of individuals. Waterman's (1988) factor called "A Different Mirror" shows open-minded and inquisitive organizations recognize that ideas may come from anyone. This is a powerful asset. Looking through a different mirror may give institutions just that vantage point they need to allow for the influx of fresh ideas.

A basic factor that Waterman describes as involving teamwork, trust, politics, and power attempts to destroy the "we/they" barrier that can be so common within organizations. Communication, the sharing of information, is the most important requirement for pulling people together toward a set of shared goals or values. Few higher education initiatives can challenge campus teamwork and trust more than outcomes assessment. Yet, it can provide opportunities to enhance these aspects through the effective use of politics and power.

A CULTURE FOR CHANGE

Renewal must be a continuous process. Stability in motion recognizes change as a positive indicator, and gives a new vantage point that helps organizations break out of former mind-sets. Waterman (1988) states that attitude makes the difference, expectations are everything, and attention is all there is to get any project accomplished. Attitudes and attention generate what things get done within organizations. Involving staff in setting realistic performance standards and measuring them regularly is a way of paying attention to priorities. The premise that there is always room for improvement is a basic concept of renewal.

Lewin (1947) uses an ice cube model of unfreezing, changing, and refreezing to describe the stages of organizational change in the following ways:

- Unfreezing involves the slow "defrosting" or unlocking of firm positions and set attitudes.
- Changing involves replacing old values, attitudes, and/or behaviors with new ones.
- Refreezing involves institutionalizing new behavioral patterns through the use of supporting mechanisms to make the change part of the culture.

It takes time for established approaches to thaw to the point of restructuring, more time for reshaping to take place, and still more time for the changes to solidify as part of the institutional culture. It is not a good idea to attempt to unfreeze everything at once, to avoid creating a heightened degree of uncertainty. Refreezing and defrosting are continuing processes in effective outcomes assessment.

Once the administrative branch of the organization has embraced the concept of assessment, it may be necessary to convince faculty members about the advantages of a comprehensive assessment program. Generally, faculty resistance to the idea of assessment is expressed in one of two ways. There is nothing the faculty does that can be measured. The faculty members in the individual programs at the institution are too busy with their duties to accept any additional responsibilities. If not dealt with, faculty resistance can result in an individual program not complying with the assessment mandate. Administrative intervention becomes necessary. A compliance response by faculty is a frequent result of this sequence.

Approaching the task from the change perspective can help guide decisions on how to structure the work involved and influence some of the training provided. It will also become apparent that organizational change takes time and some in the organization will be ready to move faster than others.

If a decision is made to assess students' learning styles, other decisions will naturally follow: the reason for assessment on a campus, a model for assessment, the instruments and methods that will be used for gathering information, how this information will be used, how the feedback cycle to the student will be accomplished, and a host of other issues. Both the institutional and program levels must confront and resolve these same issues if the effort is to be successful.

PLANNING TO PLAN

The planning of an assessment program requires knowledge of the institutional culture and distinctive college environment. An understanding of how things happen and how change takes place is essential to the design of any successful intervention strategy. Knowing who will be affected and understanding the proposed changes are significant factors in predicting results. It may be helpful to examine other departmental initiatives to determine the strengths and weaknesses of the process associated with those efforts.

Assessment must be campus and program specific to be effective. Outcomes assessment is simple, but it is not easy. The basic steps involve (a) setting goals, (b) designing instruments, (c) collecting data, (d) analyzing data, and (e) making modifications and changes. This process, while simple in theory, can be extremely time consuming and difficult in practice.

Figure 11.1   Steps to Assessment

```
-----------------------------------------------------------------------
                                                      +-------------+
                                                      Feedback
                                          +-------------+
                                          Data Analysis
                              +-------------+
                              Data Collection
                  +-------------+
                  Instrument
                  Development
      +-------------+
      Goal Setting

-----------------------------------------------------------------------
```

Figure 11.1 presents the steps of an effective assessment process. These steps should be considered as part of a circle with each area of student development receiving the appropriate attention. Each step influences both those that follow and those that precede. While it is necessary for the goal-setting phase to inform the instrument-development phase, it is likely that the instrument-development phase will cause some rethinking of your goals. These dynamic interactions will take place between and among all the steps.

VIEWING SUCCESS

By standard measures, the Cooperative Nursing Programs were rated as excellent. They were graduating classes who scored a consistent 100% pass rate on the National Council Licensing Examination. There was full employment of graduates. Large numbers of graduates went on for higher degrees, read professional journals, and became credentialed in specialities. The curricula were coherent and internally consistent.

Outcomes assessment facilitated the faculty's ability to explore the programs and to identify areas needing attention and improvement. Student retention, particularly minority retention, became the focus. A systematic use of outcomes assessment gave the faculty options for action. The No-Bad-News perspective saved hand-wringing and guilt feelings.

Program improvement did not imply a deficiency but rather a readiness for change. The No-Bad-News perspective permitted trial-and-error learning at the grassroots level and eliminated the imposition of top-down instructions.

Faculty were encouraged to do what they thought would work. They reorganized their classes, attended instructional workshops, worked with consultants, and watched minority student retention improve. Outcomes assessment provided the foundation for a positive interaction between faculty and students. Students became aware of the collaborative efforts of faculty-improved advisement, more explicit goals, clearer expectations of performance, defined criteria, and more detailed syllabi. The initiation of Learning to Learn minority nurse mentors and the exploration of Educational Biculturalism were possible because of faculty preparation for and participation in a comprehensive outcomes assessment effort.

REFERENCES

Astin, A. (1991). *Assessment for excellence.* New York: Macmillan.

Astin, A. et al., (1967). *A typology of student outcomes.* Los Angeles, CA: University Press.

El-Khawas, E. (1990). *Campus trends survey.* Washington, DC: American Council on Education.

Ewell, P. (1984). *The self-regarding institution: Information for excellence.* Boulder, CO: N.C.H.E.M.S.

Fletcher, R., & Clark, J. (1977). *Developing and using simulations.* Washington, DC: Winston.

Harris, J. (1985). Goals for higher education. *A.A.H.E. Bulletin.*

Lewin, K. (1947, June). Frontiers in group dynamics: Concept, method and reality in social equilibrium and social change. *Human Relations.*

Nolan, J. (1982). *Developing work teams.* New York: Wiley.

Seymour, D. (1992). *Causing quality in higher education.* New York: Macmillan.

Waterman, R. (1988). *The renewal factor.* New York: Bantam.

12

Measuring Initial Transcultural Nursing Retention Efforts through Qualitative and Quantitative Analysis

Virginia M. Fitzsimons and Mary L. Kelley

*T*hree years, many hours, and much effort later, we took a look at the preliminary results of our retention efforts. Because the approach was multiphasic—a learning center, minority nurse mentors, new studying methods, economic and mobility strategies, BSN and MSN mobility efforts, plus extensive faculty development—the measurement of our project will encompass a broad perspective also.

Qualitative reports confirmed the complexity of our students' lives. Essay after essay describes the struggle of harsh living situations. Our students' days are filled with caring for children, running to low-paying jobs, struggling with broken cars, and waiting in the cold and snow for buses that don't arrive. Almost to a student, there is a discussion of paying bills and making ends meet on a subsistence-only living level. Most of our students cling to margins of the working class. They acknowledge the meaning of a college degree—even the first step of an associate degree— to improve the economic status of their families. Most are the first in their families to attend college. Most have had checkered academic success in high school and college. To a person they're charged with enormous energy and drive to become nurses. The course work is identified as being very difficult, almost impossible. Clinical experiences are fraught with terror of failure and expulsion from the program. Each student understands that failure is a decided possibility. Fear is the prevailing emotion expressed; it permeates most of the narratives. The externship process and students' success with the LTL strategies were the two places where cheer and enthusiasm leapt off the pages. Students expressed enormous growth and self-confidence with these activities. Faculty perceptions in this area confirm student experiences.

NUMBERS TELL THE TALE—LEARNING TO LEARN

We looked at student retention and graduation rates at the AD, BSN, and MSN levels. Two places where students faltered were in early preclinical and early clinical courses. The math review labs offered by the Nursing Academic Support Center demonstrated retention success in the early retention efforts. Combining concrete, hands-on manipulation of the physical equipment (IV tubing, medicine droppers, etc.) with the early introduction of the nurse role model resulted in higher successful outcomes of this important course. It was common to have a 50% failure rate in Math 100. Successful completion of the course is necessary before students can take clinical courses. One unsuccessful attempt delays a student's progression by a full semester. Two unsuccessful attempts mean expulsion from the program. One typical Math 100 lab comprised 15 students who had taken the course once and failed. (One student earned a C and needed a C+; four students earned D; 10 students earned an F). After the Math lab, all 15 students passed with a main score of 2.8).

Learning to Learn was introduced into the second clinical nursing course. This particular course (a fairly rigorous, traditional Medical-Surgical nursing course) had a typical attrition rate of 50%. This course demands an application of knowledge and problem analysis. Faculty saturated the course with Learning to Learn—notebook checks, handouts, class assignments—all activities aimed at reinforcing the LTL methods. Some students resisted completely, but overall, the success of LTL was remarkable (see Table 7.1) The LTL method made a difference for the minority students in the class. With nine (47%) students passing rather than one, (6.2%) this course alone improved our overall minority student progression numbers. An additional and important variable for these minority students was the attention and support they were getting from the minority nurse mentors. Saturation and intensity of the LTL, plus mentoring, demonstrated that change is definitely possible.

RETENTION AND GRADUATIONS

Retention and graduation rates were our main targets of review because we promised higher rates of minority graduates at each level along the AD/BSN/MSN continuum. Figure 12.1 presents our preclinical associate level retention figures for the years 1992 to 1994. The data indicate a positive, progressive rise in retention figures. In years 1990 to 1992 (Figure 12.1a), the two-year retention rate of preclinical students was 39% for full-time students and 54% for part-time students. The years 1991 to 1993 (Figure 12.1b), covered the interval in which we initiated our program, and retention rose to 50% and 58%, respectively. In the years 1992 to 1994 (Figure 12.1c), retention was 49% and 57% marking a 10% and 3% improvement in a two-year period.

Graduation rates of African American students (Figure 12.2) rose from 15% to 18% to 23%. Over the same period, Hispanic student graduations moved from 8.3% to 10.4% to 9.0%. The project has made a clear difference for our African American students. Our Hispanic students' needs, however, must be reexamined.

At Kean College, we are often asked how is it that our faculty is so diverse. There is a way to do it, and it actually was easy. We invite minority faculty to join us. When a faculty line was open, we invited our potential candidate (an African American PhD community health nurse, for example) for lunch and a tour of the campus. We offered an employment package that was as attractive as we could make it. We made it very clear that she would have our respect and support. And even with competition from prestigious universities, she chose Kean College. Our faculty is 50% minority and visibly demonstrates our goals.

The Kean College Department of Nursing BSN enrollments and graduations are outlined in Table 12.1. Wide publication of our recruitment and retention efforts has resulted in a progressive positive growth in enrollments and graduations of African American and Hispanic students. From 5 African American graduates in 1992, we moved to 10 graduates in 1994. Hispanic graduations, while low in number, have risen from 1 to 3.

Figure 12.1

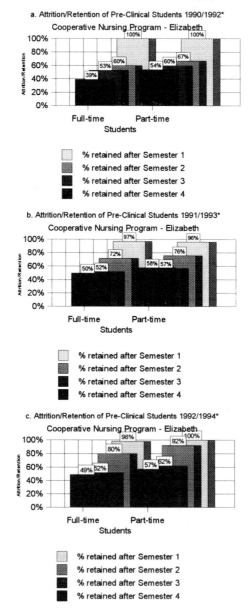

Figure 12.2

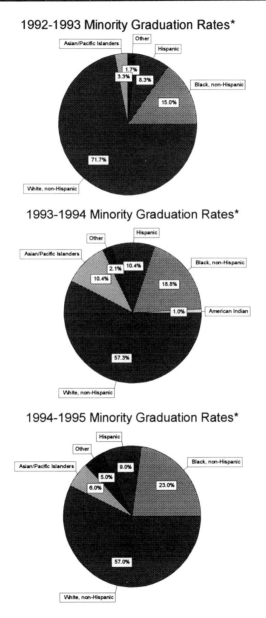

1992-1993 Minority Graduation Rates*

1993-1994 Minority Graduation Rates*

1994-1995 Minority Graduation Rates*

*Registrar—Cooperative Nursing Program—Elizabeth 8/94

Table 12.1   Kean College Department of Nursing Enrollments
and Graduations

	1992		1993		1994	
	Enrollment	Graduation	Enrollment	Graduation	Enrollment	Graduation
African American	27	5	38	7	40	10
Hispanic	14	1	11	2	11	3
White	155	27	171	32	142	29
Other	7	3	11	2	0	1

The graduate program enrollment is particularly significant. Started in January 1995, it has 18 students, 5 of whom are minority. Last year, there were 32 minorities enrolled in graduate study in all of New Jersey, and with our new numbers we have a 15.5% increase in one year. Invitations to enroll mean that we are tapping leaders and shaping our future.

TRENDS AND RECOMMENDATIONS

The improvement in retention and graduation numbers is encouraging and highlights the value of comprehensive approaches to complex problems. In particular, it is a testimony to faculty who are willing to explore change and implement curricula instructional method changes. The data recommendations to faculty and students include these suggestions:

- Attend to learning strategies (LTL) early in program.
- Identify friendship and academic networks as priorities even in the presence of time contraints; connectiveness is essential.
- Study in groups and use tutoring resources.
- Identify a role-model/mentor among faculty or senior students.
- Use a part-time program when family responsibilities are heavy.
- Keep career goals high; use mobility tracts to BSN and MSN levels.

Success is possible.

REFERENCES

Garbin, M. (Ed.). (1991). Assessing educational outcomes. New York: National League for Nursing Press.

Gronland, N. (1976). *Measurement & evaluation in teaching.* New York: Macmillan.

Knight, M. E., Lumsden, D. L., & Gallaro, D., (1991). *Outcomes assessment at Kean College of New Jersey.* Lanham, MD: University Press of America.

Munhall, P. L. (1994). *Qualitative research, proposals and reports: A guide.* NY: National League for Nursing Press.

Part Three

Educational Biculturalism Plus

13

Phenomenology: Looking at the Students' Lived Experience

Florence G. Sitelman and Robert Sitelman

THE CALL TO MEET A CHALLENGE

*W*hen the Project Director invited us to participate in a project aimed at securing better success rates for minority students who were aspiring to become nurses, we were puzzled by the role teachers of existentialism and phenomenology might play in such proceedings.

The project, we subsequently learned, included a research component that was to be divided into two distinctively different types of activities. The first was to consist of a number of research efforts, traditional in manner and quantitative in character, involving the accumulation and analysis of data culled from surveys and questionnaires or gathered from various studies and reports. The second form of research was termed "qualitative," and was to employ insights, techniques, and perspectives developed in phenomenology. This new approach, we were told, represented, if not a rebellion against traditional methodologies, then, at the very least, an effort to supplement and support them. It was felt that traditional, quantitative techniques would not be sufficient to satisfy the purposes of the project. The project directors were seeking to carve out a new direction for their research efforts, and they were turning to existentialism and phenomenology to find support. The methodology they wanted to cultivate would be distinctive, and, as it turned out, was aimed at redefining—and uplifting—their activities in the face of new challenges.

STUDENTS AT RISK

In a rapidly changing health care environment, the aspiring student nurse has to face frightening and potentially oppressive demands. This panoply of challenges involves fundamental behavior modifications for many aspirants. It requires basic shifts in deeply embedded attitudes and, at the same time, puts at risk strongly ingrained habits and learned responses for survival absorbed and integrated over a lifetime. The demands and related challenges are particularly significant for persons from culturally diverse backgrounds. These individuals are thrown suddenly into an alien if not hostile environment whose representatives assess, criticize, and judge performance and associated abilities with respect to standards of articulateness, reasoning aptitudes, powers of inference, and clarity of expression as well as required modes of discipline, perseverance, and initiative often discouraged, in the communities and households from which these students emerge.

The students who constitute the focus of the program risk isolation and hostility from their respective communities merely by enrolling in a course of study aimed at providing a professional and economic status that would remove them from those communities. Moreover, these students often arrive with a fractured self-image marked by immaturity, lack of confidence, and poor self-esteem. Thus, the threat of exile and alienation for such individuals of limited psychological and material resources makes them especially sensitive to any hint of failure, any suggestion of rejection or disapproval by the receiving culture. They will tend to exhibit high levels of passivity and inflexibility, and may appear to be less supple, agile, alert, energetic, responsive, or intelligent. They will, unsurprisingly, be quick to withdraw.

And all of this just at the very moment when the demands of the nursing profession are exploding, when the requirements are becoming more stringent, scrutiny is becoming more intense, and when standards for acceptance into the receiving community are becoming more rigorous. The prerequisites for approbation are tied to an expanding base of knowledge that generates increasing levels of expertise in an ever greater variety of academic disciplines spanning the physical and social sciences from mathematics and chemistry through psychology and sociology, in new technologies, methodologies, and procedures, in new discoveries in pharmacology, biology, physiology, in public health issues, in what is called "theories of caring" and "health and wellness" issues.

This new context in which student nurses suddenly find themselves, with its profusion of intellectual and psychological challenges, is, in fact, a hothouse for escalating self-consciousness, self-analysis, and self-critique. Heightened self-consciousness means distance from oneself. The self is divided, alienated from itself, and calls itself into question. It becomes suspicious of itself, uncertain, and bewildered. Individuals in such circumstances are prone to indecision and are less capable of strong action or effective performance, but tend to feel besieged, overwhelmed, uncertain, and defensive. A volatile anxiety quickly convertible one moment into despair the next moment into guilt and self-deprecation fills the chasm that separates the self from itself. This is a time of heightened subjectivity, of an inflamed interior. This is the female minority student, showing an abysmally high failure rate, who is the focus of this project which aims to produce increased success rates for ethnic minorities seeking to become nurses.

THE EXISTENTIAL SITUATION

The project directors asked for a preliminary discussion of existentialism before they undertook a full investigation of phenomenology's methods, principles, procedures, and techniques for use in the new form of study that they characterized as "qualitative research." And so we began with some existentialism.

Our dialogue aimed at heightening sensitivity to the particularities of the subjects of the study, a clarity not beclouded by presumptions or by inapplicable theories. Theory is helpful in concentrating perception insofar as it provides suggestions and cues for guiding our vision as we try to grasp what is before us. Theory also supplements vision by providing a framework for understanding what we see and for placing the perceived object in a set of relationships that can yield causal connection, prediction, measure and, at some point, control. But theory, though an integral part of vision, is no substitute for vision, and cannot replace it. Heightened sensitivity and clear vision must penetrate to what is particular and unique in its object; it must be specific. The clarified vision does not dissolve its object into its relationships, but brings those relationships and connections into play by giving the fullest possible exposure to the special, individual, and particular character of the object. For the nurse as researcher, perception should guide theory; for the nurse as investigator, theory should clarify perception. What the project directors sought in this exercise in philosophic theory was heightened sensitivity to the subjective conditions of a high-risk student body living on the outskirts of chaos and disruption, at the edge of failure.

The human mind tends toward abstraction. Thinking employs language, and language as we normally employ it is verbal, although it can take other forms—musical, mathematical, color, and so on. Nevertheless, except for these highly qualified and idiosyncratic modes of discourse, language is fundamentally the medium of words, which are, by their nature, general in character. And this means that as we think about something—a situation or person—using words, we tend to move away from the particularities of that situation or person to what is general and shared in common by that situation or person, to universalities of which the situation or person is but an instance. Thinking tends to distance us and allows us to "objectify" the object of our attention. Philosophers have pointed out that whereas our bodies locate us in a place and time, give us a social and historical context and individuate us from all others with whom we may or may not share various features, the human mind is an instrument of transcendence that allows the individual to rise above and beyond a situation, to be elsewhere in thought—in anticipation, reverie, memory, or daydream—than where the body is actually located.

Unlike thinking, verbalizing, or theoretizing, feeling tends to move us into our bodies and away from abstraction. It propels us into the situational moment. It is a form of immediacy. As we move from thinking to feeling, we may be conscious of a sense of "falling" associated with a movement down into the body where we are in the grips of the occasion and no longer, as it were, floating above it all. Loss of freedom and a sense of passivity are associated with this collapse into the situation, this threat of becoming one with our bodies. Our mind or spirit is an animating presence, the intellect an active force, but feelings, like desires, are depicted as drives that happen to us, forces that push and incline us. Thus we "fall" in love, "suffer" this or that emotion, "feel" this or that sensation, yearning, or passion—as if our selves and what we feel are different from each other.

Anxiety, fear, despair, guilt, and shame, like physical pain and illness, drive us toward our bodies and fix us in the moment. They are features of a pained self-consciousness that is split from itself and its body. They are marked by elements of self-rejection and are experienced as a kind of frightful hovering. They fill the void produced by an afflicted self-consciousness. They are experienced as a friction, a tearing or irritation pulsates between what would transcend and what threatens to become a collapse, a loss of self-control, and a disintegration, of a self that is divided against itself and would be other than itself. These feelings challenge thought and can plunge us into what could overwhelm us. Just give into them, and they neutralize reason and judgment, dissipate our capacity for action, and leave us overcome by what ails us. We become our immediacy when we forfeit our transcendence. But the immediate is also the contingent, the fleeting, and the flimsy. Branded by its unstable temporality, subject to its various vulnerabilities and notable dependencies, the body into which we may sink in such moments of the besieged spirit curtails our freedom, making us subject to our worst terrors and incapable of purposive action. The fall into passivity and helplessness that is connected with immersion into the body brings into consciousness an engulfing sense of purposelessness—of meaninglessness and absurdity—the painful absurdity of our own being and, therefore, of all being.

It is just these features of human experience, postulated as categories of thought, that constitute the subject matter of existentialist philosophy. Existentialism attempts to think through the human condition as embodied consciousness. Often labeled as humanism, its focus is on consciousness grounded in immediacy and conditioned by particularity. It explores the regions where reason fails us and, in the process, illuminates reason's outer limits, exposing that vast and dense geography that eludes reason's grasp and conditions its sovereignty. Spinning off the themes of situated freedom and the confrontation with absurdity, existentialism probes such states of consciousness as anxiety, dread, grief, alienation, isolation, and emptiness. It seeks to elucidate those painful elements of experience that orbit the descent of consciousness into its body. And this effort to address anxiety, terror, despair, and desperation puts philosophic thought in syncopation with teachers who wish to assist minority students in the grips of an inflamed subjectivity.

The motifs of existentialism intersect with the purposes of the nurse researcher/teacher in at least two ways. The object of concern is the individual ensnared in the moment by a subjectivity under assault and in crisis. The occasion for the high-risk and alienated student is inflamed self-consciousness. When feelings and thought are in transparent conflict, the split self reveals to a vulnerable and transient consciousness its own limited condition. To confront oneself at that level is to know oneself dependent and in passage. Freedom, meaning, and the ability to act are at risk and, therefore, in question. Anxiety, dread, despair, and alienation will color if not command the situation. But these elements of the occasion are not simply features of the student's awareness and, therefore, subjective realities external to the nurse teacher and researcher. For, as we all know, feelings are, like viruses, contagious. They also are like music permeating what they surround, and it is only through concentrated effort that we can distance ourselves from them. Situations are tense, sad, unhappy, and only through abstraction do we locate and subjectivize the sustaining feelings. Thus, the nurse researcher/teacher, confronting the student's besieged and divided subjectivity, confronts equally in herself the potential if not the actuality of a divided consciousness. The teacher, as the student, faces a potential sense of disequilibrium and alienation, the proclivity to feel threatened, defensive, anxious and uncomfortable, angry or contemptuous. There is a tempting impulse to reject students who, because of feeling threatened, and fearful of rejection, show a passive coldness if not an arrogant and truculent contempt for the teacher. In the face of a challenge to his or her integrity and sense of purpose, the teacher must struggle to maintain an integrated, undivided sense of self in order to sustain a constructive and effective concern for the student's condition. No wonder, then, that the explorations of the existentialist philosophers have struck a chord of special pertinence for faculty in pursuit of clues to unravel their own professional experience.

THE PHENOMENOLOGICAL METHOD

The thrust of the existentialist philosopher into embodied immediacy also provides the nurse researcher or teacher with the possible ground for a new beginning. The desire to carve out a new territory that will expand research is at one with the urge to return to the source, in this case, the experience in all of its peculiar and dramatic vivacity. The sensibilities of the existentialist philosopher coincide with the ambition to develop a new and different understanding of the nursing profession. Existentialism can serve as a prelude and provide a set of sustaining motifs for a new kind of nursing research that would rethink its sources by excavating and reclaiming its own ground. But such an undertaking requires a different kind of methodology with techniques that open up and illuminate the moment rather than quantify or abstract away from the situation.

And so the goal of faculty to forge a sensitivity that will support responsiveness to the assailed and fractured subjectivities of high-risk students converges with the aim of existentialists to return to immediacies. Following the trail of the great existentialist thinkers of the twentieth century, these nurse researchers and teachers find themselves in the precincts of phenomenology. Just as it is little accident that the existentialist philosopher finds hospitality and comfort in the works of the phenomenologist, nurse researchers and teachers also should find that phenomenology's language and methodology, aimed at a return to the phenomena, are congenial to their own purposes.

This turn to phenomenology represents, then, an effort to secure a foundation for a different kind of discipline attuned to the peculiar character of the subject matter and focused, in this case, on the immediacy of the embodied consciousness captured by a situation and in crisis. The endeavor is a natural extension of the project leaders' engagement with existentialist thought. It represents an effort to reclaim the phenomenon. "Qualitative research" is the label they have given to this new endeavor.

Phenomenology, or the science of the phenomenon, while rooted in early nineteenth-century philosophy, assumes its pertinence for the nurse researcher and teacher in the work of certain twentieth-century, continental philosophers who were concerned to hammer out a methodology that would, among other things, secure the foundations for the empirical and mathematical sciences. This "science of sciences" was understood, not as a competing study that would replace prevailing sciences, but as a supportive adjunct to sociology, psychology, physics, and so on. Its purpose was to supplement those sciences by providing a set of presuppositionless descriptions that would undergird the presuppositions of the natural and mathematical sciences, which rest on both a presumed terminology itself needing explication and on a preconceived "objective" reality itself subject to question.

Phenomenology, as a presuppositionless science, seeks to know its own foundations. Its practitioners characterize it as a "rigorous science" because phenomenological investigation returns to the things-in-themselves in an effort to apprehend its subject matter prior to the implementation of any abstractive, inductive, or deductive applications, or the imposition of any theoretical models. Its purpose is description, not causal analysis. Its object is the "phenomenon," not empirical data, which is already marked by presumptions, its identification and accumulation being the refined product of some theory-bound, purposive thinking. In this respect, the goal of the phenomenologist, who pursues a presuppositionless science by returning to things-in-themselves, coalesces with the program of the TLC leaders, who are attempting to apprehend the hazard-ridden immediacies of the aspiring minority students at risk and in crisis.

Such an endeavor demands a methodology and an associated terminology that will differ sharply from those employed by the abstractive and inductive models of research found in the traditional sciences. The purpose of the enterprise, at least in its initial stage, is full confrontation. The intent is to tear away the veil of theories and abstract vocabulary that would distance us from the original experience; the aim is to break through the conceptual apparatus, presumptions, and imported generalizations that blind us to the particular in all its specificity. The new science of nursing is, in this respect, a call to heightened sensitivity, a demand for increased focus.

While researchers in the natural sciences move up and away from the data they contemplate in order to uncover ever more general laws that take into account ever more disparate particulars, the phenomenologists move more deeply into the object of their study to grasp the essential character of that object. For the nurse researchers and teachers involved in the TLC project, the object of the study centers around the alienated, failing student learner. The phenomenon pursued is to be discovered in the very immediacy of that experience. But experience in its most immediate form is not normal experience as we ordinarily characterize it, for the latter is already distilled by theory and refined by a point of view. The object of our investigation is experience in its immediacy, prior to the importation of our reconstructive or deconstructive formulations. This difference between the material of phenomenological research, (i.e., the "phenomena,") and the stuff of normal experience is expressed by the phenomenologists' claim that theirs is not an empirical study. The confrontation with the phenomenon, which is more pristine and elusive and, at the same time, more dense and thickly structured than the stuff of normal experience, requires a special and highly disciplined approach—the phenomenological method.

Reflection on the history of philosophy and the growth of the natural sciences reveals the theoretical and shifting character of what is taken as subjective or objective, of what is understood as real and what is considered as less or other than real (sometimes called "appearance"). Certain aspects of what we might refer to as "primordial," "raw," "immediate" experience are over time and as a consequence of a certain kind of abstractive sorting, isolated and labeled as "feelings." They are deemed subjective and internalized in an agent or person. These elements are distinguished from other aspects of the experience that are regarded as external or objective features, located in space and regarded as part of the physical or material world. Sometimes, moreover, differences will arise over aspects of experience not deemed "feelings" which may, like feelings, be regarded, nevertheless, as subjective or internal reactions of an agent rather than as objective or external realities. Colors, sounds, smells, tastes, odors, hot and cold are examples of what are sometimes classified as subjective reactions to what is the objective reality. Furthermore, investigation into experience reveals that our understanding of what is alive, and what is not alive varies and is theory-dependent. Thus urine, feces, blood, fire, the moon, certain words or expressions are to some people, at a certain level of experience, mere physical phenomena and to others, operating at a different level of experience, living realities. Then there is the related question of powers, forces, and faculties. There are words that kill; fluids that may not be touched. Things will not only exhibit associations and tendencies, they may be rife with purposes and capacities and may themselves be moved by attitudes and feelings, the "raging" storm, the "gentle" breeze, the "angry" sea, and so on. (The point is that we actually experience the sea as angry, the storm as raging, and only later separate a physical reality from an emotional colorization, an "actual given" from a projected feeling.) What is physical and what is nonphysical or "mental" is also the product of a certain intellectual sifting and arranging that may sometimes disguise a richly textured, multilayered complex of interrelated significations not captured by our mundane discourse and ordinary descriptions, which are, themselves, the product of a highly selective perspective. Experience in its immediacy is dense with values and shot through with meanings.

Phenomenology as a rigorous and presuppositionless science rejects all forms of reductionism and resists all distinctions between the real and the less-than-real, between the objective and the subjective, the literal and the imaginary or poetic, and so forth. The latter distinctions are reductive and rest on presuppositions, whereas a rigorous science must comprehend its own foundations and, therefore, function without such presuppositions. It thus suspends questions about what exists or does not exist, what is real and what is only imagined, in order to deliver its subject matter in all of its experienced fullness to the exploring consciousness.

Reflective activity attempts to bring to light what is latent and hidden in our ordinary experience. This highly intense, rigorous, and strenuous engagement with objects in consciousness, assumed as an effort to clarify what is suppressed in ordinary experience, is contrasted with normal perceptual activity by being referred to as "intuition." The phenomenological method is adopted as a form of scrutiny aimed at securing intuitions.

It is this science of intuitions, intended to elicit what is veiled but nevertheless present and active in ordinary experience, that is employed as a model for qualitative research. Qualitative research is, then, a science of intuitions whose concern is the phenomenon, and whose aim is to make explicit what is present but hidden both in normal experience and in our ordinary accounts of it. The method is intended to generate recognition, a new awareness of what is already present but unacknowledged by us. The desire to achieve recognition, which is a critical feature of qualitative research, helps to confirm the claims of the researcher and is added apprehension. It represents an expanded awareness.

The concept of recognition suggests a notion of control. The descriptive science of expanded awareness is not uncontrolled ramblings, but is aimed at specific elicitations. It incorporates in its study of what we have called "experience in its immediacy," a rich variety of associations and relationships, all manner of connections, including those that, from a different and opposing perspective, might be regarded as unreal, mere appearance, or subjective imaginings, and, therefore, fit to be discarded in any legitimate examination of the occasion. Description, like any other conscious activity, must be informed by a purpose that can give discipline to the effort. That goal, which is the object of our search, has been characterized by the phenomenologists as the "idea" or "essence" of that which is under study. Qualitative research, then, if emulating the phenomenological method, must call for explicitness guided by recognition to uncover the essences of what it would study, in this case, the various forms of an embodied consciousness in the throes of immediacy, challenged and put at risk by the dominant culture.

An essence defines or distinguishes something; it is what makes it the type of thing it is. It refers to that feature or cluster of features in an object, activity, occasion, or event without whose presence that object, activity, occasion, or event would not be the kind of thing it is. The effort to articulate intuitions of certain phenomena by the nurse researcher or teacher constitutes, then, an attempt to produce apprehensions of the essences, that is, the defining features, of particular experiences in their immediacy as they are undergone by an embodied consciousness in crisis. The effort to intuit and describe the experience of the embodied consciousness caught in the existential moment and attended by the associated feelings of anxiety, dread, self-doubt, shame, alienation, and so on, will be subject to the workings of the imagination in at least two ways:

1. *Various workings of the imagination may help to constitute the sought-after essence of the experience under scrutiny.* Therefore, such imaginative elements are to be included in a nonreductive, presuppositionless description. What an empirical consciousness, a modern, commonsensical intelligence, might know and characterize as imaginative or poetical embellishments of an objective reality generated by a stimulated subjectivity need not be so perceived or experienced by an embodied consciousness grounded in immediacy. These features of the moment may, therefore, not only help to constitute the essential and decisive elements of the occasion, but may do so without being distinguished as somehow less than real or as "mere" imaginings. They may be experienced as aspects of the situation equally real, equally vivacious and forceful, as those features, those things, activities, and powers of the occasion that the commonsense, empirical consciousness deems real in our mundane experience. Qualitative research modeled on the phenomenological

method must then open itself to what we might think of as the poetical and imaginative features of the situation, that is, its subjective elements. And it must treat those subjective elements with the same unconditioned regard, concern, and respect that it would accord to what we normally refer to as the real or objective features of the occasion, not distinguishing them as other than real, as mere "appearance," or as peripheral in significance. It must respond to levels of signification, to tiers of meaning not normally acknowledged or recognized by the commonsense, empirical consciousness. It must see more deeply into the situation to make explicit what is only latent and hidden in ordinary experience. In pursuit of the essence of this or that experience of an embodied consciousness in crisis, the qualitative researcher aims at unqualified immediacy alive with the striated forms of the poetic imagination, dense with the values and significations of an undifferentiated subjective-objectivity. If the object is intensified focus, the goal is wholeness.

2. *The effort may call for a certain amount of imaginative "play" by the investigator.* To define and distinguish features of the occasion, and locate what is decisive in the moment, the investigator will need to vary, to add and drop, to diminish and intensify, to reshuffle and reposition the components of the situation. Such changes are intended to enable the investigator to apprehend the essential features of the situation (its defining or decisive features) as well as how varying this or that feature, or this or that congerie of features, will alter what is essential or decisive in the situation. But such variations of the components of an occasion are the work of the imagination in free play. The institution of imagined variations in the object of interest aims at grasping what is unchanging, that is, what cannot change, if the situation is to remain what it essentially is. In the free play of the imagination, questions about what is real or unreal, what exists and what does not exist, what "actual" forces or powers are in operation or not in operation are suspended for the purposes of the investigation. The components of what is decisive in the occasion must be grasped, as well as how alteration of the components will redefine what is essential to the occasion. And here, once again, the free and full play of the imagination will be critical to the effort.

Art, music, and poetry are explicit, acknowledged expressions of an engaged and disciplined imagination. What we may refer to as the "poetic imagination" provides heightened and intensified articulation of felt experience. Clarity and precision of expression are values of an exactitude that is measured by its veracity, by how true the assertion is to its object. Imagery must not only be evocative, it must also be apt, bringing to the surface what is otherwise hidden in the perception. Exactitude and aptness must express the full amplitude of the experience and give voice, among other things, to the emotive elements, the realities as felt, that help to constitute the occasion. Discipline refines its object, and sheds what is irrelevant, diversionary, and inessential. The poetic imagination aims at the essences of things and is an indispensable tool for the successful phenomenological investigation. Qualitative research, as an application of the phenomenological method, will have recourse to the poet, to the works and usages of the poetic imagination.

A SCIENCE OF NURTURING EMERGES

The divided and unstable consciousness, challenged and at risk, anxious-ridden and suspicious of itself, trembling at the edge of its own immediacy, resembles the earliest experience of the child ensnared in his or her body. The disarray and disorientation of a consciousness in crisis is reflective of the self-centered, limited awareness of a young mind not yet characterized by a mature sense of space or time or otherness. The same fragmented notions of location and distorted sense of geography, the same fixations in the moment coupled with fractured judgment and confused ideas of causal efficacy that are exhibited in the anxiety, dread, and depression of the consciousness on the verge of collapsing into its immediacy will be found in the tender and uncertain gropings of the infant attempting to steady itself. The same lack of control and sense of vulnerability coupled with feelings of helplessness and dependence that are characteristic of the child's mental life are featured in the older, but unsteady consciousness that is on the brink of plummeting inward. And, similarly, often times as not, the same need—although it may vary in form and manner—for supportive nurturing associated with a mother's relationship to her young is to be found in the dislocated student nurse, culturally as well as intellectually and physically alienated from the dominant social order that is to assess and pass judgment on her. Be it an art or a science or an art struggling to be a science, successful nursing instruction—in particular, instruction geared to the population in our study—can accurately be described as, among other things, an art or science of nurturing.

Nurturing, normally associated with successful mothering, is a critical component of nursing care, which must address the sense of disequilibrium, disarray, and fragmentation that normally attends the divided consciousness confronting illness, pain, and possible death. It entails sensitivity to and anticipation of the needs and concerns of another person collapsing into their immediacy. It is a caring that includes tending to another, providing support and nourishment that helps the other move to a fuller, more integrated state of equilibrium. Successful nurturing requires attendance to the moment. Its focus is on, not away from, its object. It must read clues, apprehend nonverbalized feelings, and grasp what is essential for another consciousness in some greater or lesser state of crisis. It must be as responsive to the emotional and the imaginary elements of an anxious and vulnerable consciousness as it is alert to physical needs and material realities. It must be intuitive, imaginative, and take in its object whole. It should not be distracted by abstraction, desensitized by theory, or constricted by preconceptions. In short, it should follow a pattern that gives voice to those very qualities of mind that phenomenological methodology puts to the test.

If these facets of nurturing are, indeed, special components of the nursing occupation, is it, then, any wonder that a new, reinvigorated nursing instruction aimed at a high-risk, challenged population should associate itself with a methodology that speaks to the distinctive values of the profession? Qualitative research is a frontier science, not simply because it represents an effort to isolate a new and different subject matter or because it embraces a pioneer procedure. It is revolutionary because it emerges as a distinctive nursing science. Aimed at carving out a science of nurturing, it affirms a methodology commensurate with itself. And in doing so, it champions those special virtues, those operations of consciousness that bespeak values and strengths of mind that have been associated with the successful teacher of the challenged, high-risk student. It is a form of study, then, that attempts to formulate a new approach to a different subject matter, and is at the same time a scientifically based expression of a nurturing profession and reflects its distinctive features. If successful, it could give all of modern instructional study a fresh turn, spread into other forms of concern, and provide a new face to social science research.

REFERENCES

Bachelard, B. (1969). *The poetics of space.* Boston: Beacon.

Edie, J. P. (1962). *What is phenomenology?* Chicago: Quadrangle Books.

Farber, M. (1943). *The foundation of phenomenology.* Cambridge, MA: Harvard University Press.

Kockelman, J. (1967a). *A first introduction to Husserl's phenomenology.* Pittsburgh: Duquesne University Press.

Kockelman, J. (1967b). *Phenomenology.* Garden City, NY: Doubleday.

Lauer, Q. (1958). *The triumph of subjectivity.* New York: Fordham University Press.

Luiipen, W. (1965). *Existential phenomenology.* Pittsburgh: Duquesne University Press.

Spiegelberg, H. (1960). *The phenomenological movement: A historical introduction.* Martinus, Nijhoff: Hague.

14

Educating Faculty in the Concept of Educational Biculturalism: A Comparative Study of Sociocultural Influences in Nursing Students' Experience in School

Dula F. Pacquiao

*A*nthropologists have argued for the centrality of value orientations in conditioning thoughts and behaviors of groups of people, presumably creating long-lasting effects on the individual's personality. Benedict (1934) has postulated the concept of characteristic purposes within a culture that provide members with consistent patterns of thought and action not shared by other societies. Values are theorized as the central organizing force that give direction to people's lives as well as meanings for their actions in any society (Foster, 1965; Goldschmidt, 1954; Kluckhohn, C. 1943).

Research in cognitive psychology has revealed that students bring to any new learning situation a body of knowledge, ideas, concepts, and understandings that they have developed from prior learning experiences. Learners use this organized structure of prior knowledge as a kind of sense-making mechanism to interpret, comprehend, judge, connect, and store new information (L. M. Anderson, 1989; Larkin, 1993). Despite the lack of agreement regarding the definition of cognitive vis-à-vis learning style, it is important to recognize that cognition is linked intimately with and deeply rooted in the affective, temperamental, and motivational structure of personality (Messick, 1984). Cognitive styles suggest uniqueness in the way people take in, process, and use information from their environment (Cropley & Field, 1969).

Greater diversity in student population in American higher education has been predicted. By the year 2000, student populations are likely to include more women, older age groups, ethnically diverse groups, commuters, and part-time students. For ethnic minority students however, increasing diversity has not been associated with proportionate rates of retention, graduation, and achievement in graduate education (Cuseo, 1992).

Demographic changes in the student population entering nursing and in the population of health care providers and recipients of health care services have been documented. The trend toward increasing cultural diversity is predicted to continue in the general population in this country. By the year 2080, it is projected that the total population in the United States will consist of 24% Latinos, 15% African Americans, and 12% Asian Americans (Cortes, 1991). In nursing, multiculturalism issues have been precipitated not only by the changing demography within the country but also by the massive influx of international nurses who were primarily recruited to mitigate nursing personnel shortages in the past decade.

Increasing demographic shifts in nursing enrollments have not been associated with proportional rise in the academic achievement of ethnically diverse students. Retention and promotion rates among this group of students continue to remain low (M. Allen, Nunley, & Scott-Warner, 1988). Their success rates in the postgraduation licensure examinations are lagging behind their white American counterparts. Recent statistics on minority representations in the health disciplines depict that between 86% and 94% of health care practitioners are whites (Werning, 1992).

In this country, there are numerous educational pathways to enter the field of nursing. One way is through the two-year associate degree program offered in community colleges. A second route is through hospital schools of nursing offering a three-year diploma in nursing. The third alternative is the four-year baccalaureate degree program offered by senior colleges and universities. A few programs offer the generic master's in nursing degree. Graduates of all these programs are eligible to take the same licensure examination to obtain the status of a registered nurse (RN) which is a universal requirement for practice.

Most ethnic minorities enter the field of nursing by way of the two-year associate degree program at community colleges, which is the fastest as well as most affordable route. Ethnic minority students are not well represented in institutions of higher learning for nursing, which limits their access to leadership positions in the profession. By the year 2000, the projected shortfall of baccalaureate prepared nurses and those with graduate degrees is as high as 50% and 66% respectively (Morrissey, 1987).

REVIEW OF LITERATURE

There is increasing awareness that cultural and educational institutions are inseparable. Studies document that for some students, the classroom is too often a place of cultural isolation with norms, values, and customs that contradict their own. Most faculty have been socialized into monocultural homes and unexamined values of the dominant culture, which provide the context for evaluating all other values and behaviors (Marchesani & Adams, 1992). Exposure to unfamiliar culture stimulates self-doubt, confusion, and self-shock that challenge the individual's self-image (Zaharna, 1989). Students with different cultural backgrounds often enter mainstream classrooms with a great deal of anxiety. Yet, as Pestalozzi (1951) has aptly pointed out, emotional security is necessary to cognitive development (Nel & Seckinger, 1993). Indeed, to many children, school is the primary contact with mainstream culture (Garcia, 1991).

Demographic characteristics of faculty in institutions of higher learning tend to be homogeneous (93% of professors are white, 70% of whom are males, 42–53 years of age) and not conducive to development of research in multicultural education (McKenna, 1989). Several studies underline the need to increase minority teachers to provide role models for students (Eubanks, 1988; Merino & Quintanar, 1988). Others suggest the need for further studies on the relationship between minority teachers and minority students' achievement (Ladson-Billings, 1992; Rist, 1970).

Differences in interactions between teachers and students attributable to race or ethnicity and gender are found to account for differences in student performance (Brophy & Good, 1984; Fennema & Peterson, 1986). Research in expectancy theory and social group theory argues that teachers' behavior toward students is influenced by their expectations of their students' abilities (Atkinson, 1964; Rogers, 1969; Rosenthal & Jacobson, 1968).

Shulman (1987) stresses the need for redefining teaching as more than mastering generic skills displayed in classroom behaviors and for examining the wisdom underlying pedagogical decisions within the teaching context. Explanations for low student performance in urban schools have frequently been blamed on the children's lack of ability, their parents, and cultural background instead of focusing on the schooling experiences of these students (Cuban, 1989).

In teaching reading and writing skills, Bartholamae and Petrosky (1986) propose that students who read submissively instead of participating in the textual content, need help in maintaining an open dialogue with their textbooks, focusing on what they remember from their reading, recognizing significance of these points, establishing connections, and making inferences. Pedagogical literature drawn from the principles of experiential tradition of active learning underlines the need to incorporate students' experiential and cultural background into the educational process (Dewey, 1938; Kolb, 1984; Piaget, 1971). Cognitive developmental literature helps account for students' difficulty in disengaging from their own personal experiences to reflect from a broader or different social perspective (Belenky et al., 1986).

Educational ethnographic literature points to the significant relationship between culturally congruent school practices and ethnically diverse students' scholastic achievement (Au & Jordan, 1981; Erickson, 1987; Erickson & Mohatt, 1982; McDermott, 1987; Ogbu, 1987; Phillips, 1983; Vogt, Jordan, & Tharp, 1987). Several authors uncover essential value differences between Anglo and other cultures with implications in students' learning and success in schools (J. Anderson, 1988; Gooden, 1993; Nel & Seckinger, 1993). There is strong evidence of institutionalized ethnocentric pedagogy with preconceived, idealized and monolithic values, behaviors, and characteristics that students should exhibit to succeed in school. These values frequently typify white American, middle-class values and experiences (Cervantes, 1984; Moll, 1988).

Sociological studies likewise document that schools perpetuate class structure in society. Bowles and Gintis (1976) contend that class structures persist through generations because schools are organized on a class basis as anticipatory socialization for the workplace. Bourdieu (1977) uses the concept of cultural capital, from which the French educational system is drawn, as the core determinant of academic success and access to social mobility in French society. In fact, cultural experiences of many poor and racial minority children are incompatible and in conflict with the cultural patterns operative within the school (Larkin, 1993).

There is a need to investigate classroom practices. Classrooms provide a highly organized, social and cultural learning environment. Its social context encompasses the dynamics of interpersonal relationships between teachers and students (Chavez, 1985; Stubbs, 1976). As intellectual and cultural mediators, teachers play a critical role in providing student access to knowledge and skills that have not been part of their previous out-of-school experience (Hernandez, 1993). Vygotsky (1978) and Wertsch (1978) find that the origins of metacognitive/self-directed development stem from social interactions between adults and children. Social interactions, especially between adults and children, are essential to learning and development.

Ladson-Billings (1989) defines culturally relevant teaching as instruction that empowers students, in contrast to assimilation teaching, which champions the status quo and transmits dominant beliefs and ideologies. Culturally relevant teaching is one that prepares the students to take social action against social structural inequality (Freire, 1970; Gardner, 1991; Sleeter & Grant, 1987).

Many studies identify varying learning styles among students. Klein (1951) distinguishes between levelers and sharpeners based on the degree of flexibility of their perception and judgment in different situations. Moore (1975) delineate field-dependent and field-independent learners as determined by the degree to which their learning is bound by situational variables. This continuum of learning styles has been applied to explain disparities between Latino and white American school performance (Ramirez & Castaneda, 1974). Frank (1983) notes that field-independent students perform significantly better in math problems, SATs, and recall tests. Kolb (1976) posits that learning is a four-stage cycle, requiring abilities that are polar opposites in two dimensions of learning (concrete to abstract and active to reflective observations). Learning style, according to Kolb, is derived from one aspect of each dimension that the learner tends to emphasize. Kagan (1964) conceptualizes a continuum between impulsivity and reflective learning styles. Ausubel (1968) formulates that individual accomplishment is a function of the person's sense of self-worth. Lack of an intrinsic sense of self-worth leads to a need to prove oneself through accomplishment. Cohen (1976) argues that while minority students often demonstrate preference for relational learning styles, schools, in general, favor and reward the analytical mode.

Several authors failed to observe consistent patterns indicating that students with certain personality traits respond better or achieve better when taking courses from teachers having corresponding personality traits (Cranston & McCort, 1985; Cronbach & Snow, 1977; Mahlios, 1981; Renninger & Snyder, 1986). DeCoux (1990) found a lack of significant relationship between learning styles and other variables as well as posed some serious questions about the validity and utility of Kolb's Learning Style Inventory. Many studies did not find significant differences between styles and student achievement (Burger, 1986; Conti & Welborn, 1986). Criticisms of learning style research focused on the existing ambiguity about the meaning of the term, the use of small samples in these studies (Guilford, 1980), lack of extensive studies dealing with various stylistic paradigms, lack of convincing evidence supporting the premise that distinguishing students' learning styles helped their performance, and failure to link issues with teachers' learning and teaching styles (Hilliard, 1989; Ladson-Billings, 1992). Kane (1984) demonstrated that the most successful students were those with flexible learning styles.

Although research does not demonstrate definitive links between learning styles and race, culture, and gender, consistent cultural and educational findings across disciplines suggest some correlations (J. Anderson & Adams, 1992). Research on traditional college programs depicts striking differences in learning styles apart from social and cultural considerations (Claxton & Murrell, 1987). Gender variations in learning styles is noted by Gilligan (1982) and Belenky and Associates (1986). Ethnic groups independent of socioeconomic differences demonstrate characteristic patterns of abilities that are different from one another (Messick, 1976). Lesser (1976) reports that students of similar ethnic background have similar patterns of mental capabilities that significantly differ from other cultural groups. Different groups' cultural value premises condition their socialization and learning styles (Kluckhohn & Strodbeck, 1961).

Most authors use learning and cognitive styles interchangeably. Others believe that learning style encompasses physiological, affective, and cognitive styles (Hyman & Rosoff, 1984). Generally, researchers agree that styles do not imply intelligence but rather pertain to the manner by which an individual processes stimuli (Even, 1982). Lack of clear definition of these terms impedes development of appropriate instruments for evaluating these concepts (Bonham, 1988). Most studies use students' achievement (course grades and GPAs) as measures of effective teaching (Thompson & Crutchlow, 1993).

Predictors of nursing students' success in the program and in the licensure examinations post-graduation are identified as GPAs, tests requiring use of English language (e.g., SATs and ACT), and grades in nursing courses (Boyle, 1986; Talarcyzk, 1989; Woodham & Taube, 1986; Younger & Grapp, 1992). However, quantitative measures of student achievement exclude various factors that are intimately linked with the lived experience of students. Tests can be assumed to measure the same types of achievement that speak minimally about the students' psychosocial backgrounds and perceptions of the learning environment affecting their school adjustment, integration, and achievement.

Tinto (1987) formulates a model delineating the longitudinal process inherent in students' departure from institutions of higher learning. According to the author, students' attributes interact with the institutional environment. Positive interactions enhance their integration and decisions to stay in school. A variety of variables are identified to affect attrition of students from colleges, such as out-of-class contact between faculty and students (Horne, 1987), financial resources, school scheduling, study skills (Smith, 1990), and time management (Astin, 1975). Several studies posit the significant influence of students' abilities and past performance in their retention and success in nursing programs (C. Allen, Higgs, & Holloway, 1988; Higgs, 1984; Hudepuhl & Reed, 1984).

Measures that were successful in promoting student retention in colleges emphasize collegewide commitment, faculty commitment and advisement, prompt and individualized attention to students, and satisfying relationships with faculty, staff, and peers (Courage & Godbey, 1992; Feldbaum & Leavitt, 1980; Thurber et al., 1989).

Student-faculty interactions in nursing schools were found to affect students' learning, self-confidence, and moral development. Positive faculty behaviors listed by students include caring, showing respect, honesty, and being a role model (Flagler, Loper-Powers, & Spitzer, 1988; Pugh, 1988; Schaffer & Juarez, 1993; Windsor, 1988). Unethical faculty behaviors included favoritism, lack of concern for students, giving unreasonable amounts of work, and showing prejudice (Keefe, 1982; Kleehammer, Hart, & Keck, 1990; Pagana, 1988; Theis, 1988).

Empirical evidence suggests the need to examine a broad concept such as cognitive style that encompasses the many variables in students' lives that are linked with their experiences at school. The study of social and cultural influences in students' cognitive style attempts to capture this vast phenomenon. Cross-cultural comparisons seek insight into existing intragroup and intergroup similarities and differences. Hence, this study is based on a qualitative investigation augmented by relevant quantitative measures of academic achievement. Qualitative research is characterized by including life events that together may yield holistic understanding of complex cognitive styles.

PROBLEM STATEMENT

Targeting three ethnic groups (African American, Filipino, and Hispanic) and white American nursing students, the study described in this chapter had the following goals:

1. Identify the sociocultural variables influencing their cognitive styles.
2. Describe their predominant cognitive modes.
3. Analyze the relationship between sociocultural factors and cognitive styles in determining outcomes of nursing programs and licensure exams.

SETTING

The study took place in an urban nursing school offering a program leading to an associate in science degree and a diploma in nursing. Located in Elizabeth, New Jersey, the school conducts a cooperative nursing program with the local county college. The College provides liberal arts and science courses to nursing students prior to or concurrent with their nursing curriculum.

Through its articulation agreement with Kean College's Department of Nursing, graduates of the school who wish to pursue their baccalaureate degrees continue at Kean College's nursing program. Kean College's Nursing Department has instituted through the Robert Wood Johnson Foundation grant, a *Transcultural Leadership Continuum* project (TLC) that promotes career mobility of minority students from the associate degree/level, through the baccalaureate, culminating in a master's degree at Kean College. The Nursing Department's master's degree in nursing is on clinical management in a transcultural context. This program targets minority students for nursing leadership roles in a variety of health care settings that primarily serve culturally diverse populations.

SUBJECTS

Participants (Table 14.1) in the study consisted of volunteer nursing students, nursing faculty, and support staff. Two levels of nursing students enrolled in the four nursing courses were invited to participate. Sixty students from the four nursing courses who met the demographic criteria responded to the questionnaire.

Table 14.1   Distribution of Student Participants

Items	Nure 131	Nure 132	Nure 231	Nure 232
Questionnaire	15	17	6	22
Additional Number in Focus Groups	6	4	0	0
Additional Number in Pre-NCLEX Exam Success	0	0	0	9
Total	21	21	6	31

Ten additional students who did not return the questionnaire participated in the focus group sessions. In addition to the 10 senior students who answered the questionnaire, 9 more gave their consent for inclusion in the examination of their achievement in the two NCLEX (licensure exams) simulated exams which were administered to all seniors prior to graduation.

Eleven faculty members and one Learning to Learn (LTL) staff person were interviewed. One English as a Second Language (ESL) counselor from the Community College was also interviewed.

BACKGROUND OF STUDENTS WHO RESPONDED TO QUESTIONNAIRE (TABLE 14.2)

The African American group of students consists of 13 females (4 Haitians, 3 Nigerians, and 6 African Americans) between the ages of 21 and 46 years. Seven respondents have attended at least 3 or 4 years of college and/or university (4 have baccalaureate degrees) before pursuing

Table 14.2   Ethnic Background of Respondents to Questionnaire*

Ethnicity	Nure 131	Nure 132	Nure 231	Nure 232
African American	4	1	3	5
Filipino	4	3	1	5
Hispanic	2	3	0	1
White American	5	10	1	12
Total	15	17	5	23

*Demographic data were obtained only from questionnaires.

nursing. Five respondents work as nurse's aides in hospitals. One subject identifies herself as a full-time student; the rest need self-employment of between 15 and 30 hours weekly for support.

Five of the six married subjects have children between the ages of 2 and 4 years. Six respondents were born outside the United States and have resided in this country for 5 to 19 years. Seven subjects identify a foreign language as the primary language spoken at home.

The Hispanic group consists of six female students in three nursing courses (NURE 131, 132, and 232). Their age range is 21 to 47 years. More than 50% of the subjects are single. Married subjects have between one to two children. Only one respondent is a full-time student. Except for one respondent, employment is outside the health care field. Weekly employment ranges between 8 and 34 hours.

Three subjects who were born outside the United States have resided in this country for a period ranging between 15 and 24 years. Two out of six respondents identify English as the primary language spoken at home. One respondent finished 5 years of secretarial school prior to entering nursing.

Filipino respondents consist of 13 students from all four nursing courses (2 males, 11 females). Their ages range between 19 and 42 years. Only one respondent was born in the United States. Those born in the Philippines have been U.S. residents for 2 to 20 years. Two respondents speak English only at home. Most of the subjects speak their native dialect in the Philippines.

Three of the five married subjects have between 1 and 4 children. Seven respondents have college degrees, three of which were obtained from American universities. Seven subjects work between 15 and 27 hours weekly, four are engaged in health fields as licensed practical nurses or unit secretaries. Except for one, all students with employment have previous college degrees prior to entering nursing school. Unemployed subjects who are single are supported fully by their parents while married ones are dependent on their spouse's income. One male subject is on a GI bill tuition program.

White American participants consist of 4 males and 24 females. They are between the ages of 22 and 51 years. Nine of the 11 married subjects have between 2 and 4 children each. Fifteen subjects work 16 to 45 hours weekly, mostly in health area fields as practical nurse, nursing assistant, medical assistant, radiology transport, unit secretary, or emergency medical technician. Only five working subjects are engaged in other employment such as waitressing, sales, and telemarketing. Nine respondents have previous experience in a university or senior college (one has a non-nursing degree).

All respondents were born in the United States and identified mixed ancestry from eastern and western Europe. Except for one subject whose language spoken at home is Italian, the rest indicated English as their primary language.

METHODOLOGY

The nature and purpose of the study were presented at a general faculty meeting in September 1993 and volunteers from faculty and staff were obtained. Students were informed of the study at each class by the researcher and respective faculty members.

The original plan for the study was to interview individual student volunteers on a weekly basis, using a tape recorder. Due to the large numbers of volunteers, the researcher decided to use a questionnaire (Table 14.3) to reach as many student volunteers as possible. Consent forms and questionnaires were distributed in each class and students were requested to return them in sealed envelopes through their teachers and/or directly to the researcher.

The first portion of the questionnaire dealt with demographic data from each student. In addition to the question of birthplace, students were asked to identify their ethnicity. Twelve open-ended questions were asked ranging from behaviors rewarded at home to those that they value in school, among their teachers and peers. One question dealt with

Table 14.3   Questionnaire

1. List behaviors or actions which are rewarded at home.
2. List qualities you admire in others.
3. Identify qualities of an ideal teacher.
4. How do you see yourself differently from your white American peers?
5. List experiences in school you found most helpful.
6. Identify those experiences in school which were frustrating.
7. How can things be better for you in school?
8. Identify ways which have been helpful in your studies.
9. Compare your learning in class and clinical.
10. Describe a class/lecture which you found to be understandable/enjoyable.
11. Describe a clinical experience you found most enjoyable/satisfying.
12. Which areas do you recognize you need help?

students' perceptions of similarities and differences between themselves and their peers (white American or ethnic minority).

Six taped individual interviews with students who were available at each weekly visit were also conducted. Weekly informal follow-up with students in the first nursing course took place. After a few weeks, students who were interviewed individually from the first nursing course sought the researcher's assistance voluntarily.

Focus group sessions held in each class included students who signed consent forms but did not return the questionnaires. Some students who were not involved with the study because they did not meet the demographic criteria participated in a few focus group sessions and provided some insights into their understanding of class material to be tested. Focus group sessions were conducted separately for each class.

The interview and focus group sessions dealt with the students' phenomenological descriptions of their school experience and the changes they perceived in themselves and in others through this experience. The researcher found that attendance at focus groups improved when scheduled prior to exams and a portion of the session was set aside to assist students in their test preparation.

Visits two to three times weekly were scheduled during Fall 1993 to build rapport with study participants and allow the researcher to be available at each group's convenience. Faculty members suggested the optimum time schedule for each group of students, accommodating their personal, work, and school commitments.

Faculty volunteers (Table 14.4) were interviewed regarding their perceptions of minority students, views of an ideal nursing student, and experiences with minority students in both classroom and clinical settings. The researcher was able to view some of the participants' written projects and exam grades.

Table 14.4   Faculty and Staff Participants*

Learning to Learn Staff	English as a Second Language Counselor	Nure 131	Nure 132	Nure 231	Nure 232
1	1	4	3	2	2
African American	White American	1 Filipino 3 White American	1 Filipino 2 White American	White American	1 Filipino 1 White American

*LTL staff and some faculty crossover courses. Faculty course placement was determined by their major course assignments for Fall semester 1993.

Some observations were carried out during students' LTL sessions. A follow-up interview was conducted by the researcher when students consented. One observation at the Skills Laboratory and an interview with one tutorial staff were also conducted. The focus of these interviews with the LTL and tutorial staff were the minority students' and the staff's experiences with them.

One interview with an ESL counselor who is acquainted with the researcher was done. This counselor was selected because of his experience in tutoring minority nursing students. The interview centered on his perceptions of their needs, measures that have been effective, and thoughts about nursing vis-à-vis other curricula.

Interview sessions lasted approximately one to two hours. Only scheduled individual student interviews were taped. At other sessions, the researcher jotted down notes.

All seniors are given two tests prior to graduation. This battery of tests simulates the licensure examination, and the results are used nationwide as exit criteria for graduation by most schools of nursing. This particular school uses the National League for Nursing and Mosby examinations. Both examinations have percentile scores comparing the students' scores with others nationwide as well as standardized norms obtained through many years of testing. Achievement of students is analyzed using the levels of cognitive domains and the core content areas of nursing. High achievement in these two tests has been documented to be proportionately related with success in the licensure examinations. Tests results of all senior students who consented to participate were included in the study.

ANALYSIS OF DATA

Student responses to the questionnaires, interviews, and focus group sessions were analyzed for recurrent themes. By using information obtained from all three methods and sets of informants, triangulation of phenomena occurred that enhanced validity and reliability of data.

Thematic analyses were done individually, for each nursing class group, for each ethnic group, and as a whole class group to discover intra- and intergroup similarities as well as differences. Examination of multi-groupings of data and informants assured further triangulation of events, thus minimizing chance occurrences and interpretation of phenomena.

Students' own descriptions and interpretations of their experiences were noted verbatim and through tape recordings to capture their contextualized perspective. Focus group session and individual interview findings were utilized to clarify further data from the questionnaire.

The same procedure was observed in analyzing faculty and staff responses. Data from individual interviews were analyzed separately and then triangulated with the group's responses. Thematic derivations of similarities and differences were done after completion of individual and group analyses.

Since the major portion of the study involved qualitative methods, the researcher's consistent weekly presence from September to December (Fall 1993) in the setting helped minimize the stranger effect on data gathering. Repeated participant observations within the naturalistic setting were aimed at preserving the integrity and genuineness of evolving events. Such protocol was essential in capturing the holistic and contextualized meanings and interpretations of phenomena.

FINDINGS: ETHNIC MINORITY GROUPS

Similarities between African-American, Filipino, and Hispanic Students

1. Core values esteemed at home influence their adaptation and interpretations of their experiences in school. Affective and relational attributes predominate their expectations of teachers and peers. Respondents have identified the strong value placed on smooth, interpersonal relations with others at home and in school in many ways:

   Generosity, loyalty, patience, willingness to help others, cooperation, sensitivity and respect for others' feelings, caring, supportive, warm, sincere, teamwork, doing things together, feelings of belonging and acceptance, feelings of being appreciated.

   Students overwhelmingly point out the positive influences in their school life by such factors as *peer support and teamwork, being appreciated by patients they took care of, and family support.* They have indicated their strong preference for personal, one-to-one, supportive relationships with teachers. They express *anxiety and feelings of intimidation when asked to speak in front of a group and repeat themselves when they are not understood.*

2. Hard work, persistence, and tenacity, which are esteemed and rewarded virtues at home, proved to be insignificant in their school achievement. Hard work as rewarded at home is equated with ability and success. Criteria for success in school are defined by diffused

rather than specific indices, merging hard work and long hours of study with achievement in examinations. Thus, application of concepts as required in the examinations is not viewed as separate and distinct from tedious reading and rereading of textbooks and rewriting of notes. Students experience cognitive and affective dissonance when their *exam grades do not reflect the degree and intensity of work they put into studying the material.* They are distressed by their teachers' *lack of appreciation for their hard work.* In contrast, their parents and family continue to reinforce the same value orientation which creates further conflict between what is perceived as hard work vis-à-vis ability (application of learning) that is demanded in exams.

Dissonance similarly results from the existing gap between accumulating factual knowledge vis-à-vis demonstrating ability to apply learning in many ways. Students go through the program unable to fathom what is expected because classroom experience appears to reinforce accumulation of factual information that is not emphasized by examinations. Students have predominately identified the *lack of assistance from their classroom teachers in establishing connections between facts with emphasis on learning and understanding important and difficult subject matter rather than cramming factual material.*

For most of these students, hard work with its correlative values of perseverance and patience, is the key to their retention and promotion in school. Examples of this hard work are:

> *Reading notes right after lecture, rewriting notes, underlining text, having two sets of notes (from the text and from the lecture), taping lectures, reading text before and after lectures, reading notes and text aloud, rehashing topics with study groups, validating understanding of material with peers, practicing skills in test-taking with computerized exams, practicing in skills lab.*

Investment of time and effort through repetitive enhancement of understanding requires hard work and persistence. Most students find the *pressures of coping with new material and written assignments for clinical courses are impediments to their ability to spend more time using the repetitive technique that has proven effective in their learning.* Equally frustrating is the drive by teachers to finish the bulk of information to be given in class instead of verifying that previous material is understood before advancing to the next lesson. Leaving much of the difficult material for the students to *learn on their own* compounds the total amount of material to decipher.

Students look for the same qualities in their teachers: *appreciation of their hard work, patience and willingness in helping them, not giving up on students who have difficulties, explaining material creatively and innovatively until it is understood, spending extra time and effort to assist students.*

3. Clinical experience is viewed as superior to classroom learning since it clarifies, demonstrates, and renders the abstract meaningful.

   Dealing with a specific situation makes the task more manageable and concrete. Seeing the effects of nursing protocols in actual patients provides the holistic meaning of classroom learning. Direct correlations between class and clinical experiences are described as learning that is *lasting, lifelike, satisfying, and meaningful.*

   Students are intimidated by their teachers' questions during clinical experiences and most of them identify *stress, anxiety, and panic as reasons for not being able to respond coherently when asked.* Nevertheless, students see the centrality of clinical practice to their understanding of the subject matter.

4. Self-confidence is important to success in the program. Ways of enhancing self-confidence include experiencing success in examinations, previous college and clinical experiences before entering nursing school, and positive reinforcements from patients.

   Students consider examinations as *most stressful, creating anxiety and panic reactions* during the test period. They are acutely aware of the possibility of being dismissed from the program after failures in two nursing courses. Additionally, they believe that success in the program largely hinges on *achievement in examinations rather than clinical performance.* They describe having a *mental block, difficulty understanding what is being asked, and a tendency to change their right answers for the wrong choice, realizing their mistakes soon after their anxiety has passed.* Students express agony over these *stupid errors.* Some identify *difficulty with vocabulary, comprehension, and reading speed* as reasons for their poor achievement in examinations.

   Previous experience in college or university appears to increase students' awareness of what is expected and enhances their confidence in dealing or negotiating with the school system. Students with college degrees tend to be more self-directed, assertive, and know how to demand retribution for discrepancies in their rights. Previous clinical experience gained prior to entering nursing as well as engagement in active nursing employment while in school improve self-confidence because students tend to be *more comfortable with the clinical skills and have more time to deal with classroom lessons.*

5. Nursing school experience creates profound changes in their personal and social life. Students believe that they are *more mature and intelligent* than their peers outside nursing. They have given up their social life because of school demands on their time. Time constraints have led to personal and family conflicts, especially for married students and those with children. Female students are torn between meeting demands from family and school. Most of their family members are unable to grasp fully the pressures nursing school extols on them.

   Students came to realize that nursing is an extremely rigorous program unknown to others outside the profession. Students with previous college degrees have stated that high achievement in other programs translates to an average grade in nursing. They have developed greater tolerance and acceptance of a C or C+ grade since entering nursing.

6. Strong individual motivation is a key to retention and promotion in the program. The Nursing program is considered extremely difficult, creating tremendous pressures and frustrations among students.

   Students' motivation to become a nurse and finish the program appears to be the sustaining factor that nurtures their continuation in the nursing program. This intrinsic motivation is reinforced by their peers and family members, hence the task of continuing in the program becomes a group effort, cushioning the impact of failures and disappointments along the way.

7. In comparing themselves with their white American peers, subjects relate that they have more responsibilities outside school, which limit their ability to use and access strategies that could enhance their achievement.

   Most subjects cite the *necessity of employment for long hours weekly to support themselves as the reason for time constraints in studying. Consistent participation in a study group with peers and using additional time to practice with computerized simulated examinations, practice clinical skills in the lab, and research in the library are labeled most helpful* by the students. All these measures entail availability and investment of extra time outside class hours.

Differences between Groups

In comparing the different ethnic minority groups, salient contrasts are noted between students in NURE 232, the last nursing course with other students in the program.

1. Seniors' expectations of themselves, teachers, and peers reflect professional values of accountability, interactive skills, and intellectual responsibility. Professional values are translated into attributes they look for in themselves and in others. In addition to affective and relational criteria, students identify more elaborate and numerous criteria pertinent to the teachers' knowledge of the subject matter, experience relevant to the topic, and ability to translate abstract formulations into comprehensible concepts.

   Correlatively, students at this level identify the need to interact with patients as a professional inclusive of abilities to explain and make patients appreciate the necessary information and skills for health promotion and restoration. Qualities that they admire in others as well as recognize as weaknesses in themselves, are requirements for taking on the professional role such as *assertiveness, standing up for what one believes, ability to persuade and convince others, feeling comfortable when speaking to a group.*

2. Seniors have increased awareness of themselves, unfolding elaborate portrayal of their strengths and weaknesses in objective and realistic terms. Recognition of communication and language difficulties have been identified to explain low achievement in examinations. Exposure to the various clinical specialties in nursing has allowed assessment of their individual potential in each one. Consequently, they were able to compare and diagnose their needs based on a wider experiential perspective. They developed further insights into their interests and lived experiences as they gained firsthand exposure to a variety of situations in each clinical specialty. For instance, providing care for patients in obstetrics and pediatrics has allowed students who are married and with children to make more sense of their own lives. An African American found the lecture on sickle cell anemia enriching since she has experienced this phenomenon in her life outside the school.

3. Self-affirmation is evident among seniors. They underscore their differences from their white American peers by affirming those values underlying these differences that are inherent to their identity and worth as an individual belonging to a particular cultural

group. Unlike other students in the program, respondents from NURE 232 express affirmation of their cultural background as unique and valuable to their being. They are cognizant of the existing differences but do not feel diminished by them. One student has aptly responded:

> *I am proud of my heritage. I am not intimidated by others. I see myself with an advantage because of my strong family support, making me strong and confident.*

They are accepting of the existing differences and find comfort in their uniqueness. One student states:

> *I don't really see myself as being different except in the color of my skin and my culture, which I think enhance me as a person because I am able to see the best in both worlds.*

Another senior states:

> *I don't really see any differences but I am aware that others perceive me as different (not as capable) and this awareness forces me to work harder at times to prove myself to them (even though I know I am capable and I don't have to prove myself at all).*

Students in NURE 231 and 232 have commented on the value of cultural discussions, having a cultural day, and exposure to various ethnic groups in school. At the same time, they object to some cultural beliefs and practices as *being made fun of by others.*

4. Seniors reiterate the importance of the theoretical basis of clinical practice. They emphasize the reciprocity between theory and clinical, realizing their combined significance rather than ranking one over the other.

   Seniors have commented that having gone over the necessary nursing skills in previous levels, they are more ready to concentrate on the theoretical aspects. *Meeting teachers' expectations of satisfactory clinical performance when students are just learning the new skill as well as coping with new theoretical content in class is considered a difficult task.*

   This group identifies the significance of strong pathophysiological background to their success. They claim that achievement in NURE 132, which introduces the application of pathophysiological concepts in nursing, generally determines the students' progression in succeeding nursing courses.

Some differences are noted in the demographic characteristics of the three ethnic groups of participants. More African American subjects are married with children and work more hours to support themselves. Many of them tend to work in the hospital as nurse's aides which is recognized as a positive influence in their learning. By contrast, employment among Hispanic students tends to be outside health care, depriving them of this additional reinforcement. On the other hand, Filipino participants tend to be mostly single, full-time students who enjoy financial support from their families and spouses. Actively working Filipino participants possess college degrees, which enable them to generate better income for fewer number of work hours.

FINDINGS: WHITE AMERICAN STUDENTS

Differences from Ethnic Minority Classmates

1. There is congruence between values rewarded at home and those esteemed in nursing school. Specific themes can be derived from the great majority of student responses:

   - Individualism: *honesty, truthfulness, straightforwardness, self-assurance, confidence, self-expression, assertiveness, self-motivation, sense of humor, outgoing.*
   - Achievement orientation: *work ethic, accomplishing tasks once started, quality of work, intelligence, good grades.*
   - Self-reliance: *independence, self-discipline, staying out of trouble, cleaning after yourself, practical, standing up for one's rights.*

   Although these students have indicated affective and relational attributes similar to those identified by ethnic minority students, they have predominately underlined values that are congruent with their teachers' expectations of a professional. Hence, cultural transition for these students from their homes to that of the professional school has more continuity than dissonance.

2. In comparing themselves with their ethnic minority classmates, a great majority of these students identified language differences. Respondents portrayed these differences in terms of the problems that these students have with *English comprehension, expressing their thoughts and feelings, and interacting with others.* A few

respondents described their ethnic minority classmates as *less out-going, less compassionate, and have different values, likes and dislikes from them.*

These themes were reiterated by their teachers who mostly identified *language and interactive skills as barriers* to ethnically diverse students' lack of achievement in nursing.

3. Respondents identified a variety of measures they implemented to improve their success in school. In addition to those strategies which ethnic minority students listed such as study groups, skills lab, rereading assigned chapters and rewriting notes, they also indicated *highly individualized and self-initiated methods such as reading other journals and purchasing additional reference books.* There seemed to be less reliance on study groups alone but a preference for self-study with group augmentation.

Similarities with Ethnic Minority Classmates

1. Expectations of an ideal teacher denote a combination of professional teaching abilities and relational, affective attributes.

Respondents from all groups identified the need for *caring, compassionate, fair, and patient teachers who take the time to assist students, listen to their problems, and have some flexibility to accommodate students' needs.* Caring teachers were portrayed as *fair, consistent, and clear in their expectations of students.* Respondents rated highly their experiences with teachers who can *provide the challenge and support for students to meet these challenges.* Teachers were admired for their *knowledge and intelligence and for their ability to make the material clear, understandable, and meaningful for students.* Respondents underscored their *feelings of disgust and denigration when intimidated, verbally abused, or insulted in front of others. Classes that were rushed with minimal time for students' questions were labeled as frustrating.*

Classroom or clinical experiences with faculty, as well as encounters outside the classroom, appeared to have significant influences in students' feelings about themselves and their total experience in school. One-on-one interactions with faculty were rated highly when done in a *caring, supportive manner.* On the other hand, inconsistent behaviors allowed for faculty and not acceptable for students were viewed as *unfair.* Students negatively regarded *lack of punctuality among faculty for classes and individual conferences.*

2. Curricular concerns were expressed by students from every group. They verbalized their feelings of being saturated by *too much content/material covered in most lectures, too much paperwork for clinical, and unreasonable expectations* of teachers regarding their clinical proficiency at each level. Consequently, respondents did not see the value of other learning experiences such as a community report during exam time. These were perceived as *unreasonably burdensome*. When carefully planned, these special projects such as cultural day presentations were considered positive experiences. Students' comments on their experiences with patients were positive.

Students' evaluations of learning experiences were highly conditioned by the way they were graded. Exams were the number one concern since most student failures were associated with them. Students described difficult exams as being *vague and unfair, and as asking off-the-wall questions.* Although white American respondents indicated lesser anxiety toward "tests" than their ethnic minority classmates, they were affected by the large numbers of failures among their peers.

Extracurricular experiences affected their life in school. Students who were involved in the student government found this to be a positive experience.

Increased congruence between students' and faculty's conceptualizations of a professional was noted as students progressed through the last nursing course. Among their needs, students identified further assistance with professional interactions with patients. White American subjects identified a higher proportion of interpersonal and caring behaviors as qualities they admired among their teachers and their peers.

FACULTY

Description of an Ideal Student

Faculty and staff offer greater homogeneity in their perceptions and evaluation of students. Three outstanding characteristics depict the ideal nursing student. Attributes that they believe to be central in the professional role of nurses include:

1. Capacity for self-direction. These self-directed students *take initiative to follow through independently, act and make decisions if*

necessary, and seek resources or assistance independently and promptly.

2. Sense of responsibility is demonstrated by *accountability for own actions/judgments, honesty and integrity in terms of own strengths and weaknesses, and thorough preparation for the task ahead.*

3. Critical thinking skills in terms of capability for *independent problem solving, common sense not to take things at face value, reflection and analysis of situation, seeing connections between concepts, determining priorities, abstract formulations, and tolerance of ambiguity.*

Experiences with Ethnic Minority Students

Although faculty make distinctions to allow for individual differences in students, their experiences with ethnic minority students center around three major impressions.

Language Problems.   Faculty identify this problem to be the most outstanding barrier in students' achievement. These students are perceived to have poor oral communication skills, slow reading ability, and limited vocabulary. These combined limitations interfere with their ability to express themselves clearly and coherently both orally and in writing. They have difficulty with reading speed and comprehension resulting in low achievement in examinations.

Incompatible Cognitive Skills and Styles.   Faculty state that these students favor *rote learning* and are predisposed to *copying rather than formulating their own thoughts, and accepting things as they are rather than thinking through the situation.* Others depict their thinking style as *rigid, circumscribed, and structured. They tend to be concrete, visual learners.*

Unassertive Interactions.   They are hesitant to *disagree, ask questions, or seek assistance from teachers or persons in authority.* This unassertive style of interaction is sometimes interpreted as *lack of initiative, compassion, or sense of responsibility. When students seek their peers' assistance rather than their teachers, they risk being misinformed. Teachers' criticisms tend to be personalized and internalized by the students.*

Faculty have delineated demographic characteristics of these students that contribute to their low achievement in school: *many existing responsibilities outside their student roles, lack of adequate support systems at home, and tendency to socialize with peers within the same ethnic group.* Others believe that their motivation for going to school may be *practical life concerns such as getting a job and making money rather than the intrinsic motivation of becoming a nurse.*

Measures recommended by faculty members to enhance these students' academic success revolve around three strategies:

1. Improve and remediate in English grammar and comprehension.
2. Accept self-responsibility for putting extra effort into studying and understanding the subject matter.
3. Develop self-awareness of own learning style and pursue measures to remedy situation actively, consistently, and promptly.

Quantitative Measures of Cognitive Styles

Of the 19 ethnic minority graduating seniors who consented to participate, less than 50% scored above the 50th percentile in both the NLN and Mosby exams. Except for two students, percentile scores in both exams were proportionally related with each other. The Mosby Assess Test provided a numerical breakdown of the 375 questions based on cognitive domains. Only two questions were knowledge questions. Approximately 79% of the total exam consisted of questions using application and analysis skills and another 29% required comprehension.

CONCLUSION

The eminent sociologist, Parsons (1968) has posited that the school is a potent socialization agent to societal norms. The American nuclear family is considered by Parsons as a necessary adaptation to changes accompanying industrialization and its concomitant social mobility. In the case of ethnic minority groups of students, their social and cultural background pose inherent conflicts toward an effective and smooth transition to the social norms espoused and valued by the school. Nursing school experience as shown in the study continues to support mainstream white American middle class ethos.

It has been identified that the American core values reflect that of the dominant white middle class Anglos (Kluckhohn, 1976), which place a premium on individualism and self-reliance (Hsu, 1983). Corollary values of individualism include those virtues underscoring the distinctiveness of the individual's personality, such as independence, competitiveness, self-expression, responsibility, and integrity. These values according to Hsu (1983) are pervasive, governing social interactions, family structure, and institutionalized norms.

It is evident from the faculty's conceptualizations of an ideal student that similar values are likewise institutionalized and fostered in nursing and considered critical to the assumption of professional nursing roles. Faculty uphold values of self-expression (language competence, assertiveness), independent thought (critical thinking), and self-reliance (sense of responsibility and self-direction). By contrast, ethnically diverse subjects in this study bring in values espoused at home underlining mutual interdependence and group centeredness. Corollary values of this core are attributes that support smooth interpersonal relations with others: sensitivity, respect, loyalty, generosity, sense of belonging, cooperation, tolerance, and accommodation of others.

The ultimate measure of students' cognitive ability is through application of learning rather than passive, rote learning. Whereas faculty esteem independent, creative, and highly individualized thought patterns, ethnic minority students on the other hand uphold relational, other-directed cognitive styles that limit expression of their innovative, individualized judgments.

Success in school therefore is a problematic achievement for students who must subjugate their indigenous learning styles and predispositions before they can immerse themselves in a different pattern of thinking and behaving. Experience in nursing school is a process of cognitive and affective dissonance causing upheavals within themselves and in their relations with others. Their challenge goes beyond intellectual pursuit, encompassing all other facets of their being. In fact, one staff member notes, *"They (ethnic minority students) tend to mimic the teachers instead of letting themselves unfold in the process."* Unfolding of personalities for this group of students heightens the conflict between their values and the norms espoused in school.

Teaching these students should make the values visible and transparent in both classroom and clinical settings. If connectedness of concepts is of value, classroom emphasis should elucidate this process for them. If students are to avoid rote learning, classes must stress the qualitative process of understanding rather than recitation of facts. As the philosopher John Dewey aptly pointed out, education is the artful discovery of connections between phenomena that begins and ends in the synthesis of the subject matter with everyday life, moving the students to greater realms of meanings. Gilligan (1982) has similarly observed that in contrast to men, women thrive on relationship and connectedness, which are fundamental to their moral and intellectual growth.

Senior students from the ethnic minority group in the study experience renewed self-confidence and reaffirmation of their identity, which influence positively their views of themselves and their relations with others. Other variables that nurture this affirmation are previous experiences in an institution of higher learning and clinical experience. Familiarity and exposure to the institutional norms outside their home environment improve their awareness of the world outside and what's expected of them.

Belenky and associates (1986) have found that among women in particular, there is a need to affirm their personal, subjective knowledge before they can bridge the gap toward the highly abstract, objective learning. According to the authors, women who validate their own innate ways of knowing become superior constructivists, creating a mix of the personal with the objective, instructing the mind with the emotive and vice versa. Constructive knowing is a prerequisite to the development of empathy.

In educating nurses, instructors should attempt to understand and accommodate their students' unique and innate personalities. It has been demonstrated in the literature that self-affirmation rather than total subjugation is a prelude to the development of superior intelligence, constructive knowing, and empathy. According to the philosopher Nel Noddings (1984), empathy is the capacity for taking others into oneself, seeing and feeling others. Empathy is basic to caring, which in nursing is highly desirable and critical to its practice. Caring has been identified by nursing scholars as the ethico-moral fabric underlying nursing practice (Leininger, 1991; Watson, 1985).

The findings of this study support the hypothesis that sociocultural influences exist affecting cognitive styles, schooling experiences, and academic success of student groups.

SEVERAL QUESTIONS ARE RAISED IN THIS STUDY

1. Should nursing education be monolithic and predicated on the premises of white middle-class American values?
2. Is superior cognitive ability measured by a singular exam that is universally applicable to all groups of people?
3. Is the paper-and-pencil test the best measure of nursing competency (licensure) when nursing is a combination of scientific knowledge base and the art of caregiving?

4. If language exists as a barrier, should other means of evaluation be devised to ascertain students' nursing capacities aside from the paper-and-pencil tests?

Another area that needs to be examined is the length of the nursing school program for ethnic minority students. Findings of this study suggest that schooling experience is not limited to acquisition of knowledge and skills in the practice of nursing. Survival and success in nursing school also include learning a new way of thinking and behaving that reflects the professional norms. Internalization of new values and norms necessitates a longer period of exposure and living in the world of different contexts and meanings. If cognition and values are intertwined, professional behavior and thought patterns are developed and manifested over time, which may not be evident early on when students are preoccupied in accumulation of facts about nursing.

1. When multiple entries to nursing practice exists, which one should be recommended for these students? On what basis is one program better than another?
2. What support systems can be developed to encourage minority enrollment in baccalaureate programs where economic returns are delayed?
3. What other strategies in school can be developed to facilitate transition of these students from their indigenous environment to that of professional nursing?

As this study suggests, success in nursing school for most ethnic minority students lies in biculturalism, which bridges the values between home and school. It is a process of self-affirmation and development that does not negate indigenous predispositions but allows flexibility and adaptation in a world of differences. Biculturalism needs an environment that fosters new values without devaluing others. Faculty and school administrators need training and skills to facilitate appreciation in every student group's uniqueness while learning to become the professional nurse to all kinds of people. Self-reconstruction for ethnic minority students is a process of self-affirmation and heightened awareness of their own values as they become this professional being who can practice in a world of multiple values and norms. Biculturalism is a process in becoming—the student becomes the adaptable professional whose behavior is shaped by nursing, by his or her own uniqueness, and by the values of others. The most significant concept here is that nursing values and norms are shaped by the people and society this profession serves. Professional values are not predetermined as the absolute good but are evolving and molded by the sociocultural forces in every society.

LIMITATIONS OF STUDY

A significant area that the study did not address is the examination of linguistic variables in cognition. Faculty and students have identified the salience of language in academic success necessitating further investigation into the relationship between language socialization and cognitive ability.

Schieffelin and Ochs (1985) posit that language socialization concerns socialization through the use of language and socialization to use language. Whereas language is a major source of information for cultural groups, it is likewise a major resource in understanding and transmitting that culture. Among British children, communication styles and forms are intimately linked to social identity formation and assumption of social roles (Bernstein, 1973). Studies have also demonstrated the existing differences between language socialization at home and in school; for some groups of children, language patterns acquired at home are not the same as those valued in school (Cook-Gumperz, 1973, 1977). Findings from this study suggest the need to examine the variable of language socialization in cognition of adult learners.

The achievement of ethnic minority graduating seniors in the prelicensure examinations reflects the continuing lag among these students in developing the cognitive operational skills that are emphasized in examinations in nursing schools and for licensure. Nursing schools aim to graduate employable nurses and are therefore vulnerable to the demands of the licensure examinations. If the value placed in these exams leans heavily on the higher level of cognitive domains, it is imperative that examinations in schools of nursing stress the same cognitive abilities. Curricular experiences must therefore explicate and make visible the process of applying concepts and synthesis of learning that promote connection between facts and enhance their meaningfulness to students whose indigenous worldviews may be different from those espoused in school.

A small, convenient, and purposeful sample was used in the study. Generalizations from the findings are limited and require further expansion and replication. This study should be examined within the context of empirical literature on the subject.

REFERENCES

Allen, C., Higgs, Z., & Holloway, J. (1988). Identifying students at risk for academic difficulty. *Journal of Professional Nursing, 4,* 113-118.

Allen, M., Nunley, I., & Scott-Warner, M. (1988). Recruitment and retention of black students in baccalaureate nursing programs. *Journal of Nursing Education, 27*(4), 107-116.

Anderson, J. (1988). Cognitive styles and multicultural populations. *Journal of Teacher Education, 39*(1), 2-9.

Anderson, J., & Adams, M. (Spring, 1992). Diverse student population: Implications for institutional design. In L. L. B. Border & N. V. N. Chism (Eds.), *Teaching for Diversity, 49,* 19-33.

Anderson, L. M. (1989). Learners and learning. In M. C. Reynolds (Ed.), *Knowledge base for the beginning teacher* (pp. 85-99). New York: Pergamon.

Astin, A. (1975). *Preventing students from dropping out.* San Francisco: Jossey-Bass.

Atkinson, J. W. (1964). *An introduction to motivation.* Princeton, NJ: Van Nostrand.

Au, K., & Jordan, C. (1981). Teaching reading to Hawaiian children: Finding a culturally-appropriate solution. In H. Trueba, G. Guthrie, & K. Au (Eds.), *Culture and the bilingual classroom: Studies in classroom ethnography* (pp. 139-152). Rowley, MA: Newbury House.

Ausubel, D. P. (1968). *Educational psychology: A cognitive view.* New York: Holt, Rinehart and Winston.

Bartholamae, D., & Petrosky, A. (1986). *Facts, artifacts, and counterfacts: Theory and method for a reading and writing course.* Upper Montclair, NJ: Boynton/Cook.

Belenky, M. F., Clincky, B. M., Goldberger, N. R., & Taule, J. M. (1986). *Women's ways of knowing: The development of self, voice and mind.* New York: Basic Books.

Benedict, R. (1934). *Patterns of culture.* Boston: Houghton Mifflin.

Bernstein, B. (1973). *Class, codes and control (Vol. 3).* London: Routledge & Kegan Paul.

Bonham, L. A. (1988). Learning style use: In need of perspective. *Lifelong Learning: An Omnibus of Practice and Research, 11*(5), 14-17.

Bourdieu, P. (1977). Cultural capital and pedagogic communication. In P. Bourdieu & J. C. Passeron (Eds.) (R. Nice, Trans.). *Reproduction in education, society and culture* (pp. 71-106). Beverly Hills, CA: Sage.

Bowles, S., & Gintis, H. (1976). *Schooling in capitalist America.* New York: Basic Books.

Boyle, K. K. (1986). Predicting the success of minority students in a baccalaureate nursing program. *Journal of Nursing Education, 25,* 186-192.

Brophy, J. E., & Good, T. H. (1984). *Teacher-student relationships: Causes and consequences.* New York: Holt, Rinehart and Winston.

Burger, K. (1986). Computer assisted instruction: Learning style and academic achievement. *Lifelong Learning: The Adult Years, 10*(2), 21-23.

Cervantes, R. A. (1984). Ethnocentric pedagogy and minority student growth: Implications for the common school. *Education and Urban Society, 16*(3), 273-274.

Chavez, R. (1985). Classroom learning environments' session. In H. Mehan, H. T. Trueba, & C. Underwood (Eds.), *Schooling language minority youth* (pp. 35-45). Proceedings of the Linguistic Minority Project Conference, Vol. I, Lake Tahoe, CA: University of California Linguistic Minority Project.

Claxton, C. S., & Murrell, P. H. (1987). *Learning styles: Implications for improving educational practices.* ASHE-ERIC Higher Education Reports, No. 4. Washington, DC: Association for the Study of Higher Education.

Cohen, R. (1976). Conceptual styles, culture, conflict and non-verbal tests of intelligence. In J. Roberts & S. Akinsaya (Eds.), *Schooling in the cultural context* (pp. 290-322). New York: David McKay Company.

Conti, G. J., & Welborn, R. B. (1986). Teaching-learning styles and adult learner. *Lifelong Learning: The Adult Years, 9*(8), 20-24.

Cook-Gumperz, J. (1973). *Social control and socialization.* London: Routledge & Kegan Paul.

Cook-Gumperz, J. (1977). Situated instructions: Language socialization of school children. In S. Ervin-Tripp & C. Mitchell-Kernan (Eds.), *Child discourse* (pp. 103-121). New York: Academic Press.

Cortes, C. E. (1991). Pluribus & unum: The quest for community and diversity. *Change, 23*(5), 8-16.

Courage, M., & Godbey, K. L. (1992, March-April). Student retention: Policies and services to enhance persistence to graduation. *Nurse Educator, 17*(2), 29-92.

Cranston, C., & McCort, B. (1985). A learner analysis experiment: Cognitive style versus learning style in undergraduate nursing education. *Journal of Nursing Education, 24*(4), 138-236.

Cronbach, L. J., & Snow, R. (1977). *Aptitudes and instructional methods.* New York: Irvington Publishers.

Cropley, A., & Field, T. (1969). Achievement in science and intellectual style. *Journal of Applied Psychology, 53*, 132.

Cuban, L. (1989). The "at-risk" label and the problem of urban school reform. *Phi Delta Kappan, 70*(10), 780-784.

Cuseo, J. B. (1992). Cooperative learning: A pedagogy for diversity. *Cooperative Learning and College Teaching, 3*(1), 1-6.

DeCoux, V. (1990, May). Kolb's learning style inventory: A review of its applications in nursing research. *Journal of Nursing Education, 29*(5), 202-207.

Dewey, J. (1938). *Experience and education.* New York: Macmillan.

Erickson, F. (1987). Transformation and school success: The politics and culture of educational achievement. *Anthropology and Education Quarterly, 18*(4), 335-356.

Erickson, F., & Mohatt, G. (1982). Cultural organization and participation structure in two classrooms of Indian students. In G. Spindler (Ed.), *Doing the ethnography of schooling* (pp. 131-174). New York: Holt, Rinehart and Winston.

Eubanks, E. (1988). *Teacher education pipeline.* Washington, DC: American Association of Colleges of Teacher Education.

Even, M. J. (1982). Adapting cognitive style theory in practice. *Lifelong Learning: The Adult Years,* 14-27.

Feldbaum, E., & Leavitt, M. (1980). *Nurses and the educational process: A report to nurse educators.* College Park: University of Maryland, Program of Health Services Delivery, Bureau of Governmental Research.

Fennema, E., & Peterson, P. (1986). Teacher-student interaction and self-related differences in learning mathematics. *Teaching and Teacher Education, 2*(1), 19-42.

Flagler, S., Loper-Powers, S., & Spitzer, A. (1988). Clinical teaching is more than evaluation time alone. *Journal of Nursing Education, 27*(8), 342-346.

Foster, G. (1965). Pleasant society and the image of the limited good. *American Anthropologist, 67*(2), 294-313.

Frank, B. (1983). Flexibility of information processing and the memory of field-independent and field-dependent learners. *Journal of Research in Personality, 17*(1), 89-96.

Freire, P. (1970). *Pedagogy of the oppressed.* New York: Continuum.

Garcia, R. (1991). *Teaching in a pluralistic society: Concepts, models and strategies.* New York: HarperCollins.

Gardner, H. (1991). *The unschooled mind: How children think and how schools should teach.* New York: Basic Books.

Gilligan, C. (1982). *In a different voice: Psychological theory and women's development.* Cambridge, MA: Harvard University Press.

Goldschmidt, W. (1954). *Ways of mankind.* Boston: Beacon Press.

Gooden, C. R. (1993, Summer). Diversity with style—Learning style, that is. *Kappa Delta Pi, 29*(4), 129.

Guilford, P. J. (1980). Cognitive styles: What are they? *Educational and Psychological Measurement, 40,* 715-735.

Hernandez, J. S. (1993, Summer). Bilingual metacognitive development. *The Educational Forum, 57*(4), 350-358.

Higgs, Z. (1984). Predicting success in nursing: From prototype to pragmatics. *Western Journal of Nursing Research, 6,* 77-93.

Hilliard, A. (1989). Teachers and cultural style in a pluralistic society. *Issues 89: NEA Today, 7*(6), 65-69.

Horne, M. (1987). *A test of causal model attrition among freshman students and an examination of the interaction of academic, social and commitment variables.* Unpublished doctoral dissertation, University of Houston.

Hsu, F. L. (1983). *Rugged individualism.* Chicago, IL: University of Tennessee Press.

Hudepuhl, N., & Reed, S. (1984). Establishing a student retention program. *Nursing Education, 9,* 19-24.

Hyman, R., & Rosoff, B. (1984). Matching learning and teaching style: The jug and what's in it? *Theory into Practice, 23*(1), 35-43.

Kagan, J. (1964). American longitudinal research on psychological development. *Child Development, 35,* 1-32.

Kane, M. (1984). Cognitive styles of thinking and learning: II. *Academic Therapy, 20*(1), 83–92.

Keefe, C. (1982, November 4–7). *The ethical decision points for the teacher in relation to student perceptions of unethical teacher behaviors.* Presented at the Annual Meeting of the Speech Communication Association, Louisville, KY.

Kleehammer, K., Hart, L., & Keck, J. F. (1990). Nursing students' perceptions of anxiety-producing situations in the clinical setting. *Journal of Nursing Education, 29*(40), 183–187.

Klein, G. (1951). The personal world through perception. In R. R. Blake & G. V. Ramsey (Eds.), *Perception: An approach to personality* (pp. 328–335). New York: Ronald Press.

Kluckhohn, C. (1943). Covert culture and administrative problems. *American Antiopologist, 45,* 213–22.

Kluckhohn, F. R. (1976). Dominant and variant value orientations. In P. J. Brink (Ed.), *Transcultural nursing: A book of readings* (pp. 63–81). Englewood Cliffs, NJ: Prentice-Hall.

Kluckhohn, F. R., & Strodbeck, F. L. (1961). *Variations in value orientations.* New York: Harper & Row.

Kolb, D. A. (1976). *Learning style inventory: Technical manual.* Boston: McBer.

Kolb, D. A. (1984). *Experiential learning: Experience as the source of learning and development.* Englewood Cliffs, NJ: Prentice-Hall.

Ladson-Billings, G. (1989, May 4). *A tale of two teachers: Exemplars of successful pedagogy for black students.* Paper presented at the Colloquium in conjunction with the 10th Anniversary Meeting of the College Board's Council of Academic Affairs, New York.

Ladson-Billings, G. (1992). Culturally relevant teaching: The key to making multicultural education work. In C. A. Grant (Ed.), *Research and multicultural education: From the margins to the mainstream* (pp. 106–121). Washington, DC: Falmer Press.

Larkin, J. M. (1993, Summer). Rethinking basic skills instruction with urban students. *The Educational Forum, 57*(4), 413–419.

Leininger, M. (1991). The theory of culture care diversity and universality. In M. Leininger (Ed.), *Culture care diversity and universality: A theory of nursing* (pp. 5–68). New York: National League for Nursing Press.

Lesser, G. (1976). Cultural differences in learning and thinking styles. In S. Messick (Ed.), *Individuality in learning.* San Francisco: Jossey-Bass.

Mahlios, M. C. (1981). Effects of teacher-student cognitive style on patterns of dyadic classroom interaction. *Journal of Experimental Education, 49*(3), 147.

Marchesani, L. S., & Adams, D. (1992, Winter). Dynamics of diversity in the teaching-learning process: A faculty development model for analysis and action. In M. Adams (Ed.), *Promoting diversity in college classrooms: Innovative responses for the curriculum* (pp. 9–20). San Francisco: Jossey-Bass.

McDermott, R. P. (1987). The explanation of minority school failure, again. *Anthropology and Education Quarterly, 18*(4), 361–364.

McKenna, B. (1989). College faculty: An endangered species (p. 10). *On Campus.* Washington, DC: American Federation of Teachers.

Merino, B., & Quintanar, R. (1988). *The recruitment of minority students into teaching careers: A status report of effective approaches.* Boulder, CO: Far West Regional Holmes Group, University of Colorado.

Messick, S. (1976). Personality consistencies in cognition and creativity. In S. Messick (Ed.), *Individuality in learning.* San Francisco: Jossey-Bass.

Messick, S. (1984). The nature of cognitive styles: Problems and promise in educational practice. *Educational Psychologist, 19*(2), 59-74.

Moll, L. (1988). Some key issues in teaching Latino students. *Language Arts, 65*(5), 465-472.

Morrissey, K. (1987). The nursing crunch is on. *Nursing and Health Care, 8,* 198.

Nel, J., & Seckinger, D. S. (1993, Summer). Johann Pestalozzi in the 1990s: Implications for today's multicultural classrooms. *The Educational Forum, 57*(4), 394-401.

Noddings, N. (1984). *Caring.* Berkeley, CA: University of California Press.

Ogbu, J. (1987). Variability in minority school performance: A problem in search of an explanation. *Anthropology and Education Quarterly, 18*(4), 312-334.

Pagana, K. D. (1988). Stresses and threats reported by baccalaureate students in relation to an initial clinical experience. *Journal of Nursing Education, 27*(9), 418-424.

Parsons, T. (1968). The school class as a social system. In ＿＿＿＿＿＿＿ *Socialization and schools* (Reprint Series No. 1:69-90). Cambridge, MA: Harvard Educational Review.

Pestalozzi, J. H. (1951). *The education of man: Aphorisms.* (H. R. Norden, Trans.). New York: Philosophical Library, Inc.

Phillips, S. U. (1983). *The invisible culture: Communication in the classroom and community in Warm Springs Indian Reservation.* New York: Longman.

Piaget, J. (1971). *Psychology and epistemology.* New York: Penguin.

Pugh, E. J. (1988). Soliciting student input to improve clinical teaching. *Nurse Educator, 13*(5), 28-33.

Ramirez, M., & Castaneda, A. (1974). *Cultural democracy, bicognitive development and education.* New York: Academic Press.

Renninger, K. A., & Snyder, S. S. (1986). Effects of cognitive style on perceived satisfaction and performance among students and teachers. *Journal of Educational Psychology, 75,* 668-676.

Rist, R. (1970). Student social class and teacher expectation: The self-fulfilling prophecy in ghetto schools. *Harvard Educational Review, 40,* 411-450.

Rogers, C. R. (1969). *Freedom to learn.* Columbus, OH: Charles Merrill.

Rosenthal, R. S., & Jacobson, W. (1968). *Pygmalion in the classroom: Teacher expectation and pupil intellectual performance.* New York: Holt, Rinehart and Winston.

Schaffer, M. A., & Juarez, M. (1993, May-June). An ethical analysis of student faculty interactions. *Nurse Educator, 18*(3), 25-28.

Schieffelin, B., & Ochs, E. (1985). Language socialization. *Annual Review of Anthropology, 15,* 163-191.

Shulman, L. (1987). Assessment of teaching: An initiative for the profession. *Phi Delta Kappan, 69*(1), 28-44.

Sleeter, C., & Grant, C. (1987). An analysis of multicultural education in the United States. *Harvard Educational Review, 57*(4), 421-444.

Smith, V. A. (1990, May). Nursing student attrition and implications for preadmission advisement. *Journal of Nursing Education, 29*(5), 215-218.

Stubbs, M. (1976). *Language, schools and classrooms.* London: Methuen.

Talarcyzk, G. (1989). Aptitude, previous achievement, and cognitive style: Relation to academic achievement in nursing courses of differing content. *Journal of Nursing Education, 45*(4), 9-12.

Theis, C. T. (1988). Nursing students' perspectives of unethical teaching behaviors. *Journal of Nursing Education, 27*(3), 102-106.

Thompson, C., & Crutchlow, E. (1993, Jan.-Feb.). Learning style research: A critical review of the literature and implications for nursing education. *Journal of Professional Nursing, 9*(1), 34-40.

Thurber, F., Hollingsworth, A., Brown, L., & Whitaker, S. (1989, May-June). The faculty advisor role: An imperative for student retention. *Nurse Educator, 13*(3), 27-29.

Tinto, V. (1987). *Leaving college.* Chicago: Chicago University Press.

Vogt, L., Jordan, C., & Tharp, R. (1987). Explaining school failure, producing school success: Two cases. *Anthropology and Education Quarterly, 18*(4), 276-286.

Vygotsky, L. S. (1978). *Mind in society: The development of higher psychological processes.* M. Cole, John-Steiner, V., Scribner, S., & Souberman, P. (Ed. and Trans.) Cambridge, MA: Harvard University Press.

Watson, J. (1985). *Nursing: The philosophy and science of caring.* Boulder: Colorado Associated University Press.

Werning, S. C. (1992, October). The challenge to make a difference: Minorities in healthcare today. *Healthcare Trends and Transitions, 4*(1), 33-46.

Wertsch, J. V. (1978). Adult-child interactions and the roots of metacognition. *Quarterly Newsletter of the Institute for Comparative Human Cognition, 2*(1), 15-18.

Windsor, A. (1988). Nursing students' perceptions of clinical experience. *Journal of Nursing Education, 26*(4), 150-154.

Witkin, A. H., & Moore, C. A. (1975). *Field-dependent and field-independent cognitive styles and their educational implications. Review of Educational Research, 47,* 1-64. Princeton, N.J., Educational Testing Service.

Woodham, R., & Taube, K. (1986). Relationship of nursing program predictors and success on the NCLEX-RN examination for licensure in a selected associate degree program. *Journal of Nursing Education, 25,* 112-117.

Younger, J., & Grapp, M. J. (1992, March-April). An epidemiologic study of NCLEX. *Nurse Educator, 17*(2), 24-28.

Zaharna, R. S. (1989). Self-shock: The double-binding challenge of identity. *International Journal of Intercultural Relations, 13*(4), 501-525.

15

Institutional Culture and American Professional Education

David M. Bossman

*T*he current literature on organizational behavior largely centers on the psychology of individuals functioning within organizations (Allcorn, 1989, 1992; Diamond, 1993; Schein, 1985). While the psychological approach to organizational behavior is normal within American culture, it fails to identify precisely how typical American organizational structures differ from those of traditional group cultures.

Hence, persons from collectivist, group-dominant cultures, either outside or within American society, will find difficulty in understanding and working effectively within institutions that operate according to American individualist modalities (Althen, 1988; Stewart & Bennett, 1991).

The psychological approach to organizational behavior misses precisely the problem experienced by members of traditional collectivist subgroups who must cope with the commanding reality in American society of personal, introspective identity. Americans routinely distrust collectives in favor of personal freedom, free enterprise, and individual achievement—a state of affairs startlingly distinctive among world cultures (Althen, 1988; Malina, 1986; Niebuhr, 1960). American organizations correspondingly place demands on individuals that persons schooled in traditional cultures simply find difficulty in achieving. Therein lies the rub.

This chapter will address the question of institutional culture within the larger social world context of individualism and will investigate the meaning of such a culture as a social setting in which group members share a set of symbols with a standard range of perceptions, interpretations, and values. The organizational cultures, accordingly, consist of individuals who freely associate themselves with the organization for personal as well as professional reasons.

Institutions viewed within a cultural context are seen to be embedded in a social world that in large measure shapes those institutions with shared social patterns (Hunter, 1991). These shared patterns (perceptions, interpretations, and values) distinguish one social world from another, and determine the operations of embedded institutions (Kluckhohn & Strodtbeck, 1961).

Institutions, then, even those fulfilling diverse operational services, conform to these overarching social systems to a notably greater extent than to the services in and of themselves. This is so because the social context helps define the social need and dimensions of the services within a given range of shared social symbols.

Recognizing this reality lays open the possibility and need for exploring how similarly defined institutions vary from one social system to another. Failing to recognize this reality blinds analysts to the full extent of discrepancies that can be expected when moving from one social world to another (Geertz, 1983).

Social world differences, as opposed to individual differences, are surprisingly neglected even within the social sciences, especially those with a psychological orientation. This reflects the cultural bias of the social scientist, who expects individuation and introspective development as a universal phenomenon. On the contrary, in collectivist or group-centered social worlds, the psychological self simply is not a driving force in how people behave.

Some, in fact, most social worlds place primary weight on social group membership and established social roles rather than on the psychological "self" (Geertz, 1983). American psychologists may easily overlook the import of this difference, assuming that throughout the world persons are individuals as Americans understand personhood: independent and introspective, with internal control and internal responsibility (Malina, 1989, 1992).

Psychologists reared and educated in introspective, individualist cultures typically project their own social world perceptions onto persons from other social worlds without imagining that humans, when socialized in traditional patterns, not only are not introspective but in fact are *anti-introspective* and oppose the determination of self from inside rather than from outside the individual (Malina, 1986).

Thus, the mature or psychologically healthy person in one culture can be perceived as the immature or psychologically unhealthy person in another. A Polish-American once exemplified this simply by asserting that what she was punished for in Poland she is rewarded for in the United States. In large measure, "maturity" depends on whether knowing oneself means effectively knowing one's social place (and corresponding social role) or one's inner self (and efforts to achieve success).

In the first—knowing one's social role—cultural perception of maturity means recognizing one's assigned place and its defined job description (e.g., father, mother, son, daughter, doctor, nurse) and conforming to its externally determined demands. Here, the individual's success lies in subordinating the self to the assigned status.

In the second—knowing one's inner self—maturity and emotional stability mean that a person makes workable choices by asserting the inner self and taking control of and being responsible for personal options. This social context sees the externally controlled person as *dependent.* The society that expects individuals to conform to social roles sees persons as *willful* if they seek self-actualization rather than conformity to role. Each view is the proper product of its social context.

These, however, are only the starting points of recognizing how social systems work and what impact they have on institutional cultures. Just as cultures lay diverse and even opposing demands on individuals, they similarly lay diverse demands on institutions and their personnel. Such personnel come to work with socially formed concepts of self, others, and their relationships and roles. The socially conditioned divergence typically begins in preschool and extends throughout life (Tobin, Wu, & Davidson, 1989).

Even biological roles—father, mother, children—take on socially conditioned dimensions that substantially, if not radically, alter how people act out personal identity and relationships with others (Malina, 1989). Similarly, social perceptions of the full range of social and professional roles differ based on foundational social world orientations, with characteristic features in the American educational system (Althen, 1988).

This chapter focuses attention on what these differences are, how they operate, and what their ramifications are in studying the institutional cultures of the professions in the United States today. The links

between social world, institutional culture, and professional education
are both clear and of commanding import when shaping educational curricula to match institutional culture, especially when students and/or
faculty come from traditional cultures or subcultures. The goal, then, is
to determine the character of institutional culture within a setting of
American culture with an eye to addressing the issue of curriculum in
professional schools.

The pursuit of this goal can be divided into three lines of inquiry:

1. Variations in social world systems.
2. How institutions reflect social world systems.
3. How education helps shape institutional culture.

These three parts will bear in mind the particular realities of the nursing
profession and the culture of American health care institutions.

VARIATIONS IN SOCIAL WORLD SYSTEMS

Social world systems can be characterized by using models that compare
various abstract features present in all social systems. The model chosen
here was designed by British social anthropologist Douglas (1986), as developed by Malina (1986) and applied for American usage (Figure 15.1).
Malina (1986) develops the categories of Douglas's grid/group model to
facilitate American understanding of foreign texts across social world or
cultural lines. Hence, the model is properly a cross-cultural analytical
tool for describing social world dynamics and their perceptual fields.

The two features that the model identifies are *social pressure to conform* (strong or weak) on a horizontal continuum, and the *degree of adherence* afforded social symbols (high/low) on a vertical continuum.
This model thus produces quadrants reflecting pressure to conform (degree of adherence): weak/high, weak/low, strong/high, strong/low. In
social worlds characterized by *strong group pressure* to conform to social
standards and *high social adherence* to these standards (with corresponding belief in their efficacy), there exists a pyramid of established
group ranks that determines the social roles people receive either by
birth or formal ascription (from above), and the relative place in society
in which each role operates. Thus, when there is strong pressure to conform, individuals consider their role as a calling, not properly sought or
freely chosen.

High adherence to an externally ascribed role or bestowed status results in a shared social sense that the role or status clearly and effectively

Figure 15.1   Model Adapted from Mary Douglas and
Bruce J. Malina (1986)

Weak Pressure / High Adherence	Strong Pressure/High Adherence
Purity: pragmatic attitude toward purity; pollution is not automatic	*Purity:* strong concern for rules to define and maintain social structures; well-defined purification rites
Rite: the individual remains superior to the rite process	*Rite:* express the internal classification system of the group
Personal Identity: individualism; pragmatic and adaptable	*Personal Identity:* internalizing clear social roles; individual is subservient to, but not in conflict with, society
Body: viewed instrumentally, as means to some end; self-controlled; treated pragmatically	*Body:* tightly controlled but a symbol of life
Sin: basically caused by ignorance or failure; hence viewed as stupidity or embarrassment; the individual is responsible	*Sin:* the violation of formal rules; focus is upon behavior rather than on internal states of being
Cosmology: the universe is geared to individual success and initiative	*Cosmology:* the universe is just and reasonable; personal causality, limited good (goods already assigned)
Suffering and Misfortune: an intelligent person ought to be able to avoid them; totally eradicable	*Suffering and Misfortune:* the result of automatic punishment for the violation of formal rules

Weak Pressure / Low Adherence	Strong Pressure/Low Adherence
PRESSURE: degree of societal pressure at work on a given social unit (individual or group) to conform to societal norms.	ADHERENCE: socially constrained adherence normally given to the symbol system – classifications, patterns of perception and evaluation – through which the society brings order and intelligibility to their experiences.
Strong pressure: conformity along with strong corporate identity, clear distinction between in group and out group clear sets of boundaries separating the two, and a clear set of normative symbols defining group identity.	*High adherence:* a fit or match between the individual's experiences and societal patterns of perception and evaluation.
Weak pressure: nebulous group identity (individualism), vague distinctions between in group and out group, high porous sets of boundaries between groups	*Low adherence:* low fit or match between an individual's experiences and societal patterns of perception and evaluation.

Purity: anti the purity posture of the quadrant from which it emerged	*Purity:* inside of the body is under attack; purification ineffective
Rite: anti the rites of the quadrant from which it emerged; effervescent; spontaneity valued	*Rite:* focused on group boundaries, with great concern to expel pollutants (deviants) from the social body
Personal Identity: no antagonism between society and the self, but the old society of the quadrant from which it derived is seen as oppressive	*Personal Identity:* located in group membership, not in the internalization of roles, which are confused; dyadic
Body: irrelevant; life is spiritual; purity concerns are absent, but they may be rejected; body may be used freely or renunciation may prevail	*Body:* social and physical bodies are tightly controlled but under attack; invaders break through bodily boundaries
Sin: as matter of personal ethics and interiorness	*Sin:* a matter of pollution; evil is lodged within the individual and society; sin is much like a disease deriving from social structure
Cosmology: the cosmos is likely to be impersonal; there is individual and direct access to Nature	*Cosmology:* dualistic; warring forces of good and evil; limited good; the universe is not good and may be whimsical; personal causality
Suffering and Misfortune: love conquers all; love can eliminate	*Suffering and Misfortune:* unjust; punishment not automatic; attributed to malevolent forces

defines persons beyond their personal ability to change their calling. This then is a system of ascribed identity (dyadic personality), limited mobility, and external control.

The strong pressure/low adherence social quadrant is a social world in which adherence to, or trust in, social symbols is low. This is typical, when the group as a whole, or to which a person belongs by birth or ascription, feels threatened by an unfriendly or hostile social environment. Then, adherence to outside norms is low, while the in-group bonds remain central to a person's identity. The persons in this quadrant are dependent on the group for their identity but the group has a low sense of social affirmation and feels in need of boundary protection.

The weak pressure/high adherence social quadrant exists when individuals experience little pressure to conform to established social determinants, hence perceive a social system that allows for and rewards personal decisions and individual achievement. Persons are encouraged to make their own life choices and take responsibility for their decisions. When individuals perceive that the system allows them and, in fact, fosters their sense of personal freedom, there exists a high degree of adherence to such a social climate. This society champions personal rights and responsibilities, with a corresponding reliance on the ability of individuals not only to control their own lives but to do so in a way that does not threaten others' realization of their own personal freedoms and that shows sensitivity to others in ways groups cannot (Niebuhr, 1960).

The weak pressure, low adherence social quadrant is a social world in which individualism exists, but individuals perceive society as threatening and dangerous. Similar to the strong pressure, low adherence social quadrant, the weak/low is a quadrant of unfulfillable or severely underrealized values. Hence, low adherence results from alienation and a sense of imminent danger from without. Individuals are socially isolated and thus feel threatened by anything outside themselves.

The strong/high and the weak/high quadrants both share the sense that while the system may not be perfect, whatever is imperfect can be adequately remedied by values inherent in the system. The strong-pressure society sees the group as the locus of power and the individual's obligation as one of loyal commitment, whereas the weak-pressure society sees the individual as capable of making personal choices that lead to fulfillment of personal goals and achievement of social success that will benefit not only the individual but others as well.

This adherence (grid)/pressure (group) model provides a superstructure for examining various social scripts that run through and govern persons and relationships within the various social worlds. These systemic scripts commonly are described as *purity* (a socially shared sense of being in place) and *pollution* (a person or thing out of place); *personal identity* (externally or internally determined); *rites* (symbolic means for crossing or reinforcing boundaries); *body* (a symbol of the society); *suffering* and *misfortune* (social sense of causes and effects); *sin* (the violation of standards); and *cosmology* (how reality holds together).

Each grid/group quadrant sees these social world scripts according to a systemic logic that persons within the social world readily recognize as "natural" or "common sense" (Geertz, 1983). In fact, the scripts flow from the basic orientation of the social world in terms of individualism versus group centeredness (group) or social adherence versus alienation (grid).

In the social worlds characterized by strong pressure to conform to group norms, *purity rules* are perceived to derive from and support the natural order. Their violation is not negotiable and *pollution* is automatic when individuals do not observe the established order of when, where, and how things are done. In the high-adherence quadrant, remedies for such a violation of established order are clear and effective. In the low-adherence quadrant, purity rules are perceived to be widely transgressed (low adherence) and remediation is ineffective (pollution prevails).

In the social worlds with weak pressure to conform, purity norms are known but less rigidly understood, according flexibility for personal circumstances and assessments. When personal adherence to recognized norms is notably low, society's purity norms are flaunted and deemed inoperative. When general adherence prevails, society's purity norms are deemed reasonable and the system is socially affirmed.

The logic of social worlds extends to a shared sense of the source of *personal identity:* In strong-pressure societies, the group (or its head) assigns identity; whereas in low-pressure societies, the individual pursues personal growth with a sense of freedom to decide. In the high-adherence quadrants, this mode is deemed effective; in the low it is regarded as threatened. Hence, persons in the strong/low quadrant often experience a sense of inexorable tragedy in life, and persons in the weak/low experience a need to isolate themselves to preserve their security from life's personal tragedies.

The logic further applies to *rites:* In strong-pressure social worlds, rites emanate from the group or its head rather than from personal choice or initiative. In social worlds that exert weak pressure, advancement rites follow from personal choice or meritorious achievement. Compare, for instance, "arranged" marriages against "romantic" marital partners. Arranged marriages reflect a strong-pressure social world; romantic partners characterize low-pressure societies. Correspondingly, advancement in social status in strong-pressure social worlds comes from those with recognized power; whereas in weak-pressure societies, it is based on certified personal competence.

The *body* is perceived to be under attack in low-adherence social worlds. In social worlds characterized by high adherence, the body is perceived as essentially healthy, improvable, or curable through established social means (a workable body of knowledge). In strong-pressure quadrants, the body is seen in harmony with the entire social order, whereas in weak-pressure societies it is seen as personal and freely put to use.

Suffering and *misfortune* in strong-pressure social worlds derive from outside the individual, perceived either as unjust (low adherence) or the result of some kind of sin (high adherence). In weak-pressure societies, suffering and misfortune either can be avoided by care and planning (high adherence) or overcome by the will of the individual (low adherence).

In strong-pressure societies, *sin* is the violation of societal norms, either because evil is lodged within individuals or society (low) or because some laws were in fact violated (high). In weak-pressure societies, sin comes from personal ignorance or failure (high) or from a matter of personal ethics (low).

Finally, for strong-pressure societies, *reality* holds together either by a just and reasonable controlling force (high) or by warring forces of good and evil (low). For weak-pressure societies, cosmology means that the universe is either geared to individual success (high) or is benign but impersonal (low).

Together, these features run through the social worlds within which organizations exist and manifest their particular appropriations of social operations. Key to the use of this model, which distinguishes social systems, is the ability to see the logical relationship of social scripts to the overall operations of the social system. Thus, individuals and institutions will have varying characteristics depending on how these scripts operate in their social worlds.

INSTITUTIONS REFLECT SOCIAL WORLD SYSTEMS

It is a matter of testing the model to determine whether and to what extent institutions reflect the social world systems in which they inhere. In general, social systems provide the context for understanding and interpreting all social realities—modes of belonging, interpreting, being effective, and adapting—that affect individuals and institutions of society. In particular ways, according to the previously defined scripts, individuals predictably relate to institutions according to social world scripts.

Belonging, or membership in an organization has various meanings within each quadrant. In strong-pressure quadrants, belonging is ascribed by those outside and above the individual. Hence, it implies the commitment and loyalty of individuals who associate membership with the granting power. Correlatively, in strong-pressure societies, the mode of being effective is associated with being in an ascribed position of power. In strong group organizations with these dominant social operations, other aspects of the model can be expected to follow. Therefore, in institutions where loyalty to the organization derives from the exercise of authority or power to extract personal commitment, there is normally a strong pressure on individuals to conform.

In societies with a low pressure to conform, the operations of loyalty and power are secondary to how individuals interpret social realities and adapt to circumstances. Hence, for weak-pressure persons, the ability to persuade (influence) and the ability to utilize goods and services (inducement) become dominant. Thus, weak-pressure unsteadiness tends to invest more energy in persuasion and inducement than in loyalty and the exercise of power.

Medical staffs in health care institutions reflect this influence. In a weak-pressure, individualistic social world, medical services can be expected to center on patient care in terms of specialized expertise (influence by certified competence) and informed consent (induced by personal trust in the certified competence), with an assurance that results will be forthcoming from an educated use of resources. In strong-pressure social worlds, patient care could be expected to consist in unquestioningly (loyally) recognizing the status (power) of the doctor and staff. High-pressure societies would normally expect loyalty, whereas weak-pressure societies would seek to establish confidence.

Educational institutions work in similar fashion. Where the power of authority operates as a dominant institutional feature, loyalty and obedience become the norms of behavior. Hence strong pressure toward conformity is key to the educational experience. This may be seen in traditional educational systems that stress group over individual values. In low-pressure social worlds, teachers and administrators operate as "leaders" who induce learning and motivate performance. The educational models differ notably in overall orientation and practice (Miller, 1983).

Social institutions that reflect their social world perceptions, expectations, and values thus fulfill social expectations that lead to socially perceived effectiveness. Those from outside a given social system may be quick to see errors in that system's institutional procedures, as exemplified in a study of preschools (Tobin, Wu, & Davidson, 1989). Even at the level of preschool, educational goals are already clear and reflect social conditions.

That this should be the case is not surprising, but it does press the educator to give special consideration to the social world of the learning system.

HOW EDUCATION HELPS SHAPE
INSTITUTIONAL CULTURE

The challenge of educators today is to recognize both the diverse social worlds from which their students come as well as the appropriate social world for which students are seeking an education. While various social worlds exist in the United States today, educators must carefully consider not only the needs of their students but also the requirements of the social institutions in which they propose to work.

Advocates of multiculturalism have sought to establish the principle that their individual cultures have an equal right to exist within the curriculum of the American educational system. This initiative alludes to the long history of injustices that have occurred during the evolution of American culture.

Educational canons established in the past necessarily reflect the values of their makers (Bossman, 1991). This means that as social awareness changes, the content of the various canons must also be open to review and change. How this is done is, of course, open to discussion. Allan Bloom (1987) and Harold Bloom (1994) have variously taken positions on retaining the integrity of the established canons, reflecting on the legacy that made this a great nation. Their orthodoxy, however, seems to render uncritical homage to the past as the ground for the present established order.

Arthur Schlesinger, Jr. (1992), on the other hand, has argued against uncritically accepting new curricula that misrepresent history in the well-intentioned but flawed effort to right past wrongs. Moreover, dwelling on the rights of subcultures to be included in the curricula can foster social fragmentation that helps no one.

Educators today must determine what kind of curriculum most fairly characterizes the truths of American history while providing all students with the means necessary to succeed in society as we now know it. This necessarily introduces a number of key issues deriving from the particular character of the American social world.

The grid/group model suggests how we can analyze these issues with some degree of realistic objectivity. First, the social world of the United States is clearly centered on personal, individual rights and responsibilities. This means that any institution that seeks to deprive individuals of personal rights, or to hinder their exercise in a way that compromises personal achievement, must be carefully examined for adequacy in American society. Education can be a useful tool for perfecting this principle in practice.

While arguments have been made for single-sex education for state military schools, the example of excluding blacks from effective social access under the principle of "separate but equal" is now soundly discredited in American society and accordingly in American educational institutions. Education here means gaining social access that will allow achieving to the standards necessary for full involvement in American society. Any educational system that caters to one particular segment of the population to the exclusion of others runs the risk of misrepresenting society and failing to prepare students for life in a complex and diverse social world.

Professions, such as nursing and social work, that are unbalanced in gender representation run a significant risk of suffering social devaluation and gender stereotyping. Individualism in American society has gradually—and as yet only partially—come to recognize the detriments of gender stereotyping and discrimination. Social advances seem to be slow to reach those professions that are predominantly staffed by women. A culture of women can well remain a subculture within an institution, thereby further limiting the access of members of the profession from advancement and social valuation. Similarly, when a profession attracts only members of minority cultures, it can be presumed to be in a state of cultural isolation. This state of affairs merits careful rehabilitation on social world grounds to allow members normal career mobility.

Educational institutions that hinder access to *the standards of American society* can be open for question on the grounds that achievement rather than group connections are requisite for success in this society. Thus, educational practices that isolate groups or individuals in terms of language, culture, or gender can, because of the particularities of this social world, be deemed substandard by denying students equal access to success.

American educational systems need as well to find ways both to identify the values that underlie the American social system—not necessarily as universally applicable but as operationally recognized in our particular social world—and be sure that these values are clearly articulated and developed for use in American institutional cultures. The flight from values has been unnecessarily tied to the question of church and state. Social values do exist and can therefore be open to examination for their constructive service to an integrated society.

Such values include learning how to be open to the realities of personal identity—gender, sexual orientation, ethnic background, religion, physical condition—and to garner the benefits of such human diversity within institutions. Education helps foster awareness of the needs and rights of others by seeking opportunities for diverse students to come together and to work together, to discover that their fellow students are striving to fulfill their personal potential while also contributing to the well-being of others. An individualistic society must necessarily value the diversity that flows from acknowledging personal differences.

The widely recognized liberal optimism of American society suggests that Americans generally value personal diversity and achievement (e.g., by supporting the "underdog" as opposed to championing the powerful), and perceive social mobility to be achievable. Institutional culture must reflect this aspect of American life by maintaining open access to upper levels of careers. Toward this end, access to the educational means for advancement is essential.

Standards and regulations, so rigid in collectivist social worlds, ought not to be neglected in American education. But individuals must learn to make judgments about how to safeguard social order without placing barriers to change and advancement. Societies that show little tolerance for divergence from past norms lack potential for adapting to new needs and pursuing new opportunities. Institutional culture in an individualist social world must allow room for growth.

These objectives focus on how to address the legitimate pleas of minority groups to share in the American system. Group-centered values may be legitimate for group maintenance and can continue to enrich the lives of those group members while being subordinated to voluntary group membership in the larger American society.

This introduces the American value of cooperative relations between all groups without the need to further in-group interests at the expense of individual rights and responsibilities. It affirms the need to recognize individual differences without setting one group against another as more or less legitimate by standards that are inimical to the American standard of personal achievement and performance.

Institutional culture, which reflects the social world of individualism in the United States, requires an educational system that prepares students for effective careers, utilizing the values and goals of the culture. The right of subcultures to exist should not be confused with the rights of individuals within those groups to learn the means to succeed in American society. Educators have the opportunity and responsibility to clearly differentiate between subcultures and the majority culture and, while duly acknowledging these subcultures, should make the norms of the majority culture accessible to all.

In the health care professions, minority nurses and doctors frequently serve the needs of their ethnic subcultures, which continue to isolate individuals in traditional ascribed (not voluntary) group enclaves even within American society. The needs of individuals in these cultural enclaves remain real, and the sensitive health care professional needs to be aware of how persons socialized in high-pressure or low-adherence social worlds perceive the various roles of professionals and family members. A cross-cultural study of such enclaves is important, especially where the subcultures are notably cohesive and defensively resistant to involvement with outsiders. An example of this is in Elizabeth, New Jersey, where nursing students largely derive from recent immigrant groups. Several questions that arise from this situation are not unusual in areas of high immigrant-group density:

1. To what extent should the culture of the patient's or professional's origin be regarded as contextually normative?
2. How can we best recognize the particularities of the subculture of the patient or professional to better serve members of that group?
3. Is there any middle ground that can recognize the reality of the subculture but allow for equipping graduate nurses not only to serve that group but to participate in mainstream patient care?

The answer to the first seems to depend on whether the professionals are necessarily tied to serving a particular group. If that is the case, then the professionals might well simply train in a culture in which that group operates the institutional system. If the professionals likely will serve a variety of persons, as is typical in the United States, then the second question needs to be addressed. How does the American professional, whether a member of a particular subculture or not, gain an understanding of patients whose identity is ascribed according to gender or group (dyadic personalities with the strong-pressure social world's normal external control)? The dyadic individual—whose identity is ascribed by another—is accustomed to external control and accordingly needs to be understood as a dependent personality. Gaining insight into the social world that produces such personalities is most helpful in leaning how to address the needs of these patients.

The third question seems to be most typical for regions of the country with a variety of subcultures that share the widespread social practice of role ascription and the norm of dyadic personalities. While social diversity has contributed in many ways to the rich ethnic legacies within American society, this has happened mainly when people have crossed over the borders of their subgroups. Bounded groups, however, tend to view outsiders as potentially dangerous, and members who venture into the mainstream are treated as traitors. Recognizing these realities, it can be a legitimate social goal to help integrate subcultures within the United States into the mainstream culture for the benefit of all. This has been the accepted practice in the past and largely has produced a rich and vibrantly integrated society. When neither the mainstream nor the subculture feels threatened by diversity, integration and sharing can and does take place. The horrors of "ethnic cleansing" operate only when persons are defined precisely as in-group or out-group members rather than as individuals.

The goal in professional education seems to be toward mutual understanding and cooperation between mainstream professionals and subculture persons. We need not champion a subculture as the answer to
American social problems, nor the mainstream culture as the ultimate in
social advancement. Neither is realistic. Rather, professional education
in American schools should recognize the reality of the immigrant base
within American society and seek to learn from diverse individuals while
recognizing the logic that maintains a strong-pressure system. On the
other hand, the logic of a low-pressure system pertains in American society, and dyadic personalities benefit here when they effectively learn
how to function as individuals—to take control of their lives, to make personal decisions, and individuate apart from group-derived roles. This
takes the courage that immigrants throughout American history have
demonstrated.

Thus, the professionals who are best equipped for service in American
society are those that have come to grips with the individualism of American social life, have taken pains to understand how other social worlds
function, and have gained insight into how to work with subculture personalities and help them integrate into the value system of an individualist social world. Failure to take this last step is likely to slow down a
normal process toward effective development among members of subculture groups and effectively keeps our nation divided along subculture
lines (Schlesinger, 1992).

A final point concerning gender-based subcultures. Whereas strong-
pressure societies normally base identity on gender (women's work,
men's work, etc.), individualist societies progressively are viewing gender as having secondary importance in personal identity. This means that
the individual is less controlled by assigned social roles or stereotyped
personality characteristics of women and men. Within the nursing and social work professions, however, where women represent the vast majority, the typical women's subculture can tend to isolate and control the
professional, who in other aspects of life would not be so stereotyped.

Although gender-role submission may appear "normal" to some, it
continues to frustrate many women in the professions, who simply reject the stereotype but find themselves in an institutional culture that is
not yet fully integrated. Recognizing such an institutional culture as a
subculture may help professional women to engage the patterns more
effectively and find means to improve the situation. The reality is that
people socialized in an external-control subgroup learn how to surren-
der control from those who have done just that. This chain of teaching
gender-subordination needs to be recognized and modified to normalize
the profession in terms of individuality with internal control and

responsibility. Both control and responsibility are internal, or personal, within an individualist society.

REFERENCES

Allcorn, S. (1989). Understanding groups at work. *Personnel, 66*(8), 28-36.

Allcorn, S. (1992). *Codependency in the workplace.* New York: Quorum.

Althen, G. (1988). *American ways: A guide for foreigners in the United States.* Yarmouth, ME: Intercultural Press.

Argyris, C., & Schon, D. (1982). *Theory in practice.* San Francisco: Jossey-Bass.

Bloom, A. (1987). *The closing of the American mind. How higher education has failed democracy and impoverished the souls of today's students.* New York: Simon & Schuster.

Bloom, H. (1994). *The Western canon.* New York: Harcourt Brace.

Bossman, D. (1991). Cross-cultural values for a pluralistic core curriculum. *Journal of Higher Education, 62*(6), 661-681.

Diamond, M. (1988). Organizational identity. *Administration and Society, 20*(2), 166-190.

Diamond, M. (1993). *The unconscious life of organizations: Integrating organizational identity.* New York: Quorum.

Douglas, M. (1986). *How institutions think.* Syracuse, NY: Syracuse University Press.

Geertz, C. (1983a). "From the native's point of view": On the nature of anthropological understanding. In *Local knowledge* (pp. 55-72). New York: Basic Books.

Geertz, C. (1983b). Common sense as a cultural system. In *Local knowledge* (pp. 73-93). New York: Basic Books.

Hunter, J. D. (1991). *Culture wars: The struggle to define America.* New York: Basic Books.

Kluckhohn, F., & Strodtbeck, F. (1961). *Variations in value orientations.* Evanston, IL: Row, Peterson.

Malina, B. J. (1986). *Christian origins and cultural anthropology.* Atlanta: John Knox Press.

Malina, B. J. (1989). Dealing with Biblical (Mediterranean) characters: A guide of U.S. Consumers. *Biblical Theology Bulletin, 19*(4), 127-141.

Malina, B. J. (1992). Is there a circum Mediterranean person? Looking for stereotypes. *Biblical Theology Bulletin, 22*(2), 66-87.

Miller, A. (1983). *For your own good: Hidden cruelty in child-rearing and the roots of violence,* (H. & H. Hannum, Trans.). New York: Farrar, Straus & Giroux.

Niebuhr, R. (1960). *Moral man and immoral society.* New York: Charles Scribner's Sons.

Pauchant, T., & Mitroff, I. (1992). *The crisis-prone organization.* San Francisco: Jossey-Bass.

Schein, E. (1985). *Organizational culture and leadership.* San Francisco: Jossey-Bass.

Schlesinger, A. M., Jr. (1992). *The Disuniting of American: Reflections on a multicultural society.* New York: Norton.

Stewart, E., & Bennett, M. J. (1991). *American cultural patterns: A cross-cultural perspective* (rev. ed.). Yarmouth, ME: Intercultural Press.

Tobin, J., Wu, D.Y.H., & Davidson, D.H. (1989). *Preschool in three cultures: Japan, China and the United States.* New Haven: Yale University Press.

Zaleznik, A., & Kets de Vries, M. (1975). *Power and the corporate mind.* Boston: Houghton Mifflin.

Part Four

Various Modes and Approaches of Economic Support for Minority and At-Risk Students

16

The Work/Study Experience: A Phenomenological Inquiry

Lynne R. Nelson

. . . nothing is known that is not in experience, or, as it is also expressed, that is not felt to be true, not given as an inwardly revealed eternal verity as something sacred that is believed. . .

(Hegel, 1807/1977)

What transforms a student into a nurse? Can we know the essence of that transformation and discover what contributes to that becoming? Can we make that process address the needs of increasingly diverse populations of intelligent, caring, and creative people? Will we be able, as we face the next century, to amend the culture of learning within the nursing profession, to address the paradigm shift within health care, to provide innovative ideas that impact the learning process and reflect our changing world? These questions suggest a phenomenological pathway to knowing outside the arena of logical positivism, where we may "no longer be present at the emergence of perceptual behaviors; rather we install ourselves in them in order to pursue the analysis of this exceptional relation between the subject and . . . (the) body and its world" (Merleau-Ponty, 1964, pp. 4-5).

THE PHENOMENON OF WORK/STUDY

The innovative work/study experience for our nursing majors allows them to increase their clinical and communication skills while receiving financial remuneration. These students are employed as externs on medical/surgical clinical units during the summer and winter academic vacations, managed by the unit registered nurses and supervised by faculty. The program is optional and provides a supplemental experience to the formal, academically oriented theoretical and clinical curriculum. The program reflects the school's belief that learning is self-directed, that variety in the type of learning experiences addresses the needs of a diverse student population, that faculty function as facilitators of learning, and that learning is evidenced by a change in behavior. Work/study gives students access to supplemental learning experiences that have been reported to increase confidence and professional maturity. In turn, the students learn to manage stress, role conflict, and frustration in the clinical setting. Students report that they have increased their clinical skills, are more organized, and can set priorities. Benefits to the participating hospital include opportunities for role enrichment for staff nurses who interact with students in the work environment. New graduates who have participated in the work/study program as students have reduced orientation time and increased productivity (Kelley, 1985). The literature reflects the success of similar work/study programs in which student nurses supplement academics with clinical work that provides income. Students report increased confidence and competence in using their communication and clinical skills (Cusack, Joos, & Simenc, 1990; Farley & Tyree, 1991; Keating, Baj, Spicer, & Ripple, 1994). New graduates who have participated in a work/study program as students acquire and use informal networking skills in searching for employment, and significantly increase their starting salaries as beginning professional nurses (Taylor, 1988).

FINANCIAL COMPONENT

Our students have major familial financial responsibilities; most must work outside the academic program to support themselves and their families, and many are single mothers. For these students, the program's financial reimbursement for their work is the deciding factor in whether or not they are even able to consider participation. Students often arrange vacation time or leaves of absence from their respective jobs to take advantage of the program. Thus, financial remuneration enables students from diverse socioeconomic backgrounds to access an experience that may be pivotal in their overall success in becoming professional nurses. The money creates the means, opens a way, and helps structure the milieu in which equality of opportunity exists.

PHILOSOPHICAL PREMISES OF THE WORK/STUDY PROGRAM

The premises of the work/study program have their foundations in the beliefs of the faculty about learning, which, in turn, reflect John Dewey's philosophy. For Dewey, the pursuit of a career, while not the exclusive purpose of education, was an important focal point of the educational process. His philosophy incorporates the belief that individuals are motivated to survive and to succeed in many areas of life, including in a career. Therefore, educators need to include the world beyond the classroom curriculum and allow students to use their intellects in "reconstructing their world and not merely become apprentices." Dewey's model opposes a dualism of vocational and academic education. It calls for incorporating intellectual knowledge within a career-driven educational process (Heinemann & DeFalco, 1990). An educational experience with a pragmatic work/study component integrates theory and application, offers students an interdisciplinary perspective, and assists them in developing and reinforcing cognitive skills, analysis, problem solving, and decision making. In addition, it assists students in creating an environment for reflective and self-directed learning, and in achieving academic, career, and personal growth objectives (Heinemann, DeFalco, & Smelkinson, 1992). The integration of intellectual knowledge with its pragmatic application in an educational process describes the standard clinical experience in a nursing curriculum. Work/study differs from the traditional clinical experience in part because it takes place outside the formal educational setting; it is an optional experience that focuses on the individual as part of the clinical working staff. The individual participates in group decision making rather than individualized nursing judgment, and focuses on the reinforcement of learning rather than the acquisition of new knowledge. Although students may learn new theory and new skills, their organizational skills and behaviors also improve during their experience.

Underlying principles of the work/study program reflect a Tyler (1950) model. Tyler's curricula utilized the evaluation of learning based on behavioral objectives. Critics of the Tyler method of curriculum development and evaluation of students charge that it tends to focus too strongly on technical training. Conversely, it has been praised for providing for regulated and quality outcomes in beginning practitioners (Bevis, 1988). "The Tyler model places a high value on effectiveness, efficiency, certainty, and predictability, and it emphasizes individualism and competition" (Diekelmann, 1988, p. 139). The extent to which the work/study program uses behavioral objectives and reflects the values inherent in the Tyler model is related to the academic environment of the school of nursing in which the program exists. Because the institutional curriculum reflects the Tyler model, students' success in the program is based on increased expertise in observable clinical and communication skills in the work environment.

Participating faculty and unit registered nurses evaluate individual student progress in the work/study program. Students also participate in self-evaluation and program evaluation using questionnaires and written narratives (Kelley, 1985).

POSITIVE EXPERIENCES FOR STUDENTS AT RISK

The work/study program has been versatile enough to allow a diverse population of academically successful students to improve their performance in the clinical setting. It has provided students who are at risk for poor performance with the opportunity to integrate academic learning into practice. Students at risk include those who have failed and repeated either a science or clinical nursing course and may also include those, who for reasons of background or perception, feel alienated from the academic and clinical worlds.

Minority students who have not developed strategies to deal with perceptions of institutional or individual racism are at risk for academic failure (Kornguth, Frisch, Shovein, & Williams, 1994). Minority students may have learning styles that are strongly dependent on the noncognitive factors of positive affiliation with faculty, and their ability to demonstrate progress may differ from usual norms of the program. For some minority students, "being in the world" is related to values of interdependence, group cohesiveness, and a sense of belonging. They value accommodation, tolerance, and smooth interpersonal relations in the learning environment, and expect them to characterize interactions in the academic and clinical settings. In the academic culture, however, dominant independence, self-expression, and competitiveness are the pre-dominate values. Highly individualized thinking and problem solving are valued over group decision making and cohesion (Pacquiao, 1994). It may be difficult for at-risk students to develop in a complicated environment while immersed in a fast-paced, strenuous academic course. Both the academic and clinical settings require a prescribed pace for the acquisition of course content, for the application of vast amounts of nursing knowledge, and for individualized demonstration of progress in learning. Students experience difficulty in adapting to a style of learning that contrasts with their dominant values, or with demonstrating the acquisition of knowledge in a manner consistent with the Tyler model of student outcomes.

The work/study program has provided students affective and psychomotor strategies for success. They become an integral part of the staff team and experience support and affiliation. This positive social system and a sense of autonomy increase their job satisfaction and reduce stress (Flarey, 1993). Minority students valuing group cohesiveness have a great opportunity to acquire and to reinforce nursing knowledge and to make nursing decisions while working as part of the health care team. Faculty are facilitators of student learning and collaborate with students to identify individual needs. Student-faculty interactions in the work/study setting reflect the values of comfortable interaction and positive affiliation. The reinforcement of skills allows students more time for developing technical expertise. They also report that they find space and silence for self-reflection and goal setting on the clinical unit. Minority students dealing with perceptions of alienation or racism have greater opportunities to develop professional relationships. Work/study offers time to develop a diverse support network. Students representing a wide range of academic abilities, levels of clinical performance, and noncognitive needs report positive growth from participation.

AIM OF STUDY, MODE OF INQUIRY

Our work/study program benefits students by increasing their competence and confidence in caring for patients, and in making connections between nursing theory and practice. Student experiences in the program form an elaborate subpattern of meanings not fully represented by the factual information. Examination of the phenomenological aspects of the work/study program does not fully explain what it is like to be a student extern in the program. The multifaceted components of reality that reflect different ways of knowing require distinctive and discrete methodologies with which to understand phenomena such as these students' experiences

(Munhall, 1988; Wolfer, 1993). Differing epistemologies need not compete or conflict, but rather yield complementary understandings which broaden knowledge (Munhall, 1982; Wolfer, 1993).

> *Thus perception and thought have this much in common—that both of them have a future horizon and a past horizon and that they appear to themselves as temporal, even though they do not move at the same speed nor in the same time.* (Merleau-Ponty, 1964a, p. 21)

Using a phenomenological framework of inquiry, the aim of the study was to describe and understand the meaning of student experiences in the work/study program. These students underwent an indefinable personal transformation with patterns that indicated the development of a greater ability in the art of nursing. With a goal of identifying and understanding the essential nature of this transformation, we sought to make connections where possible, between the subpattern of meanings for the students, the philosophical premises of the program, and the reported factual information about the students' experiences.

PHENOMENOLOGY AS INQUIRY

> *Everything changes when a phenomenological or existential philosophy assigns itself the task not of explaining the world or of discovering its 'conditions of possibility,' but rather of formulating an experience of the world, a contact with the world which precedes all thought about the world.* (Merleau-Ponty, 1964b, p.27)

This presentation of the experiences of students in a work/study program seeks to access the essential meanings of being in the world as a student extern in a work/study program. The inquiry uses VanManen's (1990) approach to phenomenological research as a framework. It avoids presuppositions, procedures, or techniques and is discovered rather than assigned as a response to the question posed. This approach calls for a hermeneutic phenomenological inquiry, which means that the process is both interpretive (hermeneutic) and descriptive (phenomenological). Any interpretive activity, however, conforms to the philosophical premise that the essences of lived experiences are their meanings, and must be reflected in language (VanManen, 1990). The activities of inquiry were also based on those developed by VanManen, including: "turning to" the phenomena, investigating the experience as lived, and discovering and reflecting on the essential themes of the phenomena. These activities suggested the process of assessing the meanings of the experiences of student externs as being in the world in a work/study program.

QUALITATIVE CONSENT

Student experiences were collected through 4 in-depth taped interviews and 16 written narratives. Informed consent in qualitative research is a dynamic ongoing process in which negotiation and renegotiation take place. During qualitative interviews in particular, participants may find themselves at points in dialogue that they could not have anticipated. Protection of the participants' human rights includes collaboration in dialogue (Munhall, 1993). Students who were taped were informed in writing of the nature of the study, that they would be taped, that confidentiality would be maintained, and that collaboration regarding their participation would be an ongoing component of the dialogue with the interviewer.

The written narratives were collected as part of the student evaluations of the work/study program. Students where informed that they need not sign their names although most chose to do so. Nevertheless, students are not identified in this work.

TURNING TO THE PHENOMENA

The students' experiences in the work/study program as externs seemed to differ from their experiences in the formal academic environment, not so much in magnitude, but in kind. Participation in the work/study did not present itself as a tutorial of the academic clinical experience, or as additional time for the absorption of course content. I recognized through informal conversations with students, and through mentoring students who had participated in the program, that a difference in experience existed although its nature was not readily apparent. The phenomenological question that presented itself was, "What are the essences of student experiences as being in the world of the work/study program?"

INVESTIGATING THE EXPERIENCE AS LIVED

Being in the world of the work/study program is described in the student experiences:

> *I had realized just how limited my previous clinical experience had been. As a student during clinical, I would arrive several hours into the shift, work with only one patient and then leave before the shift was over. There was minimal contact with the floor staff. I did not feel like a team member, more like one more interruption of the busy nurse's day.*

In my experience as an extern, I've worked the full evening shift with up to four patients, and the other nurses have come to rely on my nearly full responsibility of these patients. Aware of my relative inexperience, especially at first, the nurses have always been available to me if I required any assistance. I've taken and given reports on my patients and learned to discriminate between essential and nonessential information. I've learned to be more alert to changes in doctors' orders and become more aware of when to expect these changes. I feel more confident in my assessments—more efficient. I've also experienced reality in terms of realizing that needs must be prioritized, and that I cannot attend to everything at once. If I had not been in this program I hate to wonder what I would have missed, the measure of shock I would probably have experienced on my first job as a RN. Now, I feel confident knowing what the work of a RN really entails and still am happy that I decided on nursing as a career.

This student's experience highlights the transforming process of participating in the work/study program and crystallizes and affirms her decision to enter the profession of nursing. Other participants share similar experiences:

The experience separates you from being a student, yet you are not a staff nurse; but it gives you that feeling . . . you question, "Is this what I really want?" When I first came into nursing, I thought it would give me a sense of security; I was going to have a job no matter what. Once I was an extern, it made me feel like this is really what I want to do. I can take care of patients, I can relate to them. It made me feel good, and just that fact boosted my confidence.

Another student documents her odyssey in a transforming process:

It was very interesting. I think I got the most difficult patients (as an extern). When I got on the floor it started. I found out that this is the usual thing the staff does. There were tubes coming in and out of the patient and it was overwhelming the first week or so . . . how was I going to handle this? And I had a problem with organization and getting myself together . . . I was pacing back and forth, running . . . I was literally on top of the patients . . . counting their breaths, making sure all the time that they were not in danger. But then I started to relax, to calm down . . . to become more effective . . . to plan my day, to be more organized.

We had more autonomy (as externs). I felt that I was able to draw more from my own personal experiences (in giving patient care). I felt more confident, more independent, as if I could use my mind, my resources. . . . The biggest thing I can say is that you have that autonomy. There was also the responsibility that I felt (when) there was no clinical instructor present watching everything I did . . . I could still hear voices in my head "maintain sterile technique" and things like that.

Students share their experiences taking care of patients as part of the work/study program. They equate a growing depth of relationships with patients with working day to day and staying on the units for the full shift. In addition, students speak of their ability to relate better to patients, as having to do with the greater autonomy they perceived that they had in the situation. Some students had powerful experiences with patients and families that contributed to a professionalizing process, and which would have been unlikely except during an ongoing relationship with a patient:

During this experience as an extern, I lost my first patient, which had a great impact on me. This is something I will always remember. By going through this experience, I have learned that there are many emotions that go along with grief. I have also learned that you can show emotion while still doing your job by providing comfort to others. . . .

My organization improved greatly. I was able to prioritize care for the patients I had. Overall this has been a positive experience for me, I even received a thank-you letter from one of my patients.

I've also taken care of AIDS patients, something I've wanted to do for awhile. It definitely makes you reevaluate your life and the care you give to others. I think these experiences not only perfected my skills but helped me deal with the patient as a whole person.

Another student shared the following:

One experience that . . . I really felt good about was one patient . . . (She was) quite old and was on a respirator and she was a renal patient . . . there was a big dispute (in) the family whether to make her a DNR (Do Not Resuscitate) or not. She was there for practically my whole experience, many weeks. Towards the end, I was able to know the family well. Her sisters wanted the DNR status, but the grandchildren did not. It turned out that they were all confused as to what the DNR meant and so I was able to explain what being a patient who would not be resuscitated would mean to her. She was blind and hardly responding. When she did respond, she cried all of the time. It seemed that she just wanted to be at peace. I think that I was responsible for getting the family to jointly decide to let her become a DNR and she died not too many days after that. They thanked me, the sisters did. I felt that if I had not been an extern that I would not have gotten to know the family. The doctors and the rest of the staff had given up on trying to get the family to agree on anything.

BEING IN THE WORLD AS A MEMBER
OF THE PATIENT CARE TEAM

Students shared how a close working relationship was highly valued as a means for creating a positive learning experience, and for creating a sense of belonging that contributed to their professional growth. This is a strong motivational factor that connects with students who have alternative learning styles from that of the traditional learning environment:

> *There isn't that barrier that exists when you are a student on the floor as an extern. In the (academic) clinical, when you are a student on the floor, there is a barrier that obstructs between you and the staff. . . . When you are there as an extern, you are one with the staff. . . . The staff was close and helped one another and helped me a lot. They saw that I was interested in learning and so they were interested in helping.*

Other students shared the following:

> *There are more aspects to working than being familiar with giving patient care. Because you are dealing with staff members you get to see what (nursing) is really like. You use your own personality in dealing with staff members, you make it work with the other staff. . . . It has made a big difference for me. I really feel self-confident.*
>
> *The nurses on my unit made me feel like one of the gang. I feel confident with port-a-cath dressings, inserting catheters, and I even took part in a code where I had to perform chest compressions. The staff supported me and gave me opportunities to practice skills.*
>
> *Without the help of nurses on the unit I would not have learned as much. They pushed me when I needed it. I learned so much about oncology on my unit. My communication with patients improved and I overcame shyness. I would do this again in a heartbeat.*

BEING IN THE WORLD IN RELATIONSHIP TO
FACULTY AND INSTRUCTORS

Students shared how different their relationships were to faculty who participated in the work/study program from what they were in the formal academic clinical setting. This was not related to the personalities of any particular faculty members; in many instances, faculty who participated in the work/study program were the same people who taught in the formal class and clinical environment. All students who described experiences in the project recounted these differences:

I felt that we had more autonomy than being on the clinical floor with our instructor (in the academic setting). The instructor in the work/study program treated me not so much as a student but, as if we were already nurses. She would come in and do grand rounds with all our patients. We were to then interact with the staff during the shift.

Other students shared:

In the clinical (academic setting) you feel that someone is constantly watching over your back. It put pressure on me, it made me so nervous. I was so much more confident with the instructors in the work/study. . . . at the end of the day just reviewing notes and going over the patients with them was great.

I felt as if I could really make a difference for patients. The instructor seemed to think that I could do the work. It was like she was a big sister or something. I wasn't afraid to ask questions. She made it a great experience and it helped me to have more confidence.

The relationship between the instructors in the work/study program was characterized in many positive ways. The faculty seemed to engage in an interactive process that included the ethical practice of autonomy and caring. These values, evident within student-faculty interactions, have been suggested as contributing to the ethical decision making and caring behavior of students in the patient care setting (Schaffer & Juarez, 1993).

ESSENTIAL THEMES

The essential themes that emerged as students shared their experiences included autonomy, self-confidence, positive and enabling affiliation with staff and instructors, a sense of belonging, and a sense of increased preparedness for the care of patients. These factors reflect components of bicultural learning styles (Pacquiao, 1994) that give meaning to the experiences of some of the students. The themes, as they emerged, should not be generalized to other work/study programs or to other student participants in such programs. The experiences of these students took place within a particular milieu, and all aspects of that milieu cannot be assumed as known. These phenomenological meanings are part of the unique experiences of students in a circumspect world.

The phenomenological question: "What is it like to be a student extern in the work/study program?" not only revealed the experiences of students as being in the world but suggested the essence of their world. In turn, the context of this world gave meaning and vitality to the program.

PHENOMENOLOGY: THE HIDDEN CURRICULUM TRANSFORMS THE CULTURE OF LEARNING

The work/study program contains many elements of a phenomenological model of nursing education: "The essence of the phenomenological model is the attempt to come to some understanding of the world of Being, the lived world of people" (Diekelmann, 1988, p. 142). Traditional models use prediction and evaluation of students to measure progress. Phenomenology focuses on "the lived experience of clinicians and on introducing students into the clinical world" (Diekelmann, 1988, p. 142). Teachers and clinicians collaborate in creating an environment in which students may access meaningful experiences that link their conceptual world. The focus of student-faculty interaction includes the exploration of situational meanings (the case study format). The phenomenology model incorporates the concept that teachers are interested in maintaining a student-faculty dialogue and in mutually exploring the lived experiences of students as they learn what it means to become a nurse (Diekelmann, 1988).

Phenomenology, the hidden curriculum of the work/study program, subsumes but does not eliminate the Tyler model. The technical and cognitive outcomes of students are still valued but the learning process conforms to the phenomenological experience. In the work/study program, students develop a collaborative relationship with the faculty and are immersed in the world of clinical nursing on a day-by-day basis.

Students develop an ongoing dialogue with faculty and unit nurses in acquisition or reinforcement of knowledge. The case study format of learning is possible because students may care for a patient for an extended period, often for the duration of the patient's hospital stay. These students enjoy a greater magnitude of being in the world of the patient and family, as care is designed by excellent nursing staff. An extended patient care format also allows students to discover meaning in sustained observation of the role of the professional nurse. This view is unlike that of the formal academic clinical experience, where students may be assigned to the clinical unit for only two consecutive days and rarely spend an entire eight-hour shift there.

The phenomenology model strongly addresses the needs of a multicultural student population. The format for student-faculty interaction coincides with the needs of many students for strong positive affiliation with faculty and staff. Students who favor concrete learning can have repeated hands-on experiences, and the case study format helps them make conceptual connections within a milieu where nursing staff work together to deliver expert patient care. Minority students who value cooperation and group cohesiveness over competition can crystallize learning in a less conflictive environment.

The phenomenological model—a hidden or unstated component of the work/study program—acts as a transforming agent for many students when they most need it by creating a nexus of learning that gives meaning to their experiences and promotes their success in the formal academic environment.

CONCLUSION

The following poem was written by the author in tribute to the students who have participated in the work/study program, and to the faculty and instructors who guided their learning, and to the excellent and caring nurses who helped form the milieu of experience:

Nurse: Transforming

I reach out my hand
Steadied now my ancient fears
And all my soul is calm.
My teachers watch and guide me in my head
Make my way in confidence to your bed
All the world is bright with knowing sight,
I bring the skills to take away your pain
I dry your tears.

REFERENCES

Bevis, E. O. (1988). New directions for a new age. In *Curriculum revolution: Mandate for change* (Publication No. 15-2224, pp. 27–52). New York: National League for Nursing Press.

Cusack, J. M., Joos, L. J., & Simenc, G. L. (1990). Cooperative education: An innovative recruitment technique. *Dimensions of Critical Care Nursing, 9*(2), 119–125.

Diekelmann, N. (1988). Curriculum revolution: A theoretical and philosophical mandate for change. In *Curriculum revolution: Mandate for change* (Publication No. 15-2224, pp. 137–157). New York: National League for Nursing Press.

Farley, V. M., & Tyree, A. (1991). A work-study course in an ADN program. *Advancing Clinical Care* (Jan/Feb), 30-32.

Flarey, D. L. (1993). The social climate of work environments. *Journal of Nursing Administration, 23*(6), 9-15.

Hegel, G. W. F. (1977). *Phenomenology of Spirit* (A. V. Miller, Trans.; J. N. Findlay, Analysis). New York: Oxford University Press. (Original work published 1807)

Heinemann, H. N., & DeFalco, A. A. (1990). Dewey's pragmatism: A philosophical foundation for cooperative education. *Journal of Cooperative Education, 27*(1), 38-44.

Heinemann, H. N., DeFalco, A. A., & Smelkinson, M. (1992). Work-experience enriched learning. *Journal of Cooperative Education, 28*(1), 17-33.

Keating, S., Baj, P., Spicer, J., & Ripple, H. (1994). A collaborative work study program between nursing service and education. *Nurse Educator, 19*(1), 23-26.

Kelley, M. E. (1985, May). *Nurse extern program.* Unpublished report, Elizabeth General Medical Center School of Nursing, Elizabeth, NJ.

Kornguth, M., Frisch, N., Shovein, J., & Williams, R. (1994). Noncognative factors that put students at academic risk in nursing programs. *Nurse educator, 19*(5).

Merleau-Ponty, M. (1964a). *The primacy of perception* (H. L. Dreyfus & P. A. Dreyfus, Trans.). Evanston, Il.: Northwestern University Press.

Merleau-Ponty, M. (1964b). *Sense and non-sense* (H. L. Dreyfus & P. A. Dreyfus, Trans.). Evanston, Il.: Northwestern University Press.

Munhall, P. L. (1982). Nursing philosophy and nursing research: In apposition or opposition? *Nursing Research, 31,* 176-181.

Munhall, P. L. (1988). Philosophical ponderings on qualitative research methods in nursing. *Nursing Science Quarterly, 11,* 20-28.

Munhall, P. L. (1993). Ethical considerations in qualitative research. In C. O. Boyd & P. L. Munhall (Eds.), *Nursing research: A qualitative perspective* (pp. 395-408). New York: National League for Nursing Press.

Pacquiao, D. (1994). *Sociocultural influences on cognitive styles of African-American, Filipino and Hispanic nursing students.* Unpublished manuscript.

Schaffer, M. A., & Juarez, M. (1993). An ethical analysis of student-faculty interactions. *Nurse Educator, 18*(3), 25-28.

Taylor, M. S. (1988). Effects of college internships on individual participants. *Journal of Applied Psychology, 73,* 393-401.

Tyler, R. (1950). *Basic principles of curriculum and instruction.* Chicago: University of Chicago Press.

Van Manen, M. (1990). *Researching lived experience: Human science for an action sensitive pedagogy.* New York: State University of New York Press.

Wolfer, J. (1993). Aspects of reality and ways of knowing in nursing: In search of an integrating paradigm. *Image, 25,* 141-146.

17

Single-Parent Housing: One Economic Solution for Students with Children

Judith Mathews*

THE NEEDS OF THE SINGLE-PARENT STUDENT IN NURSING EDUCATION

The single-parent family, led usually by an ethnic minority female, is a growing segment in the U.S. population. Traditional college life routinely includes housing for the college student. With special housing arrangements, single parents can have a successful college experience while their children are supervised and safe. Exploring the economic needs of our students identified the barrier inadequate housing arrangements raised for the minority students we wanted to enter our program.

---

*Maureen Hreha and Marilyn Burke collaborated on this chapter.

SINGLE-PARENT HOUSING: ONE FORMULA FOR DEVELOPMENT AND ACADEMIC SUCCESS

Each year, qualified applicants to nursing programs include numbers of single parents. These single parents inquired about student housing for themselves and their children but withdrew their applications when only the traditional dormitory residence halls were available with no accommodations or facilities for children. The lack of appropriate contemporary housing for families prevented some qualified applicants from pursuing an education. We addressed the need, modifying our existing structures. Single-parent housing had three goals:

- To determine the requirements for converting existing student residence space into housing for single-parent students and their families.
- To plan for family living guidelines.
- To determine the appropriate support services for the single-parent students and their children.

Accomplishing the first goal required identifying physical space and planning the renovation. Addressing the second and third goals required research into the characteristics and needs of the single-parent student.

WHO IS A CANDIDATE FOR SPECIAL HOUSING?

The U.S. Census Bureau counts "other families" as a category of households. This category is defined by the Census Bureau as households not headed by married couples. Single mothers head about seven million of these families. The Census Bureau projects that by the year 2010, eight million households will be headed by single mothers. The number of these families headed by single mothers under the age of 25 will increase by 50% by the year 2010.

The 1990 census showed that households headed by single mothers are often low-income households. About 45% of single mothers with children under 18 live in poverty. These families are frequently minority families. Births to single mothers continue to occur at alarmingly high rates across all ethnic groups. Such family units are vulnerable in many perspectives, in particular, educational goals have been sidetracked. If the Transcultural Leadership Continuum (Project TLC) proposed to address the economic needs of minority students in nursing education, it had to address the single parent as well.

THE SINGLE MOTHER WITH HER CHILDREN
REQUIRES SUPPORT SERVICES

Does the single mother with children require support services? Corporate America thinks so. Single parents head 25% of today's American families ("Single Parent Support," 1994). Employers who address the issues of diversity in the workforce often find that some of those issues include family demands. Employers are willing to invest in supporting workers affected by various family issues to enable their employees' productivity and well-being. Demographics indicate that single parenting is now recognized as one of those family issues ("Dow Programs," 1993).

Single parents' needs are often addressed by employers who provide assistance such as child care programs or flextime scheduling arrangements. Dow Chemical provides day-care programs at a number of its plants to assist single parents and dual-career families (*Occupational Outlook Handbook*, 1992). SONY is another company that provides day-care facilities at some of its sites (Jorgensen, 1993). American companies are taking advantage of the diversity of the workforce and addressing employees' lifestyle concerns to enable increased success on the job. Companies want to ". . . harness the diversity of the US work force to increase productivity and profit shares" ("Dow Programs," 1993).

Single-parent college students also have needs—as students, as parents, and as individuals. Colleges that have started on-campus residential programs already know this and address these needs.

Single-parent housing, child care, and other support services for nursing and other postsecondary students are already provided at schools such as Trinity College and Goddard College in Vermont, Texas Woman's University, and St. Catherine's in Minnesota.

Individuals who work with single parents recognize that among their primary needs are relevant education, skilled counseling, quality child care, and a job that pays enough to make it financially advantageous to work. Texas Woman's University's program (Murphy-Chadwick, 1989) for single-parent students in need is a quality program of increasing demand. The school's services support not only the adult single woman student but the child of that student as well. The on-campus family population has grown yearly with a 363% increase since 1983. Single parents have a secure environment to make a home while attending classes. The accessibility of quality child care and convenient, secure housing can relieve two of the major pressures facing students with young families.

The College of Saint Catherine identified a need for special housing and additional services for its student population, which included several single mothers. St. Catherine's offers several health-related degree programs, including an associate's degree in nursing. St. Catherine's recognized the need for odd-hour day care: Single parents who must take early morning clinicals in hospitals in support of schoolwork require odd-hour day care for their children. Living with other single parents and having access to regular and odd-hour child care would reduce scheduling hassles and enable a community of support to provide connections that can serve as a safety net for students.

Housing and child care are basic requirements for the single parent in need who wants to enroll in postsecondary college and nursing programs. Additional support services allow single mothers to succeed, increasing not only enrollment but retention and successful completion of the program.

As Muhlenberg Regional Medical Center School of Nursing addressed the issues of housing for its single-parent students, it also looked at programs to support those students. Based on information from existing programs at colleges, plans were developed for three counseling approaches that would address the single parent as student, person, and parent.

THE PHYSICAL PLANT

Figure 17.1 illustrates the floor plan for a single-parent housing dormitory. There is a large common living room with a bathroom attached. A standard kitchen has a refrigerator, range, microwave, sink, and cabinets. There are four two-room family units adjacent to toilet, bath, and shower units. Two offices at the end of the hall serve as counselor space. Furnishings are simple and sturdy.

Approval of the Certificate of Occupancy requires code compliance inspections by the engineering department, insurance company, and the environmental safety officer of the town.

A HOUSING BLUEPRINT

Students admitted to the nursing program are fully qualified applicants as well as single parents (women) with extraordinary needs. Once Muhlenberg decided that the physical renovations were feasible, it developed a support services plan.

Local New Jersey shelters who provide housing for single parents were surveyed. They all affirm the necessity of providing support services such as counseling, child care, health, and family services. Their residents are from a world of poverty, abuse, and other crisis situations. Identifying the

Figure 17.1

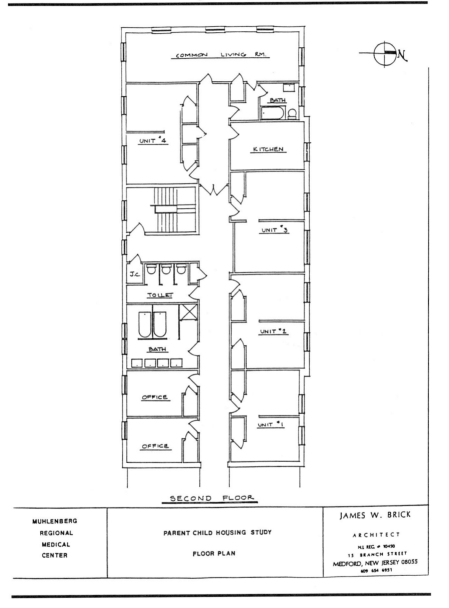

potentially successful student is not enough. The student who is a single parent may have to overcome a history of complex problems.

A comprehensive housing plan respects the single parent as a person. A personal counselor is available for scheduled individual and group counseling sessions. The sessions focus on improvement in self-esteem, problem solving, interpersonal relations, and conflict resolution within the group. This counselor helps the students adjust to dormitory living and enables each to function as an individual, student, and parent in a communal setting.

The program also supports the single parents as parents, and that effort begins with safe, dependable child care. The women have the services of the Muhlenberg Child Care Center, which provides care for children from the ages of 3 weeks to 5 years Monday through Friday. Evening child care is included and scheduled for weekday evenings twice a week within the dormitory setting. A cooperative program of babysitting was organized for weekend, odd-hour, and sick child care, and gradually assumed more of the child-care responsibilities.

The program facilitates additional parenting support by providing a family mentor. The family mentor is available formally and informally to foster the family unit and support the student as a parent. Formal sessions are presented in parenting, safety, child growth and development, decision making, goal setting, health and wellness, socialization, team building, and peer interaction. The family mentor assists in an initial orientation period for the incoming families.

Finally, this project supports the single-parent nursing student in academic and clinical training matters with an academic counselor. The counselor focuses on the individual as a student, identifying and addressing learning problems, study skills, test-taking strategies, and time and project management skills.

CONTRACT FOR DEVELOPMENT: FAMILIES TOGETHER

Accepted single parents are screened for motivation, sense of responsibility, and aptitude for college academic work before they enter the program. This screening process is in addition to a preparatory six-week period before classes begin. It is essential that both the single parents and their children are familiar with their new living conditions and expectations. This orientation period gives the families time to get to know one another before the entire class meets as a whole.

Careful screening of single-parent applicants, combined with a full network of professional support for the women and their children, enables these students to achieve their educational goals.

The program is not simply a gift. It demands from the student the ability to study and achieve academically as she copes with communal living and parenting. The program asks that the woman return to her community as an educated nurse ready to serve as role model of achievement and independence.

REFERENCES

Dow programs address child care, dual-career couples, and other work-family issues. (1993, October 23). *Chemical & Engineering News,* p. 47.

Healing's bedside revolution: Health care reform could further expand role of nursing. (1993, December 31). *Washington Post,* p. A1.

Health-care reform should bode well for nurses. (1994, January 11). *Wall Street Journal,* p. A1.

Hennenberger, M. (1994, August 21). For nurses, new uncertainties: Managed care means fewer openings, specialized needs. *New York Times,* p. 45.

Jahn, B. J. (1990). *An investigation of changes in perception of career mobility with advanced formal education by registered and vocational nurses.* Unpublished doctoral dissertation, East Texas State University, Texas.

Jorgensen, B. (1993, September). Diversity: Managing a multicultural work force. *Electronic Business Buyer,* pp. 70-76.

Murphy-Chadwick, N., & Brocksimmons, G. (1989). *Family Housing and Services* (ERIC ED316148). Washington, DC: American Association of State Colleges and Universities.

New Jersey Administrative Code. (1988, November 7). *Manual of Requirements for Family Day Care Registration* (Provider edition). Trenton, NJ: New Jersey Dept. of Human Services.

North, D. (1987). AFDC goes to college. *Public Welfare, 45*(4), 4-12.

Occupational Outlook Handbook (1992-1993 Ed.). Chicago: VGM Career Horizons.

Patterson, M. (1993, July 14). Single motherhood on the rise. *The Star Ledger, 1*(15). Newark, NJ.

Scott, J. (1989). *Traditional and Reentry Nursing Majors: Motivational Factors, Vocational Personalities, Barriers and Enablers to Participation.* Muncie, IN: Ball State University.

Single parent support. (1994, September). *Small Business Reports,* 20.

Single parents. (1993, December). *American Demographics, 1,* 36-37.

Part Five

Preparation for a Master of Science in Nursing: Moving Minority Nurses Toward Leadership Positions

18

Mentoring African-American College Students: A Dean's Experience

Betty W. Barber

THE NEED AND IMPORTANCE OF MINORITY MENTORING

*M*entoring provides support and guidance that facilitates the mentee's realization of his or her dream or goal. A mentor is a trusted person who believes in and supports the mentee through advice, resources, research, and sharing of self and experience. Mentoring is person-centered.

Both traditional and nontraditional college-age students must accomplish major developmental tasks to become successful adults. Chief among these tasks is the adoption of a personal set of values—a moral and ethical framework for determining the direction of life goals, as well as accountability for actions. In forming their set of values, students very often identify those values learned at home, in school, and in church, or acquired from significant persons who have served as mentors and role models in their lives.

An African American nursing major who enters a predominantly white college might feel culture shock, especially during the first weeks on campus, when brought together with individuals and groups of different races, cultures, sexual orientations, and beliefs. Some minority students feel a tremendous pressure to outperform their classmates in a conscious effort to beat the stereotype of being less qualified (Gibbs, 1990). The persistent theme from many black professors is that predominantly white institutions are often less congenial and less sensitive to minority concerns.

Too often, behavior, beauty, and linguistic expression are judged and defined acceptable in terms of dominant group standards. Persons with mannerisms outside these norms may be regarded negatively as inferior or unacceptable, and often are perceived as lacking social and professional competence.

AN AFRICAN AMERICAN DEAN'S EXPERIENCE

As an African American Dean at a state college who has served on the faculty of three predominantly white institutions, I have observed and participated in the educational experience of African American nursing students at these institutions. Approximately half of the students whom I served were adult learners. Both minority and nonminority adult learners exhibit a higher level of fear than their traditional counterparts. In addition, there are recognized qualitative differences between the experiences of black students and white students in higher education. Minority students have a significant number of education-related fears that need to be addressed by academic counselors.

In dealing with the fears of minority nursing majors, it was important for me, as their mentor, to recognize that the majority of these students use academic services sparingly and are most reluctant to participate in counseling. Because they tend not to reveal much information about themselves, these troubled students seldom initiate a discussion of fears. When I bring up the subject in a tactful manner, however, they usually begin to share their concerns. To deal with this kind of situation, the mentor or advisor must shift from a passive stance to a proactive, more open approach. Such a strategy is even more effective when combined with a formal outreach support program. Satisfaction with academic counseling is critical to retention, making the mentor's sensitivity to socioeconomic and cultural influences a core issue.

BARRIERS AND SOLUTIONS

Because minority nursing students commonly feel socially isolated and alienated from the majority student population, they tend to congregate together and disassociate themselves from the majority student body. In discussing this behavior, some minority students have related that when nonminority students substantially outnumber them in all their classes, they experience a sense of personal discomfort. On the other hand, they expressed a sense of strength, pride, and ethnic identity when they meet together in their own small groups. The challenge for the mentor is to support the students in their apparent need and choice to form their own identity group while helping them discover the value of positive interactions with the dominant group. Positive minority role models, multiracial friendships, and common educational goals can help the students develop personal comfort in all their subsequent interracial and intraracial relationships. Mentors should encourage students of all racial or ethnic groups to examine their own cultural biases and beliefs to ensure that they respect the beliefs of others from different backgrounds.

When I am innovative and empower the students in a caring and goal-directed way, my minority students feel secure and confident. As their mentor, I demonstrate to them my high standards and values as a professional and an academic leader.

REFERENCES

Allen, W. R. (1987). Black colleges vs. white colleges: The fork in the road for black students. *Change,* pp. 28–31.

Gibbs, N. (1990, May). Bigots in the ivory tower: An alarming rise in hatred roils U.S. campuses. *Time,* p. 104.

Green, M. (Ed.). (1989). *Minorities on campus: A handbook for enhancing diversity.* Washington, DC: American Council on Education.

19

Master of Science in Nursing Curriculum Development: Clinical Management with a Transcultural Focus

Susan Warner Salmond

THE TRANSCULTURAL FOCUS

*T*he Master of Science in Nursing in Clinical Management with a Transcultural Focus at Kean College of New Jersey was designed to prepare clinical leaders who could guide others with a vision that values diversity. Our contemporary society is a culturally diverse community of individuals with many different national, regional, ethnic, racial, socioeconomic, and occupational orientations that influence interactions in health care settings (Kreps, & Thornton, 1992). Nurses and other health care workers are challenged to learn about the effects of culture on individuals' perception and expression of their symptoms (Geist, 1994). Managing patients is only one aspect of the clinical leader's role. The remainder of the role is in guiding a diverse workforce. Valuing diversity as a paradigm for managing people requires awareness of the impact of core differences, management experimentation, and institutional reform.

Another objective of the Transcultural Learning Continuum Grant was to educate minority nurses to assume positions of clinical leadership in the community. The MSN in Clinical Management with a Transcultural Focus can prepare these nurse leaders, but the vision of the program includes all cultural groups, dominant and nondominant, so that the nursing leaders of all cultural backgrounds learn to manage in a multicultural world.

The MSN curriculum is the only existing graduate nursing program in nursing administration that uses a transcultural paradigm in all its core courses. The faculty believe that nursing leaders must be grounded in a strong leadership, communication, and clinical foundation; however to guide and mentor multicultural staff, they also need bicultural leadership skills. Developing these skills requires integration of transcultural nursing content with the nursing courses. This scholarly base of practice is necessary to prepare the nurse leader to manage biculturally. Although some of the students represent minority cultures, this does not make them transcultural nor does it make them ready to lead biculturally. In reality, students of all cultural groups most often have a monocultural background that upholds a singular value orientation and consequently minimizes or negates diversity. Our program focuses on biculturalism, a process in which the individual affirms his or her own unique self while learning to address the needs of others who may have different values.

Transcultural nursing can be defined as "the comparative study and analysis of different cultures and subcultures in the world with respect to their caring behavior, nursing care, and health-illness values, beliefs and patterns of behavior with a goal of developing a scientific and humanistic body of knowledge in order to provide culture-specific and culture-universal nursing care practices" (Leininger, 1991). Leininger's theory of culture care is used in this program to discover the meanings and ways to give care to people with different values and life ways. Human care may vary transculturally in meanings, expressions, patterns, symbols, and other ways. Transcultural understanding develops awareness of how the values, feelings, and attitudes of people in other cultures influence their behavior. To achieve transcultural understanding, we can observe behaviors and define the values and attitudes that undergird those behaviors (Gaston, 1993).

Transcultural nursing leaders use culture care theory to establish the philosophy of patient care as well as to support and nurture multiculturalism in their organizational structures and practices. A *bicultural nursing leader* uses transcultural knowledge in interpersonal relations and problem solving, affirming individual uniqueness through the development of a participative, cohesive team. Ongoing negotiation and accommodation at the personal and organizational level create a reasonable fit between the individual's personal values and those of the profession and organization. Thus, the organization evolves into a dynamic culture shaped by the continuous interplay of its diverse subcultures.

THEORY COURSES: APPROACHES TO LEARNING

The development of bicultural nursing leadership requires that the professional nurse acquire insight and appreciation of multicultural value orientations. With an understanding of these different viewpoints, the bicultural nursing leader looks for strategies that will transcend these differences and transform them into creative solutions to problems. Nursing courses that integrate transcultural nursing content include seven theory courses: Nursing Science, Nursing and Organizational Theory, Organizational Communications in Transcultural Health Care Systems, Computers in Health Care, Fiscal Management, Nursing Research Proposal Development, and Nursing Research Proposal Implementation. These courses highlight *bicultural general skills,* or knowledge and ability, that enable students to be aware of and search out the specific areas in which people are likely to be different, to learn quickly about differences, and to respond satisfactorily to people from a variety of cultures even without detailed information about the culture in question (Simons & Walton, 1992). Individual assignments and some course content target *culture-specific skills* and involve knowing the customs, habits, communication and behavior patterns, even the language of a specific group, especially when the nurse regularly deals with people of that group.

Developing a curriculum that values diversity requires not only attention to course content, but also to teaching methods and strategies. Although educators have typically been cognizant that students have different preferred learning styles, classroom experiences have not reflected this multi-learning-style approach. The dominant style in many collegiate classrooms is the traditional, didactic lecture, which is no longer considered a culturally neutral approach to teaching (Adams, 1992; Leininger, 1994).

Many theorists contend that culture helps shape and structure students' learning styles (Claxton, 1990; Powell & Anderson, 1994). There are two cultural orientations to learning, an analytic style and a relational style. The analytic style involves breaking things down into their components. A relational style is more holistic and situates meanings and knowledge in global constructs. Anglo and Asian students favor an analytic approach, whereas Hispanics, Native Americans, and African Americans respond to a relational style that utilizes holistic thinking and cooperative learning strategies.

A teaching approach that uses both individualistic and group-centered learning techniques, will assist the student in bridging the bicultural dilemma and provide the faculty with a broader set of experiences for determining the students' abilities.

The teaching strategies discussed in the following chapters go beyond the traditional method and use alternative teaching modes that encourage active student involvement as contrasted with passive listening and note taking. In reality, high-quality teaching for a diverse population operates on the same principles as good teaching practice for all students; it places students in the role of active learners (Adams, 1992). All of the required content is actually taught, but it is accomplished in an interactive way, with students discussing the content and ideas and faculty filling in where student interaction does not cover an area.

This approach requires a new set of process skills for many faculty. Whereas lectures require an organized, rational, step-by-step analysis or presentation of material, experiential approaches require spontaneity and the abilities to get students to interact; draw information from students about their personal experiences; draw information from students about responses to a planned, interactive experience; and supplement the student-generated information with other theoretical content not covered. In my experience, this has required more preparation, rather than less; however, the classroom has had more dynamism and excitement.

CLINICAL EXPERIENCES

The program includes two 2-credit clinical courses, which accompany a 3-credit theory course, and finally, there is a synthesis 5-credit clinical course. These clinical experiences are designed to provide the students the opportunities to both observe and practice new sets of bicultural leadership skills.

Education of bicultural nursing leaders is based on the premise that learning for adult students is grounded in their lived experience, which integrates their developmental, cultural, social, occupational, and prior learning experiences. Our focus in developing clinical leaders was to use these experiences as a starting point in finding and shaping their identity as part of an organization and as a professional nurse.

Clinical experiences are aimed at understanding the people within an organization as well as the organizations themselves. Over time, organizations evolve into a dynamic, but tenacious culture shaped by the interplay of all the subcultures of individuals and groups internal to the organization as well as individuals, groups, and forces external to it. The culture of today's health care organization is influenced by community demographics, health care reform, socioeconomic and political forces as well as by the staff demographics and client population, interprofessional group interaction, and intragroup relationships. Bicultural leaders must be able to understand, assess, and modify this organizational culture. By placing students as participant observers in organizations undergoing significant transition, they are immersed in a real-life learning environment where they can observe the interplay of the internal and external forces and participate in shaping changes in the organization.

The final 5-credit course places the student in the role of leader and change agent to guide the implementation of transcultural clinical services. The supporting theory courses and earlier clinical courses all serve to prepare for this final project where the student performs in the role of a bicultural nursing leader.

OUR NEW PARADIGM

The mind-set of diversity flows out of understanding who you are and then being open to the experience of others. The MSN program is uniquely designed to move the students through this process. The skills and competencies necessary to perform as a bicultural leader require, first and foremost, that managers know that we interact with and manage *people* with a wide array of worldviews and lifeways. The new paradigm of bicultural leadership or ethnorelative leadership refers to being comfortable with many standards and customs and having the ability to adapt behavior and judgments to a variety of interpersonal settings (Bennett & Deane, 1994). In this way, leadership facilitates the process whereby all groups manifest their uniqueness while sharing a commitment to a common vision of the organizational mission and goals for the future.

REFERENCES

Adams, M. (1992). *Promoting diversity in college classrooms: Innovative responses for the curriculum, faculty and institutions.* San Francisco: Jossey-Bass.

Claxton, C. (1990). Learning styles, minority students, and effective education. *Journal of Developmental Education, 1,* 6-9.

Gaston, J. (1993). Cultural orientation in the English as a second language classroom. In T. Gochenour (Ed.), *Beyond experiences: The experiential approach to cross-cultural education* (pp. 97-100). Yarmouth, ME: Intercultural Press.

Geist, P. (1994). Negotiating cultural understanding in health care communication. In L. Samovar & R. Porter (Eds.), *Intercultural communications* (pp. 311-321). Belmont, CA: Wadsworth.

Kreps, G. L., & Thornton, B. C. (1992). *Health and communication: Theory and practice* (2nd ed). New York: Longman.

Leininger, M. (1991). *Culture care diversity and universality: A theory of nursing.* New York: National League for Nursing Press.

Leininger, M. (1994). Transcultural nursing education: A worldwide imperative. *Nursing and Health Care, 15*(5), 254-257.

Powell, R., & Anderson, J. (1994). Culture and classroom communication. In L. Samovar & R. Porter (Eds.), *Intercultural communication: A reader* (pp. 322-331). Belmont, CA: Wadsworth.

Simons, G., & Walton, S. (1992). Diversity: Where do I go for help? In G. Simons & B. Abramms (Eds.), *The questions of diversity* (p. 925). Amherst, MA: ODT Inc.

20

The Master of Science in Nursing Curriculum: Integrating Diversity Content within an Individual Model's Paradigm

Susan Warner Salmond

*T*he emphasis of the graduate program is in preparing clinical leaders who have an expertise in transcultural nursing and the skills to practice in bicultural settings. To this end, the curriculum was designed to address leadership content from a transcultural perspective. For each leadership content area, we critiqued the applicability of the approach for diverse cultural groups. It became clear that much of the literature addressed approaches that would be most effective with mainstream American culture, or the group that is predominantly white, middle-class males. These approaches may not achieve the same responses with other cultural groups, and strategizing other approaches is a major consideration of our program.

Preparing bicultural clinical leaders requires that students gain insight into their own cultural background as well as into other cultures. This intervention facilitates an awareness of cultural similarities and differences and how these differences may influence behavior and communication. The majority of the students who enter the program assume that people are enough alike to permit the student to judge situations from an ethnocentric framework. This viewpoint can miss important signs and symbols needed for accurate interpretation of events. By focusing on differences, in a comparative framework, students become more willing to accept the anxiety that accompanies "not knowing" what to make of a situation and begin to judge the situation from a more comprehensive, open position that allows for both tolerance and appreciation of diversity.

Integrating diversity content within an individual model's perspective is based on the premise that diversity is about individual differences and that a fundamental goal is to understand these differences and to recognize their strengths relative to productivity and innovation in the workplace (Miller, 1994).

Being able to judge a situation or communicate from a bicultural perspective is the hallmark of the transcultural leader. Culture consists of the shared beliefs, values, and attitudes that guide the behaviors of group members. Cultural self-awareness is not a simple process because culture is internalized as patterns of thinking and behaving are presumed to be "natural"—simply the way things are (Stewart & Bennett, 1991). Becoming aware and appreciative of how individuals from different cultures direct their lives helps leaders simultaneously gain a deeper understanding of their own culture. Armed with this insight, the transcultural leader is likely to have more successful communications, intervene more effectively in conflict, and promote team building that maximizes the strengths and uniqueness of the differing cultures and cocultures.

The teaching methods to assist students to better understand their own cultural world as well as the cultural world of others initially used a self-reflection or self-evaluation strategy—cultural comparative technique. In this way, students were constantly looking at their own styles and then identifying how their styles may be perceived from the perspective of other cultural groups. Specific teaching strategies targeted intrapersonal, interpersonal, and group or organizational diversity issues, because all of these levels are important in transcultural leadership. The interactive approaches described within this chapter include (a) use of themes as an organizing principle, (b) ethnocomparative approaches and assignments, (c) use of the Myers-Briggs Typology self-assessment inventory, and (d) an organizational diversity audit assignment.

THEMES AS AN ORGANIZING FRAMEWORK

The strategy of using themes as an organizing principle to examine the worldviews and cultural constructs of different cultural groups provided a framework that is referred to in all of the major courses. The assumption underlying this approach is that what people believe and value will affect their behavior. Through understanding and comparing values and beliefs, it is possible to better understand behavior and to more effectively communicate and work with people who have different worldviews.

The conceptual scheme proposed by Florence Kluckhohn (1976) was used as the organizing model. Kluckhohn orders cultural value orientations within the framework of common human or universal problems. She identifies five basic human problems (posed as universal questions in Table 20.1) to which people from all groups across time have had to find some solution. These five questions encompass what humans believe about life, the self, the world, what they have created, and human interaction.

For each question, Kluckhohn proposes that three possible typologies may represent the group's underlying beliefs (see Table 20.1). Each typology constitutes a worldview that guides behavior and attributes meaning to human experience.

The shared values within the worldview serve as rules for relationships, for communication, and for knowledge (Brink, 1976). These rules become internalized through socialization. They have never been formally taught but are inherent in the things that parents and other socializing agents do and say. This is why people from a particular culture can't easily explain when asked why they behave in a certain way. It is the norm that we are not even aware we have learned and therefore consider it innate and natural, and assume that all people must act similarly (Storti, 1994).

To analyze the value orientation of a specific group, we need to identify which typology best represents the group for each question. Table 20.2 elaborates on Table 20.1 by presenting some of the internalized rules that define the different typologies.

The value orientation of a culture reflects pervasive dominant values as well as variant values that exist at the same time. Frequently, these variant values represent the beliefs of specific subgroups within the culture that are defined by factors such as gender and ethnicity. Comparing dominant and variant themes within the same society or across cultural groups can promote a greater understanding of issues of diversity.

Understanding the value orientations and defining characteristics of these different typologies makes it possible to predict behavior without knowing the specifics of each culture or subculture as well as to identify

Table 20.1   Five Basic Human Needs and 3-Point Typology Variations

Basic Human Problem	Typology Variation 1	Typology Variation 2	Typology Variation 3
What are the innate predispositions of humans? (Basic human nature)	Evil and unalterable or Evil and perfectible	Neither good nor bad and either invariant or subject to influence	Good and unalterable or Good and corruptible
What is the relation of humans to nature?	Humans subjugated to nature (Inevitability, Fatalism)	Humans in nature (Humans in harmony with nature)	Humans over nature (Natural force are obstacles to overcome)
What is the significant time dimension?	Past (Emphasis on past time, traditions, ancestor worship)	Present (Little attention paid to the past, and the future is seen as vague and unpredictable)	Future (Oriented to what can change and what can be)
What is the valued personality type? (Action and motivational systems)	Being (Spontaneous expression of desires)	Being-in-becoming (Emphasizes self-realization, self-development of all aspects of the self as an integrated whole)	Doing (Demand for action in the sense of accomplishment)
What is the dominant modality of the relationship of humans to each other?	Lineal (ordered position)	Collateral (group-centered)	Individualistic

areas where cultural conflicts are likely to occur. This is a *culture general skill;* it enables the user to be aware of and search out the specific areas in which people are likely to be different, to learn quickly about differences, and to respond satisfactorily to people from a variety of cultures, even without detailed information about the culture in question (Simons & Walton, 1992).

Table 20.2   Defining Characteristics of the 3-Point Typology Variations

---

What are the innate predispositions of humans?

Evil	Neither good nor bad	Good
* Puritan view of humans * Humans must impose strict control and self discipline * Humans cannot be trusted * Humans must prove their worth	* Most cultures view on humans * Human nature as a mixture of the good and the bad	* Humans (within own group) have to be protected from others * Humans can be trusted at their word—no need to prove self

What is the relation of humans to nature?

Humans subjugated to nature	Humans in nature	Humans over nature
* Fatalistic viewpoint * External events are beyond control so don't plan rigidly * Some parts of life can't be changed but must be endured * Acceptance of suffering and pain * World seen as chaotic * Decision making follows planning but has a degree of spontaneity and trial and error	* All natural forces and humans form one harmonious whole * One is an extension of the other, and both are needed to make the whole	* People can control the obstacles put in their way "Where there is a will, there is a way" * People as master of their own fate: thus no reason for being unhappy by a given set of circumstances, just have to change it * No excuse, save laziness for being beaten * Will search for a way to fix things, including pain and illness * Scientific, mechanistic view of the world * Rational, objective, planned, decision making

What is the significant time dimension?

Past	Present	Future
* What has worked in past guides the present and future * Not risk takers * Resistant to change * Failure may be seen as shameful	* Dynamic interaction with whatever is happening now * Time has a more general meaning * Being late may be hours late * Prioritizing may be counterproductive to interpersonal-relationships	* Value change and what can be different * Risk takers * Newer is better * Being late is 10 minutes * Priority setting is automatic

(Continued)

Table 20.2 (Continued)

What is the valued personality type?

Being	Being-in-becoming	Doing
* What you do is incidental to who you are * What defines a person is personal qualities * Social relations paramount to working relations * That which "is" largely taken for granted and considered as something to be enjoyed rather than altered	* Value on ideas * Value on self-development for the sake of development * Aesthetic development * Task completion may be secondary to full development of the individual	* Judge people on their role and the quality of their work * You are largely what you do * Doing something can make a difference; people can actively influence events * Centrality of work to a person's happiness

What is the dominant modality of the relationship of a human to other humans?

Lineal	Collateral	Individualistic
* Value hierarchy * Respect for traditions and status * Presumption that underneath superficial differences, people are deeply different * Interaction dependent on social class * Behave appropriate to your station	* Primary group always present to support you * Children raised with value on reliance and support of the family and role identity within the family unit followed by the sense of personal identity * Typical to consult and defer to family for major decisions * Honor of the group paramount * Value cooperation * Competition may threaten group harmony * Avoiding public shame of prime importance; saving face is the directive	* Belief that you must be self-reliant * Personal accountability for own actions, roles, etc. * Dependence suspect * Self-oriented, narrow interpretation of family group * Others expected to perform individually without cooperation or unnecessary assistance * Egalitarianism and meritocracy are guiding beliefs * Muted class-consciousness * Deemphasis of status * Direct consistent communication

This understanding and appreciation of the underlying values and beliefs that influence behavior enables our students to go beyond knowledge changes and reach the realm of attitudinal change.

ETHNOCOMPARATIVE STRATEGIES

The next level of focus shows students how individuals demonstrate the different value orientations in their behavior and explores how these behaviors may be misunderstood without an understanding of value orientations. It was in this process that the rather theoretical and dry information presented in the "themes as an organizing framework" began to take on new meaning.

Two learning strategies provided students with opportunities to understand the emic point of view of a situation. An emic perspective is an insider's view; it represents the experience of the people within the cultural group. An etic perspective is an outsider's view of a situation. In the etic position, a set of values, beliefs, and understandings external to the group are imposed onto the interpretation of the experience. Storytelling and critical incident review were used to discover the emic perspective.

Storytelling

The students' assignment was to select and interview a family from a cultural group different from their own. The guidelines for selecting families included multigenerational representation; preference that someone from the family be a first-generation immigrant if appropriate to the group; and no family or close friend groups. The students helped one another by referring them to people they knew or worked with who might be willing to participate.

To prepare them for this experience, students were given an overview of ethnography as a method and received specific information regarding qualitative interview techniques. The aim was not to have a rigid, structured interview but rather to ask general questions whereby the family members told their stories. This theoretical overview did little to alleviate student anxiety, and the faculty realized that students needed more practical and experiential support to effectively accomplish the assignment.

To the fear of "how do I start" and "what do I say," faculty generated sample questions that students could use to initiate the interview (see Table 20.3). Additionally, students were paired with students of different backgrounds and given class time to interview each other. Students were surprised at the ease of conducting these interviews and at how much their respondents had to say during the process. As the dyads reported back to the class, they were able to relate portions of the story and pull out the value orientation that was probably the guiding rule of behavior. This increased their confidence and prepared them for their family interviews.

Time was set aside in class for reporting back on the family interviews. Students enthusiastically participated in discussions surrounding what they had learned about each culture, how it differed from mainstream American culture, what differences existed in underlying values, and how these differences could either be appreciated or set the stage for conflict if they were misunderstood. As students presented the different cultures, they made comparative tables similar to the one presented in Table 20.4. These tables proved extremely valuable in promoting discussion of differences.

Table 20.3   Sample Questions to Initiate Storytelling

Topic	Possible Questions
Family Background	What was it like when you were growing up? What do you remember of your grandparents/your parents?
Preferred Personalities	Who are the people you tend to like and admire? Who are some co-workers you like and admire?
Transitions	What were some of the saddest episodes that you remember in your life? Will you describe a time that you were extremely happy about an event, an accomplishment? Will you describe a time/event that you were very angry?
Future	What do you dream of for yourself? What do you want to be? If you had to change anything, what would it be?
Rituals	What special occasions do you celebrate? How do you celebrate these occasions?
Health	When people got ill in your family, what did they do? How do you remember your grandparents/parents taking care of sick people? When you are not feeling well, what do you do, whom do you go to? What qualities do you look for in a caregiver?

Table 20.4   Ethnocomparative Table

Identified Worldview	Filipino Presentation	Mainstream American Presentation
Basic Human Nature	Good * No need to prove self or give elaborate explanations—take me at my word * Role of leader is to protect the group	Evil * Trust is earned * People must prove themselves to be respected * Control assures compliance
Humans to Nature	Humans subjugated to nature * There is much in life that we cannot control and it is accepted * Part of life is unhappiness, illness	Humans over nature * Nature is just another obstacle that can be controlled * Humans have control over illness * People are master of their fate
Significant Time Dimension	Present * All attention focused on the present with little attention to details such as being on time * Disrespectful to stop the interaction of the present to get to a future spot * Task oriented; get the present job done now	Future * Punctual by the clock * Appointments order the individual rather than individuals ordering their appointments * Looking for possibilities, change * Priorities based on everything that must get done in a certain period
Valued Personality Type (Action and motivational systems)	Being * Social relations more important than working relations * Value tradition and the way things have been * More comfortable with ambiguity * Can wait for results	Doing * People seen first as their role and what they have accomplished * If there is an identified problem, take the initiative to solve that problem * Outcomes tangible, useful products

(Continued)

Table 20.4   (*Continued*)

Identified Worldview	Filipino Presentation	Mainstream American Presentation
Relationship of Humans to Other Humans	Group centeredness and lineal * Interdependence is paramount * Loyalty to the group is expected * Generosity to the group is important * Harmony is critical * Strong in-group consciousness * Hierarchial relationships and responsibilities * Euphemistic communication * Strong sense of identity as part of in-group	Individualistic * Self-identity is important * Self responsibility is inherent in worth * Integrity is expected * Rational, empirical approach to solving problems * Independence expected * Direct communication

Critical Incident Strategy

The second strategy that was used with great success was the critical incident technique. Initially, faculty prepared common workplace scenarios (health care) in which value differences led to misunderstanding or miscommunication. Students were broken into small groups and given a sample critical incident. They were asked to analyze what was happening, what was the source of conflict, and what could be done to deal with the situation.

Once again, this technique brought value orientations to life. The critical incidents presented situations in which the behavior would be viewed as unacceptable or incongruent with expectations if interpreted according to dominant American values (etic perspective). However, by interpreting the situation according to a variant worldview that is prevalent in the depicted culture or group (emic perspective), the behavior, although perhaps still hard to believe, would begin to make sense. Figure 20.1 provides a representative sample scenario and analysis used in the class.

As students discussed the incidents, they expressed a range of emotions. One student expressed anger when she said, "This really makes me

Figure 20.1 Critical Incident Analysis

Situation:
D.C. is the nurse manager on a 35-bed orthopaedic unit. D.C., a white female, has been in a leadership position for the past 10 years. D.C. is sitting in the conference room waiting for the RN staff to arrive for a scheduled 2 pm meeting. It is now 2:15 pm and no one has arrived. The door opens and L.F, a Filipino Staff Nurse walks in smiling and says "hello". She looks around and sees that none of her colleagues have arrived and asks "Am I the only one?". D.C. responds in a slightly irritated voice saying, "Yes, you are the first and it is already 2:15." L.F. glances back at the door. D.C. says "Please don't leave now. When the others come and you are not here, I will be looking for you and we'll never get started." L.F. smiles and without saying a word, walks out of the room.

Questions:
1. What is happening? Give the etic and emic perspective.
2. What could be done differently to satisfy both parties?

Etic Analysis:
D.C. is amazed and can't believe that L.F. just walked out after being told not to! This is insubordination! D.C. sees that she has clearly communicated to L.F. She expects compliance and if there is a problem, she expects direct communication regarding what the problem is (i.e., there is a patient care problem which L.F. must attend to but she will return in 2 minutes).

Emic Analysis:
L.F. is very uncomfortable. D.C. is annoyed and it would be more comfortable if L.F. just got out of there until her other colleagues were ready. It would be disrespectful to say anything directly to D.C. about the conflict, after all she is the manager. What is proper is to maintain a pleasant demeanor so as not to indicate discomfort or displeasure. L.F. will attempt to find her colleagues and come back as a group.

Possible Bicultural Resolution:
D.C. must understand the underlying cultural expectations related to hierarchy, euphemistic communication, and group-centeredness. L.F. must understand the underlying cultural expectations of direct communication and individual accountability.
D.C. could ask L.F. to get her colleagues so that the meeting could start in a more timely fashion. In this situation both individuals needs would be met. At a later time, D.C. could mentor L.F. to assist her in expressing directly what she is planning to do (i.e., let me go and check what the others are doing and I will be right back.).

---

mad. I have been a manager for six years and had these same problems all the time, why didn't someone explain this to me before? Why didn't one of my staff talk to me?" To this lament, the group responded by discussing that until recently there had been such a strong ethnocentric view of interaction and leadership that cultural variations were not truly recognized as legitimate differences. Staff as well as patients were expected to think and act in the same way.

Another student's response was summarized in her statement, "I always knew we were from different countries, but now I feel we are from different planets!" This prompted a discussion as to how alien a different worldview appears. The discussion was greatly enhanced by students sharing their personal experiences. Several students had immigrated from different countries (Philippines, Caribbean Islands, Canada) and were able to share their perspectives of the difficulty in adapting to the norms of a new country. Other students described their awakening understanding of colleagues whose behaviors reflected different worldviews.

These experiences helped students recognize the need for both dominant and nondominant groups to become bicultural (be able to understand different worldviews, flex one's own style to accommodate others, and establish expectations that are acceptable to both parties). They also began to realize that this was a long-term and complex process.

SELF-ASSESSMENT INVENTORY: MYERS-BRIGGS TYPE INDICATOR

The use of the Myers-Briggs self-assessment inventory was a valuable learning strategy because it promoted self-reflection and demonstrated differences that we subsequently used in group discussions to illustrate how differences could create conflict or innovation. The Myers-Briggs Type Indicator (MBTI) is based on Carl Jung's premise that much of what is seemingly random variation in behavior is quite orderly and consistent and due to basic differences in the way individuals prefer to use their perception and judgment (Myers & McCaulley, 1990).

The MBTI was considered the appropriate instrument because it met the learning goals of both management and diversity education. Specifically the MBTI facilitated:

- Examination of differences in a nonthreatening manner.
- Exploration of fact that "likes" feel more comfortable in communicating with likes.
- Exploration of how differences could create miscommunication and conflict.
- Discussion of the role of culture in fostering development of certain types and discouraging development of other types.
- Discussion of team building and gaps in team abilities if representatives from different types are not part of the group.

- Discussion of how to flex one's communication style to get a point across more effectively.

The MBTI is a self-report instrument that depicts psychological type by measuring preferences along 4 separate indices which direct the use of perception and judgment. Each pole of the index depicts a certain personality attribute. Because of its polar nature, the index facilitates discussions of similarities and differences. Table 20.5 describes the poles of the 4 indices and the defining characteristics of these points. Although all people use all of the attitudes and functions, each individual differs in assigning priorities to them. A theoretical overview of the meaning and process of the MBTI will be presented followed by the teaching methods used to experience and discuss the differences highlighted in the MBTI.

FOUR FUNCTIONS

Jung's theory proposes that everyone uses four different *basic mental functions* or *orienting functions* which direct the use of perception and judgment. These four functions include two irrational functions, sensing (S) and intuition (N), which guide perception; and two rational functions, thinking (T) and feeling (F), which guide judgments. There are 16 psychological types based on the priorities they give to each function and in the attitudes (introversion or extroversion) in which they use each function.

Perception refers to the way people may become aware of things, other people, events, or ideas. It includes information gathering, the seeking of sensation or inspiration, and the selection of the stimulus to be attended to (Myers & McCaulley, 1990). Perceiving functions are labeled *irrational* because they are attuned to the flow of events and operate most broadly when not constrained by rational direction. Jung describes sensing and intuition as the two forms of perceptions. Sensing directs conscious mental activity toward seeking the fullest possible experience of what is immediate and real. Intuition directs conscious mental activity toward seeking the furthest reaches of the possible and imaginative.

Judgment includes all the ways of coming to conclusions about what has been perceived. Jung describes thinking and feeling as the two types of judgment functions. Judgment encompasses decision making, evaluation, choice, and the selection of the response after perceiving the stimulus. Termed *rational,* thinking and feeling are directed toward bringing life events into harmony with the laws of reason (Myers & McCaulley,

Table 20.5   Myers-Briggs Typology Indicator

Index	Description	Presenting Style
Function		
Sensing Perception (S)	Perception observable by way of the senses Senses establish what exists at the present moment	Enjoying the present moment Realism Acute powers of observation Memory for details Practicality
Intuitive Perception (N)	Perception of possibilities, meanings, and relationships by way of insight Perception by way of the unconscious in the form of a "hunch," ability to see patterns, or make creative discoveries Permits perception beyond what is visible to the senses, including possible future events	Imaginative Theoretical Abstract Future oriented Creative May be so intent on pursuing possibilities that they may overlook actualities
Thinking Judgment (T)	Makes decisions by linking ideas together and making logical connections Emphasizes cause and effect Is impersonal	Analytic ability Objectivity Concern with principles of justice and fairness Criticality Orientation toward time that is concerned with connections from the past through the present and toward the future
Feeling Judgment (F)	Makes decisions by weighing relative values and merits of the issues; by attending to what matters to others Understands personal values and group values More subjective than thinking	Understand people Greater focus on the human as opposed to technical aspects of a problem Need for affiliation Capacity for warmth Desire for harmony Time orientation that includes preservation of the values of the past

Table 20.5   (*Continued*)

Index	Description	Presenting Style
Attitude		
Extroversion	Attention drawn outward to people and objects in the environment Perception and judgment focused on people and objects Show their best function to the outer world	Awareness and reliance on the environment for stimulation and guidance Action orientation Possible impulsiveness Frankness and ease in communication Sociability
Introversion	Attention is drawn from the environment and directed into the inner world of concepts and ideas Perception and judgment focused on concepts and ideas Show their second-best function to the outer world saving their best function for the inner world of ideas, therefore may be initially underestimated	Interest in the clarity of concepts and ideas Reliance on enduring concepts more than on transitory external events Thoughtful Contemplative detachment Enjoyment of solitude and privacy
Orientation to the Outer World	J-P preference points to the function used in the extroverted attitude, for both extroverts and introverts	
Judgment Dominant	Behaviors characteristic of persons who use either thinking or feeling in their outer life (have extroverted either their thinking or feeling function) For thinking-judgment types (TJ), decisions and plans are more likely to be based on logical analysis For feeling-judgment types (FJ), the decisions and plans are more likely to be based on human factors	Move quickly through perception to reach conclusions Perceptions tend to be shut off as soon as they have observed enough to make a decision Concerned with making decisions, seeking closure, planning operations, or organizing activities Seen in their outer behavior to be organized, purposeful, and decisive Prejudice comes from judgment with a lack of perception

(*Continued*)

Table 20.5   (*Continued*)

Index	Description	Presenting Style
Perception Dominant	Behaviors characteristic of persons who use either sensing or intuition in their outer life (have extroverted either their sensing or intuitive function) For sensing-perceptives (SP), the information is more likely to be the immediate realities For intuitive perceptives (NP), the information is more likely to be new possibilities	Remain longer in the observing attitude Attuned to incoming information Open, curious, and interested Seen in their outer behavior to be spontaneous, curious, and adaptable Open to new events and changes Aiming to miss nothing Procrastination comes from perception with a lack of judgment

1990). Thinking directs conscious mental activity toward seeking rational order and plan according to impersonal logic, whereas feeling directs conscious mental activity toward seeking rational order according to harmony among subjective values.

Although everyone uses each function, type theory proposes that one of the four functions is the dominant function. This dominant function serves as the "captain of the personality" (Myers & McCaulley, 1990). The other goals are important but are secondary to and serve the goals of the dominant function.

ATTITUDE

The *attitude* index describes the person's preference for introversion or extroversion. Good type development fosters the ability to extrovert and introvert comfortably but assumes a natural preference of one type over the other (Myers & McCaulley, 1990). A well-developed introvert can deal ably with the extroverted world when necessary but works best, showing most interest and satisfaction, with ideas. Similarly, a well-developed extrovert can work effectively with ideas, but most enjoys being action oriented and in the world of people.

ORIENTATION TO THE OUTER WORLD

The orientation to the outside world index describes the function that each type person uses in dealing with the outside world, the extroverted part of life (Meyers & McCaulley, 1990). A person who prefers judgment (J) favors their judgment function (thinking or feeling) in dealing with the outer world. A person who prefers perception (P) is more comfortable with using a perceptive process (sensing or intuition) for dealing with the outer world. Since extroverted actions are by definition more apparent in behavior than introverted activities, the J-P attitude is often one of the earliest recognized (Myers & McCaulley, 1990).

Four-Letter Type

When a person responds to the MBTI scale, preferences are recorded for extroversion (E) or introversion (I), sensing (S) or intuition (N), thinking (T) or feeling (F), and judgment (J) or perception (P). The letters for the chosen preferences appear in the type formula in this order: E or I, S or N, T or F, J or P. The four-letter type formulas stand for a complex set of dynamic relationships between the functions, the attitudes and the orientations to the outer world (Myers & McCaulley, 1990).

Dominant and Auxiliary Function

For each individual, one function will be dominant, and this dominant function will be used within their preferred attitude of introversion or extroversion. The auxiliary function develops to balance the unrepresented attitude. Thus, for the extrovert, the dominant function is focused on the outside world and the auxiliary function is exercised in the inner world. For introverts, the dominant function will be employed in the inner world and the auxiliary function will be spent in the outer world. It is through the interplay of the dominant and auxiliary functions that balance is reached so that the individual has both judgment and perceptive skills and the skills in living in both the outer world and the inner world (Myers & McCaulley, 1990).

To differentiate between dominant and auxiliary functions, the 4-letter typology is examined. Different rules are applied based on the preferred attitude (E or I). For extroverts, the J-P index points to the dominant function; and for introverts, the J-P index points to the auxiliary function. Table 20.6 gives examples of this process.

Table 20.6   Rules for Determining Dominant and Auxiliary Functions

	Extroverts	Example	Introverts	Example
1	Refer to J-P Index which is the fourth letter. This tells you the preferred mode for interacting with the outside world.	ESTJ ESTP	Refer to J-P Index which is the fourth letter. This tells you the preferred mode for interacting with the outside world.	INFJ ISTP
	If Judgment is the preferred orientation, it points to the third letter since it is the judgment function.	ESTJ	If Judgment is the preferred orientation, it points to the third letter since it is the judgment function.	INFJ
	If Perception is the preferred orientation, it points to the second letter since it is the perceptive function.	ESTP	If Perception is the preferred orientation, it points to the second letter since it is the perceptive function.	ISTP
2	The J-P Index indicates which of the functions is extroverted. The other preferred function in the 4-letter code is introverted.	ESTJ T is extroverted S is introverted ESTP S is extroverted T is introverted	The J-P Index indicates which of the functions is extroverted. The other preferred function in the 4-letter code is introverted.	INFJ F is extroverted N is introverted ISTP S is extroverted T is introverted
3	For individuals who are extroverts (1st letter E), the extroverted function is dominant and the introverted function is auxiliary.	ESTJ T is extroverted and dominant S is introverted and auxiliary ESTP S is extroverted and dominant T is introverted and auxiliary	For introverts, the extroverted function is auxiliary and the introverted function is dominant.	INFJ N is introverted and dominant F is extroverted and auxiliary ISTP T is introverted and dominant S is extroverted and auxiliary

Table 20.6   (Continued)

	Extroverts	Example	Introverts	Example
4	The tertiary function is the opposite of the second or auxiliary function	ESTJ S is auxiliary so N is tertiary	The tertiary function is the opposite of the second or auxiliary function	INFJ F is auxiliary so T is tertiary
		ESTP T is auxiliary so F is tertiary		ISTP S is auxiliary so N is tertiary
5	The fourth or inferior function is the opposite of the first or dominant function.	ESTJ T is dominant so F is inferior	The fourth or inferior function is the opposite of the first or dominant function.	INFJ N is dominant so S is inferior
		ESTP S is dominant so N is inferior		ISTP T is dominant so F is inferior

Tertiary and Inferior Function

All four functions are used by individuals although only two—the dominant and auxiliary are noted in the typology. The tertiary function is the opposite pole to the auxiliary function. The fourth function, or inferior or least-developed function, is the polar opposite of the dominant function. This is illustrated in Table 20.6.

EXERCISES TO PROMOTE DISCUSSION ON MBTI RESULTS

Students were given time to complete the MBTI. Faculty assisted to make sure that scoring was complete and that all students had the 4-letter code that represented their personality type. Different experiential exercises were then used to promote comparison and discussion.

Determining Groupings: A Focus on Similarities and Differences

Students who were familiar with each other were asked to go to the person in the class that they consider most like themselves and to see if their typologies matched or were very similar. Students were instructed to continue this process until they found their match or a very similar match. If the students were not a familiar group, the instructions were similar except that there was no initial prejudgment as to whom they thought was most like themselves. Although students showed some hesitancy initially, they became quite animated in finding their matches. There was much laughter as students said, "I knew you were an extrovert" or "You're kidding, I didn't think you were an introvert."

Students were then asked to form groups based on their Extroversion or Introversion findings. In two groups, they were told that extroversion and introversion represent an attitude or an orientation to life. They were asked to discuss among themselves what this meant to them and how it looked to them. Following this small group discussion, each group reported back to the larger class. Without needing to give further definition, students easily identified the elements of introversion and extroversion. The extroverts identified themselves as people-persons preferring to be doing something with people or something with objects in the environment. They felt that they were more spontaneous in interacting with others and did not enjoy long hours of working independently or research for reports or school assignments. The introverts described anxiety when interacting with people and hesitancy in initiating dialogue; they were very comfortable when working alone and could work for hours on reports or schoolwork and feel stimulated rather than drained. Both groups noticed that there were variations in intensity in how strong of an extrovert or introvert one was and that this influenced their preferences as well.

Class discussion then focused on how each individual could interact in both attitudes but with different "comfort zones." Furthermore, students discussed how they might misperceive a person of a different type or even how they would avoid someone of a different type. One strong introverted student remarked that she went out of her way to avoid one student who was a strong extrovert because the person just seemed "so overwhelming." This generated more discussion about how a strong extrovert might be misperceived as acting like an insincere politician, while a strong introvert might seem to be arrogant, stuck up, or perhaps lacking in social skills.

Students were then put through a series of rotations whereby they formed into four groups and discussed similarities and then returned to face the other groups and discuss differences. Groupings were done according to: attitude and J-P orientation and combinations of perception and judgment. What became obvious in this process was how misunderstandings and conflict could occur among people with dissimilar typologies. Students discussed strategies for flexing their style to become more effective communicators. Whereas initially, the attitude of many students was "That's their problem if they are going to be like that," as the exercises continued, the students began to realize that they have a type that interacts with another type; for communication and interaction to be effective, they need to be aware of the differences in style and make adjustments accordingly. For example, one of the students who was a ISTJ had previously annoyed a student who was a INFP. The group analyzed the previous conflict and the contrasting styles: Although they were both introverts, the ISTJ person tends to be persevering, hard to change, practical, matter-of-fact, present oriented, organized, and realistic; whereas the INFP tends to be flexible, future oriented, willing to change, enthusiastic, independent, and somewhat unconventional. For effective communication to occur, they must both understand what the other values and both must attempt to flex their style to improve their dialogue. Role-playing of the previous conflict situation then illustrated this process. The students enthusiastically participated in this process and generated several other examples for role-playing.

After completing these exercises, students not only had a greater awareness of the people they had a difficult time interacting with, but now understood why that difficulty existed. With this knowledge, they could develop strategies to minimize conflicts. Instead of assuming it was the other person's problem, students could now see their personal role in the process.

Once students appreciated the two-way dynamics of interaction and acknowledged that they were clearly part of the process, the discussion was transitioned back to diversity by comparing this realization to the concepts of ethnocentricity. Within ethnocentricity, we assume that others think and act as we do and therefore place external blame on others for behaving differently. We identify the problem as the other person's responsibility to become more like us. The need to understand and flex when interacting with people with different typologies was compared with the previously discussed notion of biculturalism—the need to understand and flex our approach when interacting with an individual with a different worldview.

MBTI, Worldview Values, and Role Preferences

The students were again broken into small groups. The faculty member initiated a discussion on whether the students saw a possible relationship between MBTI types and different worldviews. They then discussed the role of socialization in reinforcing or diminishing certain MBTI types as well as the connection between preferences for certain types and roles

Table 20.7   MBTI, Worldviews, and Roles Hypotheses
Generated by Students

Gender	More men will be judgers over perceptives.
	More men will be thinkers over feelers.
	More women will be perceptives over judgers.
	More women will be feelers over thinkers.
Leaders	The preferred style would be TJ.
	Sensors are valued over intuitives.
Group-centered	People who value group-centered values will demonstrate preference for feeling type.
Individualistic	People who have strong individualistic values will demonstrate preference for thinking.
Doing	Americans with a value on doing will have stronger preference for extroversion.
	People who value doing will have a stronger sensing function.
Entrepreneurs	Preferred style would be TP.
	Intuitives are valued over sensors.
Change	People with a P orientation are more comfortable with change than those with a J orientation.
Teamwork	People/cultures who value teamwork have stronger preference for FP orientations.
Value on individual versus Value on role	People/cultures who place greater emphasis on the person would have stronger F orientations than T orientations.
Orientation to time	Sensing types will have stronger present-orientation.
	Intuitive types will have stronger future orientation.
	Feeling types will have stronger past orientation.
Creativity	Intuitives will have a stronger creative ability.

and occupations. With this general overview, students were then asked to work in their groups to generate hypotheses about the relationship between MBTI types and worldview value groupings. Going from group to group, students shared one hypothesis at a time. The faculty member confirmed some of the hypotheses that had been validated through research and identified others that had not yet been tested. Students were then given specific out-of-class assignments to perform a review of the literature on one of the hypotheses and bring back the data to present in class.

This continued the discussion at a higher scholarly plane. Having more validated research data allowed for discussion of assumptions compared with tested data.

MBTI Types and Team Building

The final exercise related to use of the MBTI was a discussion of how the MBTI could be used in team building. The group now realized that strong teams have a representation of different types. Students were given a hypothetical group assignment consisting of multiple tasks and were then asked what MBTI types would be especially suited for the different tasks. This further reinforced the need for diversity and also exposed how gaps could be left on a team lacking that characteristic.

Perhaps the most telling part of the impact of this experience was that students who had always paired together to work on projects (usually because they were just alike) now said they would pick differently and would match themselves with someone with different skills. The final discussion focused on how pairing with different people would probably engender more disagreement but that, through disagreement and discussion, the final product would likely be better. This is in fact the value of diversity. On a diverse team, the leader can expect more discussion, more disagreement, and overall an improved outcome.

ORGANIZATIONAL DIVERSITY AUDITS

Diversity work enables people of different origins and backgrounds to work together successfully and to value and take advantage of their differences (Simons & Walton, 1992). Diversity in the marketplace requires a diverse workforce that can perceive the differing demands of niche groups and supply the energetic creativity to meet those demands (Miller, 1994). A critical question in evaluating diversity within an organization is the degree to which people who join the organization must conform to its culture for success versus the degree to which the organization should broaden itself to include others (Cobbs, 1994).

To address group or organizational diversity, students were given the assignment of performing an organizational diversity audit, either within the institution where they worked or in the institution where they were doing a clinical affiliation. The diversity audit was limited in scope because implementing a comprehensive audit would be an unrealistic course assignment and because, at this point in their development, students did not have the array of knowledge and skills necessary to perform a complete audit.

The faculty member narrowed the focus of the audit to include (a) comparison of the population served versus the provider population, and (b) interviews of dominant and nondominant groups to identify the degree of individual assimilation versus organizational accommodation.

DIVERSITY AND ORGANIZATIONAL PERFORMANCE

The first task was to compare the population served with the total provider population. The question to be answered was "How does diversity in the organization at present reflect the diversity that exists in the patient population and community at large?" For our purposes, the provider population was defined as all organizational personnel who had patient care contact. This included personnel from medicine, nursing, hospital administration, dietary, allied health support services (physical therapy, occupational therapy, respiratory therapy, etc.), laboratory support, radiology, transport, housekeeping, and volunteer services. Students were assigned to gather diversity demographics on age, gender, and ethnicity. Although this exercise can be done with "guesstimates," for our purpose within clinical management, we wanted students to find actual data by using organizational sources. Data were collected over a 6-week period.

Students were instructed to prepare a "business report" that included the demographic data in graphic and narrative form followed by a list of diversity issues or questions that emerged from the data. Prior to the due date of the report, students worked in cooperative groups during class to discuss and analyze their data and generate some of the diversity concerns. This actually expanded the students' ways of thinking, and the final diversity issues concern list proved quite comprehensive. Sample diversity issues included little representation within the professional provider group of the many ethnic groups represented in the community and patient population; lack of male representation within the nursing population; lack of female representation within hospital administration and department head level other than nursing; presence of a glass ceiling; communication and cultural differences of professional staff who had immigrated from the Philippines, Caribbean, Central and South America, India, Russia, Poland, Iraq, and Africa; and lack of respect across professional disciplines of which each represents a distinct culture.

DISCOVERING AND COMPARING DIVERSITY ISSUES WITHIN DOMINANT AND NONDOMINANT CULTURAL GROUPS OF THE ORGANIZATION

Another organizational diversity assignment was to assess the issues surrounding diversity in the organization from both representatives of the dominant culture and a specific cultural group that is not part of the dominant culture. This assignment could be completed individually or in pairs and could be done as one-to-one interviews or as small focus group sessions. Students could select any nondominant culture group that was represented in the organization.

Students and faculty discussed the purpose of the audit (degree of individual assimilation versus organizational accommodation and clarification of different groups' perception of diversity issues) and together generated questions that could be used. These questions were shared with the organizational representative to get approval to gather the data. Questions for the nondominant group targeted learning about differences between one's country and culture of origin compared with the United States; identifying what they enjoy about the United States, and the organization; describing what they find difficult in the United States and in the organization; classifying people they found that were easy and difficult to get along with; determining common misunderstandings that existed between people in the organization and people in their group; describing what the organization had done to support them; and clarifying what they felt they were expected to change to meet the expectations of the organization. The dominant group members were asked similar questions; however, they were asked to focus on working with members from the nondominant group.

Once again, students enthusiastically reported their findings. Most of the students concluded that individuals were expected to accommodate the organization (both staff and patient groups!) rather than the organization accommodate the nondominant groups. This led to rather lively discussions regarding ethnocentrism, stereotypes, biases, and organizational accountability. Recognizing that they had only a limited amount of information, the students concluded that most of the health care organizations in which the audits were performed had done little to accommodate or appreciate diversity. It appeared that the melting pot paradigm was still very much alive.

Another valuable lesson from this experience came from analyzing the similarities and differences of the perceptions of dominant and nondominant groups. Many of the identified concerns related back to a difference in worldviews that was not understood by both groups. Problems included in-group preferences; discomfort when others speak primary language; intercultural communication gaps related to different meanings attached to nonverbal communication; conflicting views of patient care; differences in time orientation leading to lack of prioritization; deference to hierarchy over individual accountability; and, feelings of lack of respect.

There were no mechanisms in place within the organizations for dialogue about these concerns, so the problems just seemed to widen. Cultural or diversity training had not been done nor had any programs been given to clarify expectations. All students could see the value of diversity training and diverse workgroups to begin problem-solving some of the identified issues. Those students who had performed the audit within their organization of employment verbalized plans to attempt to address some of the issues.

SUMMARY

Faculty can play an integral role in both facilitating success for diverse student groups and promoting diversity through experiential approaches. A willingness to evaluate your own teaching style for cultural biases is the first step. Once this is done, decide on the culture-general skills as well as the culture-specific skills that are essential for students within your area of specialization. With those outcomes in mind, you can design experiences to develop in students the appreciation of diversity, the skills to interact in a diverse world, and an awareness of the many issues of diversity that exist in our homes, communities, workplace, and society.

REFERENCES

Adams, M. (1992). *Promoting diversity in college classrooms: Innovative responses for the curriculum, faculty and institutions.* San Francisco: Jossey-Bass.

Brink, P. (1976). *Transcultural nursing: A book of readings.* Englewood Cliffs, NJ: Prentice-Hall.

Brislin, R. (1993). *Understanding cultures's influence on behavior.* Philadelphia: Harcourt Brace.

Cobbs, P. (1994). The challenge and opportunities of diversity. In E. Cross, J. Katz, F. Miller, & E. Seashore (Eds.), *The promise of diversity* (pp. 25–31). New York: Irwin.

Gochenour, T. (1993). *Beyond experience: The experiential approach to cross-cultural education.* Yarmouth, ME: Intercultural Press.

Kavanagh, K., & Kennedy, P. (1992). *Promoting cultural diversity: Strategies for health care professionals.* Thousand Oaks, CA: Sage.

Kluckhohn, F. (1976). Dominant and variant value orientations. In P. J. Brink (Ed.) *Transcultural nursing: A book of readings* (pp. 61-63). Englewood Cliffs, NJ: Prentice-Hall.

Kreps, G., & Kunimoto, E. (1994). *Effective communication in multicultural health care settings.* Thousand Oaks, CA: Sage.

Miller, F. (1994). Why we chose to address oppression. In E. Cross, J. Katz, F. Miller, & E. Seashore (Eds.), *The promise of diversity.* New York: Irwin.

Myers, I., & McCaulley, M. (1990). *A guide to the development and use of the Myers-Briggs Type Indicator.* Palo Alto, CA: Consulting Psychologists.

Simons, G., & Walton, S. (1992). Diversity: Where do I go for help? In G. Simons, & B. Abramms, (Eds.), *The Questions of Diversity* (p. 925). Amherst, MA: ODT Inc..

Stewart, E., & Bennett, M. (1991). *American cultural patterns: A cross-cultural perspective.* Yarmouth, ME: Intercultural Press.

Storti, C. (1994). *Cross-cultural dialogues.* Yarmouth, ME: Intercultural Press.

21

Beyond the Individual Paradigm: Confronting Social Justice Issues

Susan Warner Salmond

*T*he original strategy for integrating diversity content into the MSN curriculum was based on the individual differences model, which emphasizes development of understanding between different individuals and groups. As the classes evolved, faculty realized that although this paradigm created greater understanding, it did not lead to attitudinal changes that would enable students to perform effectively as bicultural leaders. Active debates occurred when students presented viewpoints of nondominant cultures about the use of non-English and the presence of "isms" in the workplace and academic setting. Instead of responding positively to these debates, many students were upset by them. Comments such as *"Certainly progress has been made, why can't you see that this is*

America and if you want to live here and work here then you have to live by our rules?" "If people would work hard, then the opportunities would exist," and *"I don't want to work with her if she is going to feel that way"* illustrated that faculty needed to intervene to address many of these issues.

The teaching strategies that had highlighted the individual differences model paradigm had resulted in decreased ethnocentrism of the group. Students were better able to understand how other groups organized their reality. When reviewing case examples, these students were able to judge the situation from more than one frame of reference and interpret it more accurately. But although we had addressed differences and minimized ethnocentrism, some students with dominant American values still showed a tendency toward *cultural imposition* or the expectation that everyone should conform to the majority, whatever their personal beliefs (Herbert, 1995). Cultural care preservation, accommodation, and repatterning were not applied to dealing with the needs of staff as they were in taking care of patients.

Students also had difficulty discussing their opinions and feelings about different forms of oppression (racism, sexism, ageism, ableism, etc.), prejudices, and biases, especially when they anticipated that conflict might occur. Faculty and students were anxious about their ability to handle the inevitable conflict, anger, frustration, and confusion that would occur in the workplace.

As faculty were committed to preparing bicultural nurse leaders, these issues, and the requisite skills to deal with them, needed to be integrated within the curriculum. In addition to recognizing differences and injustices, students needed to address them also. Understanding the nursing staff as well as the community it serves requires an insight into peoples' experiences with oppression. The leader of a diverse workforce and diverse community must possess the skills to discuss these issues, appreciate the differing viewpoints, and evaluate systems and practices for noninclusion.

A social justice paradigm takes the value differences described within the individual differences model but views them within the context of group dominance, social power, and privilege. The heart of this approach was to define what oppressive practices or experiences were, where they were, how they work, what mechanisms perpetuate them, and how to eliminate them (Cross, Katz, Miller, & Seashore, 1994). By targeting these topics, students could emerge with greater confidence and competence to participate in diversity management within health care.

PREPARING FOR DISCUSSIONS

Step 1: Do I Really Want to Do This?

One of the biggest barriers to confronting some of these topics within the classroom was my thought, *What will I do if it gets out of control?* I had always prided myself on facilitating an energetic, scholarly discussion on key topics in order that students left feeling good about what had occurred and feeling stimulated about the process. Coming to grips with the reality that doing my job effectively might mean that students would leave feeling frustrated, angry, or confused seemed contrary to my normal practice. It was threatening. *What would they think? Would I be able to handle it? Will people not want to be part of this program if we tackle some of these issues?* These were questions that I had to confront in developing my teaching strategy. What helped most in this process was my strong commitment to bicultural leadership and the belief in the difference that leaders could make if they were bicultural. My goals were to share information and establish a knowledge base about the dynamics and manifestations of social oppression; to develop insight into the origin of each person's values and social identity; to gain an appreciation of how these values influence our perception of others leading to prejudice and stereotyping; to facilitate students' awareness of other perspectives and people's experiences of prejudice and discrimination; to examine students' own biases and the real-world biases implicit in organizations and policy decisions; and to identify, develop, and practice intervention skills that students can use to intervene on their own behalf and serve as allies for members of targeted social groups.

Step 2: Establishing Classroom Norms

Recognizing that most of the students come from monocultural backgrounds (no matter what their cultural background), I could not assume that they would be initially receptive of other cultures and social differences. Consequently, my first thought was to create a learning climate that was safe, respectful, confidential, and comfortable. I developed ground rules for classroom communication. When presenting these to the class, I began by saying that discussing these topics could be difficult. I asked students to examine why they perceived these topics as potentially volatile. Responses validated that these issues were linked to their basic values, that they felt they would be put on the spot, and that discussion might tap into their emotional side, which they try to keep self-contained in the classroom. Students then participated in setting the ground rules for classroom discussions. We developed rules regarding mutual respect, confidentiality, nonconfrontation, honesty, careful listening, and speaking for oneself but not for others.

Step 3: Planning the Approach

When teaching within the individual differences paradigm, we had successfully drawn on experiential learning theory and cultural learning styles for planning course material. I took this same approach with the exception that I planned for and allotted more "processing time" to the different experiences that we would use. It is in this time that students reflect on the personal and social implications of a learning activity. Consequently, I carefully sequenced discussion questions to facilitate students' reflection on what they observed in the case discussion, simulation, or experience.

Step 4: Plan for Support

To effectively accomplish my educational goals within the core content of the MSN curriculum, it was necessary for all faculty to participate. Key issues needed to be identified for the different courses so that throughout the program faculty modeled their openness to deal with sensitive and complex issues. Faculty examined the courses and selected key issues that they would explore. The group also suggested teaching strategies including drawing on other personnel on campus who could offer unique expertise in either the discipline or process.

Perhaps most important in the support structure was creating an opportunity to discuss what was happening in class and "how did it go?" Faculty began meeting on a weekly basis, not just as part of a regular faculty meeting but more informally over lunch. We used one another as sounding boards and obtained valuable feedback on what was happening with faculty and with the students in the classroom. This process served to develop a more committed philosophy and more cohesive work team.

INCORPORATING DIVERSITY AND
SOCIAL JUSTICE INTO THE CURRICULUM

Melting Pot versus Salad Bowl

To discuss diversity from a perspective that confronts prejudices, it was necessary to begin by addressing the paradigms that have been used to represent the United States' multicultural uniqueness. A debate was staged with one side assigned to argue for cultural assimilation and the other side for cultural pluralism. The metaphors of "melting pot" (where assimilation is the goal) in contrast to metaphors of "salad bowl," "stew pot," or "mosaic" (where interweaving and maintaining some individual characteristics become the goal) were used as points of comparison. Students could select the side that they wanted to be on and were fairly evenly split between the two groups. No content was provided on the topic prior to the debate; rather the intent was to draw out what students saw as salient points to each paradigm. These perspectives could then be used in further discussion.

Those speaking of the melting pot spoke of the pride that has been associated with the paradigm and the effectiveness of the paradigm for millions of immigrants. People came to this country, worked hard, bettered themselves, raised their standard of living, and melted into society. Over time, these people adopted the language and the culture of the founding fathers and were assimilated into a single, homogeneous culture. For many students, the melting pot symbolized what they felt made our country unique, and they indicated it is what they have always believed.

Those speaking of the salad bowl paradigm noted that melting required immigrants give up their cultural heritage and that cultural heritage is a portion of people's identity and strength. Others pointed out that melting could never occur for some individuals because of skin color and that consequently, it was noninclusive. Furthermore, they argued that focusing on and capturing our differences may make us stronger as an organization or as a society. This group argued that by highlighting our differences, rather than trying to obscure them, we can increase our competitive strength.

After the debate, faculty guided students in an historical examination of the context of both paradigms, considering the groups for whom either of the paradigms had advantages and the groups for whom the paradigms did not bring advantage. Students looked at who the immigrants were (predominantly Western European up until the 1960s) and how this affected the value of the paradigms. The impact of technology was examined for its influence on diversity paradigms.

Although all students supported the concept of valuing differences, shedding an assimilation paradigm was more difficult. After discussing the issues, what seemed apparent was that they did not see a common goal or common vision associated with the mosaic paradigm, whereas they thought it inherent in the melting pot paradigm. When faculty presented the mosaic with an emphasis on sharing a common vision of our future while enabling all cultures to be proud of and celebrate their uniqueness, there was little discomfort.

Leininger's (1991) strategies of cultural care preservation, cultural care accommodation, and cultural care repatterning were then examined within this paradigm. Students identified the need for cultural care preservation and began to examine the context that would call for negotiation or repatterning. Students could see that negotiation and repatterning may be called for in individuals, groups, and organizations. Everyone could see the strength of a mosaic paradigm for common goals that are not monoculturally defined.

Stereotypes, Prejudice, and Racism

We educated students on the topic of stereotypes and prejudices by combining theoretical content with many different experiential activities. Students also examined how stereotypes, prejudices, and different "isms" result from an ethnocentric viewpoint.

When a person's own culture is considered central to all reality, the values, assumptions, and behavioral norms of that culture are elevated to levels of absolute truth (Stewart & Bennett, 1991). This ethnocentrism shapes people's identity. If they believe their own culture or way of doing things is the "truth," then they will form a naturally narrow and defensive identity. This ethnocentric perspective results in a tendency to perceive members of other cultures in terms of stereotypes. *Stereotypes* are a simplified, generalized labeling of certain people or social groups. Stereotyping, or generalizing, is a coping mechanism for avoiding cognitive overload by combining and condensing a variety of stimuli into manageable categories. Stereotyping becomes faulty when individuals compare characteristics assigned to a social group with their own culture based on the assumption that their own is normal, natural, and better. The resulting judgments often ennoble one group while degrading a different group (Stewart & Bennett, 1991). This is the world of prejudice.

Prejudice is a special category of stereotyping that implies bigotry. It is defined as a preconceived judgment or opinion formed about a person, situation, or object without sufficient justification, knowledge, thought, or reason. Prejudice often results in the marginalizing or disadvantaging of an individual or group. *Racial prejudice* refers to judgments based on racial/ethnic/cultural group membership before getting to know the person. *Racism* combines prejudice with the power to do something based on those prejudiced beliefs. The action taken denies one social group access to opportunities or privileges while perpetuating privileges to members of another, dominant group. The privileges ensure gains in psychological feelings, social status, economic position, or political power (Pederson, Draguns, Lonner, & Trimble, 1989).

Prejudice and racism are often used as similar terms but they are different. A person who is prejudiced becomes judgmental. Strategies for dealing with prejudice deal with consciousness raising, learning what it feels like to "walk in someone else's shoes," and assisting individuals to face up to negative beliefs. Racism involves behaviors that systematically produce adverse consequences for ethnic minorities. Much racist behavior is unknowing or unintentional and can be either individual or institutional. Individual racism may be manifested when an individual believes that ethnic minorities are inferior and assigns the care of minority patients to less qualified staff members. Institutions demonstrate racism by deliberately setting fees above the affordable range of most ethnic minority clients, thus excluding them from treatment, or by using standardized psychological tests without considering subcultural group differences and biases in test construction and interpretation.

Other "isms" certainly can be found within society and within the workplace. Sexism, heterosexism, ableism, ageism, and all the rest are present in both subtle and not so subtle forms. The impact of oppression toward these groups is lack of integration and lack of exposure. Protected, segregated, and shunned by society, people within oppressed groups must learn coping skills to survive in a hostile environment. They are often made to feel "less than" the dominant group and become targets for ridicule culminating in negative identities, low self-esteem, and low self-confidence. Identity development is impacted when the ascribed characteristic is not valued by the dominant group. From a theoretical perspective, understanding the process of gender identity development and development of a racial identity is helpful in confronting issues of oppression.

Edith Folb (1985) contends that descriptions of the dominant culture, in fact, are describing those in power, those who dominate the culture, those who historically or traditionally have had the most persistent and far-reaching impact on what we think and say, on what we believe and do in our society. Dominant culture does not necessarily refer to numbers, but to power. Blanchard (1993) agrees with Folb and hypothesizes that change and violence are a result of one culture (dominant) being pushed to recognize what has always been there; unrecognized (nondominant) cultures wanting to share power.

Members of the dominant culture often have difficulty describing their cultural backgrounds and take their dominant cultural background for granted as the norm. In contrast, those individuals from nondominant cultures are usually quite aware that their culture exists within a context and are most aware of the nuances or the differences in their cultural background. During cross-cultural interactions where there is both a power difference and a value difference, individuals, especially those from the dominant culture, must be sensitive to the feelings that may surface, the needs that these feelings create, and the behaviors that people use to cope with these feelings.

Hardiman & Jackson's model of racial identity development (1992) was used as a model for understanding the developmental process of forming a racial identity in which racism and domination are internalized to an identity that is affirming and liberated from racism. They describe five stages of consciousness or worldviews and the corresponding behaviors that may be observed in this developmental process. These models are applicable to all races, and vary based on the degree to which the person has been exposed to oppression. An understanding of this identity development and the different stages is very useful in understanding behaviors such as anger and questioning. By responding to and understanding each student's developmental stage, we can help students to grow at their own pace in the formation of racial identities that celebrate uniqueness.

Experiential Exercises to Examine Stereotypes, Prejudice, and Oppression

In addition to theoretical discussions and readings on these topics, we used several different experiential activities.

The goals for addressing stereotypes were to examine the stereotypes that individuals hold, begin to understand how and why stereotypes are formed, recognize that stereotypes are often invalid and lead to misunderstanding and blocks in communication, and appreciate the feelings that are associated with being part of a stereotyped group. In a labeling game, a sticker was placed on the student's forehead making it impossible for the person to see what was written on it. One or two words on the sticker labeled the individual. The labels identified common patient types, characteristics, or situations such as: "patient on Medicare"; "patient on Medicaid"; "patient with AIDS"; and "non-English speaking patient." Students were instructed to interact with the patient as if they were in the hospital situation. After interacting for about 10 minutes, each participant had to guess their label and give the data they used to determine their labels. They further discussed how others responded to them and how this made them feel. Feelings of inferiority, self-devaluation, anxiety, and discomfort were identified.

In another strategy, each person wrote down three to five things he or she thought of when each of the ethnicities represented in the class was named. These items were recorded directly into a computer, reviewed, organized, and then printed out to be distributed to the group. Students were asked to read the responses and to comment on what was written about their particular ethnicities. This was followed by a discussion that asked such questions as "Why did you write the things you did? Where have your ideas about different cultural groups come from? Have people from these groups experienced this kind of typing before? What did it feel like? How did it impact your opportunities?"

The Scissors Game (Hopkins, 1993) demonstrates people's feelings and "felt needs" in a cross-cultural interaction where they do not understand the implicit rules or norms of behavior or are unfamiliar with those norms. In this simulation, participants sit in a circle. The facilitator holds a pair of scissors and passes these around in the circle in one of three positions: "closed," "crossed" (partially open), or "open" (wide open). Each time the scissors are passed, the passer must say how he or she is passing the scissors. The receiver must then say how he or she is receiving the scissors: closed, crossed, or open. The facilitator validates whether the receiver is accurate or not in the interpretation and states how the scissors were actually received or passed. Participants are encouraged to observe carefully as each person receives the scissors to discover the code. The essence of this game is that the communication code is not exactly what it appears. The scissors are passed and received according to how the legs of the sender and receiver are being held, not by the position of the scissors. As the game continues, the facilitator encourages those who understand the code to be helpful (nonverbally) to those who do not. Frustration will increase as more and more participants discover the code. The game ends when everyone has broken the code.

The debriefing of these exercises is the most important aspect of the learning. In response to the scissors game, some students were excited and challenged while others felt anger and alienation. Both reactions are common to many cross-cultural interactions and the similarities were discussed. As we discussed the feelings, we examined the simultaneous felt needs: the need to be understood, the need to belong among those who understand the code (in-group), the need not to appear foolish, the need to go beyond the obvious to reach understanding. After exploring these feelings, we discussed the similarity between this situation and intercultural interactions.

Identifying *triggers* that signal oppressive attitudes toward a group was another strategy we include in the different courses. We decided on this strategy when an in-class conflict pointed out the triggering process.

In class, an African American student told her classmates in an angry, accusatory fashion that the seating arrangements of students within the class suggested racism. The students who were confronted became quite defensive and rather indignant. They denied the presence of any purposeful actions but argued that they were warmer on that side of the room and that they felt comfortable with each other. They said that they thought the other student was overly sensitive and she claimed in turn that she was not—that in fact many racist incidents had occurred in the class.

When I was informed about this situation, I recognized it as a trigger situation. Instead of ignoring the episode, I raised it with the class at a later meeting. I began by letting the students know that I had been told about the incident and that I thought it was important to discuss it. This was important not only to model effective communication but to model development in intercultural sensitivity.

Triggers were defined as recurring phenomena such as certain words, phrases, concepts, or actions usually communicated by members of the nontargeted group about a targeted group or individual that signal an oppressive attitude toward that group. People who are members of a targeted group (a group that has experienced oppression) develop a sensitivity to certain negative cues. They have been subjected to them, suffered from them, discussed them, and thought about them (Weinstein & Obear, 1992).

Although the person suffering from the trigger may be acutely aware of it, most often the person delivering the signal has no realization of doing so. The people sending the cues have been effectively and monoculturally socialized to consider their language or action "natural." Thus, they are unaware of sending a signal and are shocked when someone takes offense.

Some triggers are overtly apparent: "A woman's place is in the home"; "Blacks seem to want to stick together." Other triggers are more subtle: "I don't see race as the issue, we're all human beings"; "I always hear Jews making fun of themselves"; "they aren't the only ones who suffered"; "they're just not as qualified."

Triggers may immediately stimulate the defenses of the person and can elicit the kind of intense emotional response that occurred in the classroom situation. If not dealt with effectively, a trigger argument continues with a painful and unproductive debate of increasing intensity. It can also lead to the shutdown of group discussion ending in stifling silence and barely controlled frustration.

We used the in-class conflict to look at the trigger process. The African American student had experienced repeated situations where white students had grouped together and excluded minority students. This was a trigger to her. I asked the student to present some of her experiences. Other triggers were identified by all the students as they looked at their own experience. Many trigger situations between physicians and nurses were identified as well as triggers related to gender, health behaviors, race, and hierarchical position. It was agreed that during class sessions anyone in the group who identified a trigger should call out "trigger," and the situation would be cataloged for future discussion. Later in the semester, the group analyzed the different triggers and all students identified an increasing sensitivity to potential triggers for different groups.

The final assignment given to students in getting them to experience the world of prejudice and oppression was to have them read novels that described the experience and to present the story back to the group as if they were the individual. Some of the books reported on included *Makes Me Wanna Holler,* by Nathan McCall; *True North,* by Jill Ker Conway; *Samurai and Silk,* by Haru Matsukata Reischauer; *Skin Deep,* edited by Marita Golden and Susan Shreve; and *On Gold Mountain,* by Lisa See. This gave them an in-depth emic perspective on the particular cultural group as well as an emic perspective on prejudice and oppression.

A CLEARER VIEW

A comprehensive curriculum that combines the individual differences paradigm and the social justice paradigm appears to target the critical issues of diversity that effective transcultural leaders must understand. It is not necessary to see the world in the same way or agree on everything. It is imperative, however, to have the skills to further this discussion as well as the willingness and abilities to look at noninclusionary policies. The goal is not to achieve "the better management of human resources," a familiar discourse that privileges managers over the rest of organizational subjects, but to find and understand ways of ensuring equality and justice in organizations where this is a vision of inclusion (Holvino, 1994). This vision must be based fundamentally on respecting diversity and treating one another with dignity. But most importantly, this vision must be based on the belief that diversity is strength (McGrory, 1994).

REFERENCES

Batchelder, D. (1993). Using critical incidents. In T. Gochenour (Ed.), *Beyond experience: The experiential approach to cross-cultural education* (pp. 101–105). Yarmouth, ME: Intercultural Press.

Blanchard, K. (1993). Cultural adjustment, power, and personal ethics: Three critical incidents. In T. Gochenour (Ed.), *Beyond experience: The experiential approach to cross-cultural education* (pp. 107-112). Yarmouth, ME: Intercultural Press.

Cross, E. Y., Katz, J. H., Miller, F. A., & Seashore E. W. (1994). (pp. 215-216). New York: Irwin.

Folb, E. (1985). Who's got room at the top? Issues of dominance and nondominance in intracultural communication. In L. A. Samovar & R. E. Porter (Eds.), *Intercultural communication: A reader* (4th ed., pp. 119-127). Belmont, CA: Wadsworth.

Gaston, J. (1993). Cultural orientation in the English as second language classroom. In T. Gochenour (Ed.), *Beyond experience: The experiential approach to cross-cultural education* (pp. 90-100). Yarmouth, ME: Intercultural Press.

Hardiman, R. & Jackson, B. (1992). Racial identity development: Understanding racial dynamics in college class-rooms and on campus. In M. Adams (Ed.) *Promoting diversity ending in college classrooms: Innovative responses for the curriculum, faculty, and institutions.* San Francisco: Jossey-Bass.

Herbert, P. (1995). Theoretical foundations of transcultural nursing. In Andrews & Boyle (Eds.), *Transcultural concepts in nursing care* (pp. 3-47). Philadelphia: Lippincott.

Holvino, E. (1994). A vision: The agitated organization. In E. Y. Cross, J. H. Katz, F. A. Miller, & E. W. Seashore (Eds.), *The promise of diversity: Over 40 voices discuss strategies for eliminating discrimination in organizations.* New York: Irwin.

Hopkins, D. (1993). Tisouro: Creating felt needs. In T. Gochenour (Ed.), *Beyond experience: The experiential approach to cross-cultural education* (pp. 149-153). Yarmouth, ME: Intercultural Press.

McGrory, J. (1994). Discard the melting pot: Diversity is strength. In E. Y. Cross, J. H. Katz, F. A. Miller, & E. W. Seashore (Eds.), *The promise of diversity: Over 40 voices discuss strategies for eliminating discrimination in organizations* (pp. 213-214). New York: Irwin.

Miller, F. (1994). Why do we choose to address oppression? In E. Y. Cross, J. H. Katz, F. A. Miller, & E. W. Seashore (Eds.), *The promise of diversity: Over 40 voices discuss strategies for eliminating discrimination in organizations.* New York: Irwin.

Pederson, P., Draguns, J., Lonner, W., & Trimble, J. (1989). *Counseling across cultures.* Honolulu: University of Hawaii Press.

Stewart, E., & Bennett, M. (1991). *American cultural patterns: A cross-cultural perspective.* Yarmouth, ME: Intercultural Press.

Weinstein, G., & Obear, K. (1992). Bias issues ending in the classroom: Encounters with the teaching self. In M. Adams (Ed.), *Promoting diversity ending in college classrooms: Innovative responses for the curriculum, faculty, and institutions* (pp. 39-50). San Francisco: Jossey-Bass.

22

Learning Transcultural Leadership through an MSN-Level Clinical Experience

Susan Warner Salmond and Dula F. Pacquiao

*T*ranscultural leadership requires an awareness and understanding of values, feelings, and attitudes of people in another culture and the ways that these characteristics influence behavior. Or, reversing it, transcultural understanding requires observing behaviors and defining the values and attitudes that undergird those behaviors (Gaston, 1993). A new paradigm of "bicultural" or "ethnorelative" leadership refers to being comfortable with many standards and customs and having an ability to adapt behavior and judgments to a variety of interpersonal settings (Bennett & Deane, 1994). In this way, leadership facilitates the process whereby all groups manifest their uniqueness while time sharing a commitment to a common vision of the organizational mission and goals for the future.

Transcultural nursing leaders use culture care theory to establish the philosophy of patient care as well as to examine their organizational structures and practices to support and nurture multiculturalism. A *bicultural nursing leader* uses transcultural knowledge in interpersonal interaction and problem solving. Developing a participative, cohesive team affirms individual uniqueness, as does approaching problems and opportunities from a multicultural perspective. Ongoing negotiation and accommodation at the personal and organizational level create a reasonable fit between the individual's personal values and those of the profession and organization. Thus, the organization evolves into a dynamic culture shaped by the continuous interplay of all subcultures of individuals and groups within.

Bicultural nursing leadership requires that the professional nurse develop insight into and appreciation for multicultural value orientations. This nursing leader recognizes that most conflict situations in the organization stem from a clash in values between people or groups such as different health care providers, professional and nonprofessional staff, American-educated versus internationally educated staff; different ethnic groups; members of different socioeconomic groups; nurses and patients (over beliefs about health and illness); or administration and staff. In any of these situations, the bicultural nurse leader commits to a strategy of problem definition that assists each group to understand the underlying conflicting values and looks for ways to transcend these differences and transform them into creative solutions to problems.

THE CONTEXT OF BICULTURAL LEADERSHIP

An initial goal of the clinical experience was to examine the characteristics of organizations as a culture and to appreciate the challenge of implementing a multicultural philosophy within the confines of a bureaucracy. By its very nature and purpose, a bureaucracy demands efficiency, task-oriented outcomes, and universal sets of rules for conducting its business. Inherent in this focus is the consequent impersonalization of interactions. Hierarchical structures lead to centralized management that promotes distancing between levels of personnel, creating a gap between organizational goals and mission and individual unit operations.

In contrast to other bureaucracies, health care organizations have as their focus the delivery of humanistic services. There is a dichotomy between universalism and humanism. Humanism calls for individualized, caring approaches to people. Universalism minimizes differences and calls for standardization and task-oriented ways of approaching people.

Compounding this contradiction between bureaucracy and humanistic care is the increasing diversity in the constituency of client and provider population along with simultaneous pressures from fiscal constraints and regulatory agencies. It is within this paradox that we ask nurses to become leaders!

To help students understand and deal with this complexity, we have designed strategies that move them in a step-by-step process of bicultural development. Every step has a concurrent classroom and clinical component. It is our philosophy that clinical experiences give life and meaning to classroom theory and knowledge. Through analysis of actual clinical situations, we develop in our students the skills to navigate within the complex realities of health care today.

THE PROCESS OF BICULTURAL DEVELOPMENT

Our approach to bicultural development in the clinical practicum was to have students develop a planned change program as a participant-observer. There was no set definition as to the type of desired change, but students were asked that it be a situation in which a conflict of values was inherent in the situation. Situations were quite varied and included resolution of a conflict over professional nurse and nursing assistant responsibilities, the implementation of new or revised standards of care, and the planning of a new program for mentorship.

UNDERSTANDING WORLDVIEWS

Students were asked first to describe what their change projects would be. Most students presented a rather detailed description of the problem leading to the necessity for change and an evaluation of what was happening in the situation. Faculty then began to question the students. What was the basis of their assumptions? How had they reached the conclusions that they had already formed? The purpose of this questioning was to illustrate to the students how their personal perspectives influenced their perception and interpretation of the organizational and interpersonal problems. They were looking at the situation as an outsider and interpreting the observable events. This *etic* perspective, however, is often not valid. To get at the heart of a problem and to facilitate planned change, it is necessary to gather insight into the *emic*, or insider's, perspective. Bicultural leaders must be open to and observant of their inner reality as well as the outer reality without reacting, judging, and evaluating. By attending to our own feelings and perceptions as well as noting our tendencies to react without grasping the totality of the situation, we can stop the buildup of habitual responses and open space for new reactions to occur that reflect change, growth, and learning.

Faculty expected the students to gather the emic perspective from the groups or individuals involved. This step is often neglected in the real world, and the etic perspective is frequently used to judge the situation. This approach devalues the individuals involved and often results in inaccurate problem definition. This would explain why it is estimated that managers spend about 40% of their time solving problems that are not the true problems! Appreciating the full context of a situation requires understanding both the emic and the etic perspectives. This approach is required for all staff to feel valued and listened to and serves as the foundation for collaboration as the conflict resolution technique.

The emic perspectives were gathered through direct interview. Students were advised that an effective method for gathering emic data is to approach any situation as a student/stranger with minimal preconceived notions so that a new way of understanding is possible. What the students found in each situation was that problems approached in this manner were more complex than they had originally assumed. They were able to see more clearly how they had made assumptions and where those assumptions were correct and incorrect. The faculty then assisted the students in using transcultural nursing knowledge to understand the different emic worldviews.

This process can be illustrated by describing one of the situations handled by a student. The particular conflict involved a clash regarding compliance with assigned break times. On one unit, a group of Asian nurses had consistently missed their break times and gone at a time other than scheduled. Although the nurse manager had spoken with these nurses, there was no change in behavior. The other nurses on the unit were very angry with the situation and wanted something to be done. Initially, the student reported that the Asian nurses wanted to go on breaks together and were not sensitive to the imposition it placed on the remaining staff. Furthermore, she identified that these nurses were not accountable to the expectations placed on them by the nurse manager. Although the student did not state it outwardly, her implicit suggestion was that the nurses were selfish and irresponsible. She suggested an intervention plan that would assign the same break times to some of the Asian staff so that they could go to lunch together and the remaining staff could make it to break on time. The majority of the group saw this to be a bicultural strategy.

The clinical faculty member questioned the student regarding the situation. How had she arrived at the conclusion that the nurses were delaying their break time to go together? She identified that this had been her past experience with Asian nurses and it is what the nurse manager thought was happening. Why did she assume that the Asian nurses were not sensitive to others? She judged this to be so because the nurses were inconveniencing other nurses by delaying their ability to go to break on time and by not following the established break times. The student gathered the emic data between this class session and the next.

In the class discussion of the emic data, the student presented additional information that was not available when she made the etic judgment. The student presented that the Asian nurses thought that it was rude to leave a patient in the middle of a task (bath, dressing change, treatment) and that it was very difficult to stop in the middle of something that they had started. One statement was, "I know what I have to get done and I make sure it is finished so that I don't have to bother others to do my work." From this perspective, the different worldview was apparent and it certainly would be not correct to apply the label of selfishness. The portion of the etic perspective that was more accurate was that the Asian nurses did identify discomfort in going to the cafeteria with non-Asian nurses as they didn't know what to say. What was most interesting in the presentation is that the student was able to see the etic perspective of the Asian nurses toward the non-Asian nurses in this situation as reflected in the statement, "Those nurses don't care about what needs to get done or how much we will have to do for them—they just leave when it is time for their break. I think that is rude." The emic perspective defined by the non-Asian nurses was more accurately interpreted by the student (who is of the same cultural background). The non-Asian nurses interpreted break time assigned at 10 to mean 10. They saw the need to get to break on time for the smooth operation of the unit. Their etic interpretation of what was happening with the Asian nurses was reflected in the comment, "I think it is selfish and irresponsible when others think they can do things differently."

The next step in this analysis was to apply transcultural nursing knowledge to these emic perspectives. Faculty asked the students to examine the situation for differing values. Analyzing this problem situation against a background of transcultural knowledge about each group revealed the value orientation underlying each group's behaviors and perceptions. For instance, Asian nurses value group-centeredness with consequent ingroup versus out-group consciousness. Their time orientation is based on a combination of the past and present. Hence, setting priorities that are clearly geared toward the future is less important than the goal of maintaining relations with others. Therefore, total completion of a task promotes harmonious relations with patients. The Asian nurses evaluated "good practice" as the completion of designated tasks prior to leaving the unit.

On the other hand, the American nurses' individualistic ethos values universal rules applicable to each individual rather than different rules for different groups. The non-Asian nurses had a more lineal interpretation of time and were future oriented. They felt that "good practice" was abiding by the schedule to facilitate the operations of the unit.

This in-depth awareness of the emic perspectives helped the student to see the complexity of what initially had seemed to be a straightforward problem. This situation illustrates the mutual influence between the emic and etic worldviews of participants. In fact, etic interpretations are conditioned by the individual's indigenous, emic knowledge about the world. A person's emic and etic worldviews are naturally ethnocentric, and left on their own, will heighten the conflict and prejudices or stereotypes about other groups.

MODELING TRANSCULTURAL INTERPRETATION

Having the ability to interpret the emic and etic perspectives requires a strong foundation in transcultural knowledge. The bicultural leader not only must possess culture-general skills but must have culture-specific knowledge regarding each group on the unit. The leader's effectiveness will be measured by the ability to communicate and educate the staff on the similarities and differences between groups as well as the abilities to coach staff in analyzing situations from this transcultural perspective. Once the leader and staff can comfortably examine situations from this viewpoint, the leader can develop her staff in arriving at solutions to problems that reflect of a true bicultural perspective.

The next phase in the development of bicultural leadership skills was to develop the students' ability to discuss the differing group perspectives with the staff and to generate problem-solving solutions that accommodate their emic perspectives and the goals of the organization.

Students were given the opportunity to role-play the situation of presenting the emic worldviews to the staff. They were uncomfortable with how to present the viewpoints, especially since the Asian perspective was new to them. They were concerned that some of the staff members would negate the others' viewpoints and they were not certain they could handle this in the group setting. The students understood that this negativity most likely stemmed from an ethnocentric interpretation of events and felt that an introduction stressing the difference in perceptions between individuals and the need for respectful listening might facilitate the process. This was practiced in role-play with other students taking on different roles. This approach minimized some of the anxiety and prepared students to handle the situation.

TRANSLATING BICULTURALISM INTO PRACTICE

Having transcultural knowledge does not assure that biculturalism will be actualized in practice. There are two remaining steps to this process of actualization. First is bracketing, followed by bicultural strategizing.

Bracketing requires that the individual put aside his or her own habitual ways of looking at or dealing with situations. It is a conscious, deliberate process that permits the person to move outside his or her own monocultural worldview and become open to opportunities for innovations. Failure to do this means that transcultural knowledge remains dormant and the real potential of valuing diversity will not be actualized.

It is imperative that health care organizations achieve high-quality humanistic care. This universal goal must remain constant as bracketing occurs. Within an organization, bracketing requires that the nurse put aside preconceived notions about what constitutes quality practice to generate bicultural strategies for dealing with organizational conflict, planning, and change. Bicultural strategies capture the salient characteristics of the multicultural mosaic that constitutes the organization. The outcome is achievement of high-quality care but with genuine advocacy for diversity.

Bicultural strategizing in nursing practice can be drawn from Leininger's (1991) sunrise model of culture care. She has identified three modalities for guiding nursing judgments, decisions, or actions to provide cultural-congruent care that is beneficial, satisfying, and meaningful to people. These three modes are cultural preservations and/or maintenance, cultural accommodation and/or negotiation, and cultural repatterning or restructuring.

Cultural preservation refers to those assistive, supporting, facilitative, or enabling actions and decisions that help people of a particular culture preserve relevant values so that they can maintain their well-being. Cultural accommodation includes actions and decisions to help members of a cultural group adapt to and negotiate with a new and different environment in a way that can benefit them. Cultural repatterning involves helping individuals and groups reorder, change, or greatly modify their lifeways to evolve new ways of functioning that consider their indigenous value orientations while addressing the organizational goals.

As we expected the students to work in their clinical setting to strategize bicultural solutions to their identified problem/change projects, it was important to prepare them for this task. By using case scenarios from their actual work experience, we guided students in selecting appropriate bicultural organizational strategies for the problems presented. To help them choose appropriate strategies, we formulated guiding questions that explored the nature and impact of the problem on the organization.

An example of a problem that was presented was the tendency of Filipino registered nurses as a group to speak in their native language, Tagalog. The situation arises when there is a predominantly Filipino staff on the unit, and it has been labeled a problem by non-Filipino staff, nursing managers, clients, and doctors. Students were guided in defining the situation from both emic and etic viewpoints. Key questions that were used to assess the nature and impact of the situation on the organization included, *Are there new ways of looking at the situation that are mutually beneficial to the organizational goal, patients, staff, and the individuals involved? If allowed to continue, what impact will it have on the organizational goal, patients, staff, and the individuals involved? How will changing the situation benefit the organizational goal, patients, staff, and the individuals involved?* Responses to these questions guided the students in selecting strategies that achieve either cultural maintenance, accommodation, or repatterning.

An appreciation for the Filipino emic worldview offered another perspective of examining the situation. A significant characteristic of Filipino culture is a strong sense of group-centeredness that is associated with distinguishing in-group members from outsiders. Integral to their cultural identity and sense of group loyalty and belonging is the ability to use their native language and, in some cases, dialects. The expectation among members of this in-group is that when conversing with each other, appropriate, respectful communication will be, in fact, conducted in the Filipino language or dialect. With this cultural understanding, the students were able to modify their own etic view of intolerance for any communication not in English. This modification was in fact a repatterning of their etic view that allowed them to envision other solutions and support cultural preservation.

Once the need for cultural preservation was appreciated, students were able to define the negotiated context of the interaction. For example, during lunch breaks or in the staff lounge with *only* other in-group members present, speaking in Filipino was considered acceptable. When the interaction impacted on team work and team relations as well as the delivery of quality care to clients, students saw little room for accommodation of this behavior; repatterning was then the modality chosen.

CLINICAL EXPERIENCE OUTCOMES

After many of these critical incident analyses, students were required to return to the clinical setting to present their emic findings and to facilitate bicultural strategizing with the staff. Although they had been prepared through role-play and critical incident evaluation, anxiety was high. Students were supported by the presence of clinical faculty during the presentation. This gave the student the required support, and more significantly, there was an expert present to provide feedback and to provide further data or interpretation when the student required it.

As anticipated, there is a significant amount of resistance when someone describes a worldview different from the listener's own. Hearing it once will not convince staff that it is real, but being in the presence of bicultural leaders on an ongoing basis will make the difference. Programs such as the MSN in Clinical Leadership with an emphasis on Transcultural Nursing will prepare nurse leaders who can develop a climate that supports diversity. At the completion of this clinical experience, students realized that managers cannot assume that fair treatment always means the same treatment. This showed that students had moved from an ethnocentric stage of leading into an ethnorelative stage of leading.

REFERENCES

Bennett, M., & Deane, B. (1994). A model for personal change. In E. Y. Cross, J. H. Katz, F. A. Miller, & E. W. Seashore (Eds.), *The promise of diversity: Over 40 voices discuss strategies for eliminating discrimination in organizations* (pp. 286-293). New York: Irwin Press.

Gaston, J. (1993). Cultural orientation in the English as a second language classroom. In T. Gochenour (Ed.), *Beyond experience: The experiential approach to cross-cultural education* (pp. 97-100). Yarmouth, ME: Intercultural Press.

Leininger, M. (1991). *Culture care diversity and universality: A theory of nursing*. New York: National League for Nursing Press.

Part Six

Administrative Metaphors: Tugboats and Transitions

23

Of Tugboats and Transitions

Virginia M. Fitzsimons and Mary L. Kelley

TUGBOATS

*H*aving grown up in port cities, we understand tugboats. Those mighty little movers know where they are going and how to get there. Sleek, huge, oceangoing ships are moved and turned, then eased into narrow slips by the tugboat. The amount of energy exchanged and expended is a powerful statement regarding change. Many times, as we proceeded with this project, we felt like tugboats coasting and pushing, pulling and turning. Our groups consisted of four huge institutions, each with its own mission, history, structure, politics, traditions, staff, and students— and each was in a different, but nearby, city. Our students come from 32 countries around the world, and we serve the largest number of American-born minorities, African Americans and Hispanics, in New Jersey. We became the administrative tugboats moving our huge, complex agencies toward project objectives.

CHARTING OUR COURSE

Preparing the grant for the Robert Wood Johnson Foundation, Inc., was a complex business. As we developed the proposal, we realized it was like writing a curriculum—how to move this group of persons from here to there. Learning, defined as a change in behavior more or less consistent over time, was surely going to occur. At a minimum, *we* would learn and change.

The hectic process of presenting the proposal also prompted us to clarify our goals, compose interesting graphics, and attempt to be reasonably articulate during presentations. Questions flew back and forth, terms were defined (Learning to Learn, Educational Biculturalism, Transcultural Nursing); fringe benefits for 1996 were calculated; travel plans developed; and fiscal formulas completed in just a few swift weeks. Then the announcement—our initial success—we would be starting our minority student project. Thank you, Robert Wood Johnson Foundation, Inc.

ADMINISTRATIVE FEELINGS

After celebrating the news of our grant award, we quickly reviewed our data on promised graduates. There had been so many fast changes during the last few weeks of grant-related development that our uncertainty in regard to numbers seemed quite reasonable. As we looked over our final tables though, we knew that what we had promised was manageable.

We were also quite astonished at the wide range of responses from others. Some wished us well, offered support, and wanted to board one of our boats. Others were less than enthusiastic, attempting to stir up the waters. There were a few little tugboats out of control. We managed to chug these hazards out of our waters and we fueled up.

ADMINISTRATIVE PREDICTIONS

We had predicted that Learning to Learn (LTL) and the Nursing Academic Support Center would be the main foci—and they certainly were important. We implemented Learning to Learn on the two levels where minority students were most vulnerable: during developmental courses and the second clinical nursing course. This streamlined package of academic behaviors made a difference. Students passed in greater numbers, and faculty reported that the LTL environment (language, behaviors, and attitudes) offered the students a culture for learning. Academic thinking and organization moved the students into a level of success that pleased, yet shocked them. For some students, success was as difficult to cope with as failure had been because personal relationships changed. Learning, growth, and success are a complex matrix affecting family, intimacy, and work. The student's entire "place" in his or her cultural community shifted when class grades improved. Why was one woman beaten by her husband when she earned a 90 on an important exam? Why did another student sabotage herself during an important semester? As administrators, we have asked ourselves, "How much can we control?"

We predicted that LTL would improve retention; it had a terrific national track record. It's the usual approach to count and measure, to be empirical, to be scientific. And in keeping with that policy, we moved quantitative measurement into each objective. We decided, however, to stay innocent about what we were looking at and let the phenomenon of the huge complexity reveal itself. And it did.

Educational biculturalism became our most valuable approach. We are thrilled with the knowledge we gained about the diversity of learning. More than that—we have begun to understand how culture and subculture influence learning and why the classroom of professional studies must not use the mask of political correctness. Rather, students are there to identify assumptions, acknowledge biases, question beliefs about professional behaviors, engage in difficult discussions, and discover avenues for change. We all participated in learning and understanding the dynamics of the interactions. Feelings are affective domain; thinking is cognitive. Dialogue about differences began our understanding, and we enlarged it by using solid, tested theoretical models. Our tugboat pushed on those differences, and culture became the primary channel to our dock.

We certainly knew where we wanted to go. Our goals addressed evaluation and value complex, the highest level of the cognitive and affective domains. High-level change, many people, four distinct agencies, four years to accomplish our goal: these are the variables that made us see tugboats as a metaphor. Real change is difficult and resisted. Resisters don't give in: They get tougher. All persons need skills to change and that change comes erratically. Exploring and risk taking require energy and a certain amount of courage.

A CHAMPAGNE LAUNCHING

The day our Nursing Academic Support Center opened, we hosted a spectacular party with a shoulder-to-shoulder crowd, the press, politicians, administrators, faculty, and students. Attracted by this extensive publicity, students came and the program started. The celebration of the Center's opening was also a rite of passage for the project because it represented a physical presence on the campus with a significant display of nursing symbols, history, and texts.

INNOCENT TUGBOATS

In a sense, we proceeded as tugboats do. We knew our destination and we knew the mass that had to be moved. As tugboats never know *exactly* how they will move a ship (the tides, winds, currents, and water traffic all factor in), we also were dealing with many unknowns. Not having undertaken a particular type of project before demands that participants take a discovery approach. And this permits enormous freedom. Freedom became our tide.

We gathered each faculty and explained grant objectives, discussing how they might participate. Although we were uncomfortable in our new administrative position, we found faculty members were receptive, open to the possibilities of real change, and eager to participate.

LUNCH HELPS

The liberal arts faculty needed a total orientation to project goals. There was some resistance. Our laid-back mode, created by our "freedom tide," made them wonder whether we were without process or goals. Faculty wanted detailed specifics—what courses, which sections, how much, how many? We answered, "We don't know—we're exploring." We had threatened territorial waters. We understood. We drew back and looked for a safer approach.

Lunch was the answer. Instead of a large full faculty meeting, we met with the department chairpersons. We engaged in a dialogue and encouraged our luncheon guests to air their concerns. We got to know each other better and were able to reiterate our discovery mode. Many questions should be asked. And there won't be answers—only more persistent questions. It worked.

We visited each campus. Each faculty was asked to consider various objectives. On the Kean campus, for example, the faculty was very experienced in Outcomes Assessment and Learning to Learn. Several had won national awards and each was familiar with an open collegial approach. Having a philosopher for ethical concerns, a statistician for method development, a psychologist for cognitive learning development, and so forth, were most valuable and supportive resources.

OK, FULL SPEED AHEAD

We were on our way. Faculty were willing to be trained in Learning to Learn. We identified the early courses to measure and hired our minority registered nurses who served as mentors and role models. Freedom works. Three years later, we have met and exceeded all our goals. We assembled really bright faculty and staff, told them our goals, and said, "This is what we'd like to accomplish." And they accomplished it.

Learning and retention are up. Learning to Learn offers a formal, structured approach to giving and to receiving instructional information. This proven American cultural way of approaching classes and content is a homogeneous system that becomes a common denominator for our educationally heterogeneous groups. Its focus is at the high cognitive levels of application and synthesis areas that confound many at-risk minority students. It also moves the learner to a high affective domain level of value complex. The learner is offered a new set of behaviors, is asked to assume these new behaviors, and to apply them consistently in new situations.

The Nursing Academic Support Center is the focal point for minority students in the early science course level. It is imperative to raise career expectations from the associate degree to at least a bachelor, and preferably a master of science, degree in nursing if there is to be minority representation in leadership positions. Each student needs to see his or her future in the person of a successful professional. They need to talk with that Hispanic or African American mentor or role model and hear that the education to become a professional requires enormous discipline and acquisition of the culture (beliefs, behaviors, languages) of the professional and the profession. Each student should aim to be a leader.

OUR CAMPUS

Certain things became clear as we worked with students. The major variable between success and failure lay in the student's perception of an internal (versus externally driven) locus of control and the self-perception of being goal-directed and proactive (versus powerless or a victim). We examined our American classroom and made modifications to accommodate other perspectives. Identifying the public as our constituency sharpened our focus on the task: to educate competent nurses who could meet the demanding health needs of the emerging century. Faculty truly understand their role in monitoring practice standards.

Students struggle with the difficult curriculum and challenge its validity. We initiate them into a new culture—professional nursing—and they feel the heat and sparks of that change. We all learned that instead of one culture replacing another, the learner becomes bicultural (or multicultural).

Knowing our goal—competent, caring, well-educated professional nurses—kept us on course.

MAPPING SUCCESS

Structural tutoring and role models validated the minority students and verified that their goals were attainable. We learned that introducing Learning to Learn and writing skills early in the developmental courses was particularly effective (we strongly recommend introducing LTL in elementary schools, at the third-grade level). Learning to Learn helps students cope with the volume of content. It assists them to organize and creates "incubating space" or a safe territory where there is no judgment—just learning. The LTL method breaks academic work down into manageable parts. Students like the reinforcement of higher grades and predictable exam questions. Innovative applications of LTL information maps lead to new views of clinical experiences.

ENGINE POWER

Student empowerment is a powerful energy base. Problem solving rather than complaining were targeted behaviors. Group activities have a different meaning for adult learners and become socialization opportunities as well as a mechanism for defusing stress. Because student fear was out of proportion to reality, decompression sessions became a needed part of student life goals.

For our faculty members, the No-Bad-News approach to outcomes assessment served as a valuable resource. There were no penalties, no punishments, for identifying problem areas. This approach may be useful for licensing and accrediting bodies. On the other hand, bad news—presented in terms of the need for positive change—fuels improvement.

Retention improvement demands that faculty qualitatively explore the students' experiences from a multidimensional perspective and combine a humanistic understanding with the standard number-crunching of quantitative measurement. Retention programs must also recognize that economic needs are student priorities. Work/study opportunities and single-parent options are important options that help keep students in school.

SAFE HARBOR

Graduate study matures the nurse and provides a community with a health planner who understands quality care, innovation, and diversity. Within our Transcultural Learning Continuum, much learning took place as we moved along. Changes in the currents and the tide stirred up the waters on some of the days. Most days, however, the sun shone on us and our progress was swift and sure.

Change occurred—especially for the tugboats.

Index